An Illustrated History
of the

NORTH CORNWALL
RAILWAY

BY
D.J.Wroe

A Norman Wilkinson poster commissioned by the Southern Railway in 1947. It shows Pentire Head near Padstow. (National Railway Museum)

IRWELL
PRESS

Connecting from the 1.00 p.m. Waterloo to Plymouth, the 5.51 p.m. Okehampton bowls along with two 'P' Sets, one for Padstow and one for Bude. 'T9' No. 30709 rather shabby, though her handsome looks show through, was in the last months of service on the North Cornwall and is seen approaching Maddaford Moor on 8th May 1961. (S.C. Nash)

FOREWORD

"On behalf of the Inhabitants of Padstow and neighbourhood, I have the pleasure of congratulating you on being able today, for the first time, to travel by railway with the Honourable Mrs. Prideaux-Brune and your family the whole distance from Prideaux Place, your ancestral Desmesne on the north coast of Cornwall, to your Metropolitan residence, thus happily realizing the consummation of your ardent labours and your long cherished desires." Thus, on the 6th of April 1899,in the twilight year of the last century,ran the address presented to my Great Great Grandfather Charles Glyn Prideaux-Brune. To our ears this may sound a little stilted but through it all shines the optimism and confidence of the Victorian world so soon to be shattered by the modem age and -ultimately - Dr. Beeching!

This work, so meticulously researched by David Wroe, re-lives the glamour and gallantry as well, sometimes, as the greed and the graft which led to the realization of a dream. This book tells a real life saga and is unputdownable.

Peter Prideaux-Brune
Padstow 1994

In Memoriam

David Wroe's unexpected death on 27th October 1994, aged just sixty three, meant not only the loss of a much loved husband and father but also of a great source of inspiration, enthusiasm and a mine of fascinating recollections and information to so many people interested and involved in railways past and present. We hope that this book will prove a lasting memorial to his life and work.

Published by
Irwell Press
P.O.Box 1260,
Caernarfon, Gwynedd, LL55 3ZD
Printed by Amadeus Press, Huddersfield

ACKNOWLEDGEMENTS

It is not difficult to cull a history of a particular railway from books, newspapers and preserved documents but it would be nothing without the help of the people who worked on it, remembered it in its heyday, or simply used it or its services as a matter of course. The North Cornwall Railway, now long departed from the scene, necessarily produces a list of contributors to whom I am much indebted. Three friends should first be mentioned: Lloyd Goodman (Launceston), Tony Fairclough (Wadebridge) and Frank Sluman (Padstow). If they did not know about it, they found someone who did! Keeping me in the right columns of the timetables mazes were Roger Whitehouse (Keele), Bryan Gibson (Plymouth) and Eric Youldon (Exeter). Then there were the railwaymen headed by Charles Mitchell of Wadebridge - formerly PW Inspector there, Roy Wilce - engine driver (formerly of Wadebridge), Bert Harding (Otterham), Sid Keat (Delabole), Sandy Armstrong and Peter Hamley (St. Kew), Arthur Wills (Launceston), Jim Baker (Wadebridge), Roy Rickard, Alan Blackburn, Graham Hatton and Monty Phillips. Assistance was readily forthcoming from North Cornwall itself - John Williams and Bryan Dudley-Stamp (Bude), Sally Holden (Delabole), Harry Bolt (Warbstow), Wilfred Weeks (Canworthy Water), John and Sue Middleton (Camelford), James Evans (Callington), Sybil Dickenson (Widemouth Bay), Nigel and Kay Bowman of the Launceston Steam Railway, V. Tobutt of the Wellington Hotel (Boscastle), Mark Prout (Port Isaac), John Fry (Tintagel), Peter Ascott (Tintagel), Bob Gregson (Wadebridge), Rev. Barry Kinsman (St.Issey), Mrs Hilda Hambly (Wadebridge), Cyril Arthur and Brian Tunbridge (Launceston). On the Devon Side: Jim Spry and Elizabeth Burley (Ashwater), David Osborne (Silverton), Carl Schrade and Maurice Osborne. Dr Harris and Mrs Knight (Cornish Biographical Index, Redruth), Lt.Col. Williams (St. Tudy) and Mr Peter Prideaux-Brune generously assisted in tracing the lives of the backers and Directors of the NCR Company.

Members of the South Western Circle will recognise their contributions: John Nicholas, Mike King, G.A. Jacobs and George Reeve. Photographs are credited where shown, but Dick Riley, Ron Lumber, Peter Gray, Chris Knowles-Thomas and Sid Nash have allowed me the pick of their work. One could not forget the gratitude owed to the late H.C. Casserley for his invaluable photographs taken in the 1920s onwards, and I would particularly like to thank R.D. Penhallurick of the Royal Institution of Cornwall for his unstinting help. Details regarding coaching stock derive from research by Gordon Weddell and David Gould.

My thanks are due to the Devon and the Cornwall County Record Offices, Library of West Country Studies at Exeter, Cornwall Libraries and Art Department, Croydon Reference Library, Winchester County Library, the National Railway Museum and British Rail (Western and Southern Regions). Reference has been made to books and publications, but one in particular: R.A. Williams's, The London & South Western Railway (Volume II) which is the lead into the North Cornwall Railway's conception and birth. 'The LSWR In The Twentieth Century' (with J.N. Faulkner) has also been consulted, but the early background of the Company comes from the Minute Books in the Public Record Office, Kew. The local newspapers of the period provide much interest: The Cornish & Devon Post (which incorporated the Launceston Weekly News), the West Briton, the Cornish Guardian (Bodmin) and the Western Morning News.

Finally, Bert Moody, Reg Randell, George Pryer, John Mann, and Tony Cooke receive my special thanks for their specialised assistance with layouts and dates. Mrs Rachael Roberts and Mrs Maureen Collins cheerfully typed the drafts and final versions of my scripts and Paul Rouet assisted in the later stages.

At this distance in time some of my interpretation of events are necessarily included and, although every effort has been made to authenticate dates and times, any errors and omissions must remain my responsibility.

D.J.Wroe, 1994

CONTENTS

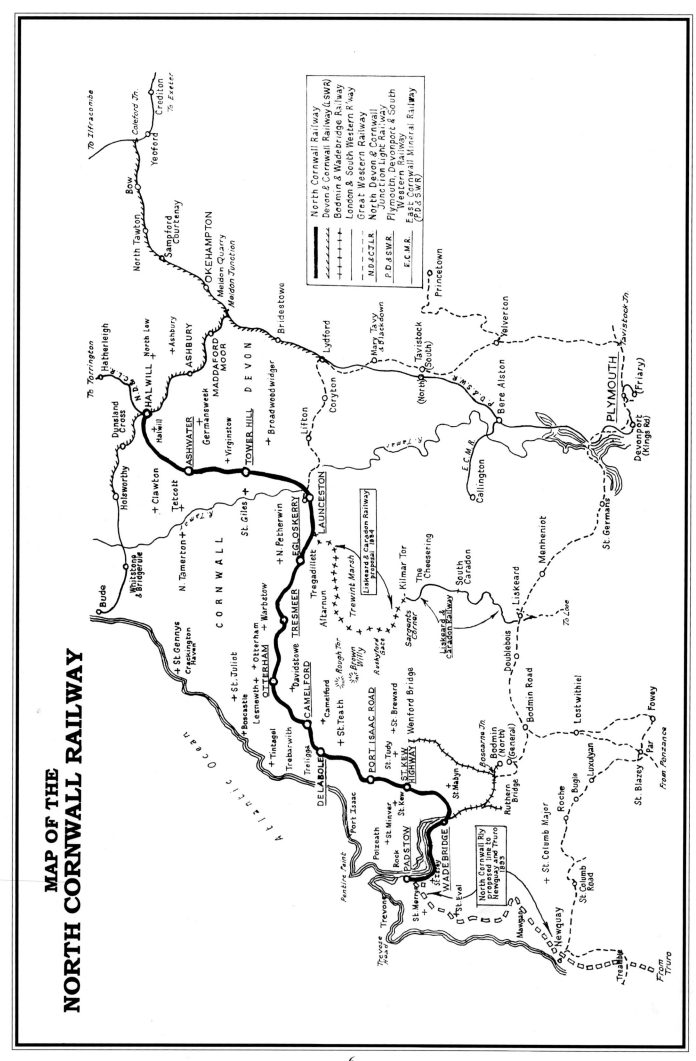

MAP OF THE
NORTH CORNWALL RAILWAY

6

INTRODUCTION

With hardly a tree in sight on the landscape, which here directly faces the Atlantic Ocean, the North Cornwall breasted the summit at Trewanion, 860 feet above sea level (centre-horizon). The 1.00 p.m. Padstow to Okehampton had come up over from Camelford and was coasting into Otterham behind 'N' Class No. 31859 on a hot August afternoon in 1964. The bogie van brought the national newspapers to North Cornwall on the previous night, and was now being returned to Clapham Junction. (P.W. Gray)

A quarter of a century on leaves few memories of the "North Cornwall", a meandering railway from Halwill Junction in West Devon to the River Camel Estuary at Padstow on the Cornish Coast. Some may recall a 'West Country' Class 4-6-2 engine edging its way round Slaughterbridge, by Brown Willy, with two or three coaches from the 11.00 am 'Atlantic Coast Express' from Waterloo. Few will remember a pair of Adams 0-6-0s struggling up the Carey Valley with a cattle special for Halwill and Exeter. Photographs of recent years show T9 4-4-0s with the Up 'Perishables' at Camelford say, or Tresmeer. Empty platforms, guard looking at his watch. Rabbits for the London or Birmingham markets were a staple in the 1930s and until the myxomatosis disease of the 1950s. Fish from Padstow once vitalised the line. Why did the North Cornwall come to exist? Railway politics of the 19th Century offer some clues. The London & South Western's ambitions west of Exeter; the Great Western guarding its territories; local promoters creating proposed lines with some certainty of support from one or both of those Companies. The North Cornwall seems to have made a good bargain

with the LSWR, and in the end (unusually) maintained its nominal independence until grouping in 1923. In the background were the railway contractors ever looking for business. How much lobbying occurred will never be known. The bigger contractors still had much work in the 1870s when the North Cornwall was conceived. The Settle & Carlisle (Brassey's) was under way for instance, and in Devon the LSWR was forging its competitive way to Plymouth. Here the works were undertaken by lesser names such as Relf. It was he who was awarded the first link from Okehampton westwards to North Cornwall. He completed the Devon & Cornwall Railways (an LSWR protege) line to Holsworthy, opened in January 1879.

Once the North Cornwall obtained its original Act of Parliament in the 1880s, nobody foresaw it would be nearly 20 years before it was completed. A peculiar situation had arisen at Wadebridge quite early in as far as the LSWR was already there before its North Cornwall satellite arrived. The ancient Bodmin & Wadebridge Railway of 1834 was acquired by the South Western Directors, not quite legally in the Parliamentary sense, in 1845.

The GWR was most annoyed knowing it to be a pawn in the LSWR's designs in West Cornwall. By the time the NCR reached Wadebridge in 1895, however, much of the rancour had disappeared.

Prospects of tourism emerged in the promoters' ideas for the line. Along the North Cornish coast only Newquay and Bude, which were to grow into resorts, actually fronted the Atlantic Ocean. Neither was of any size in the 1880s, the former a mineral outlet and a fishing port, the latter imported coal etc. into a tiny harbour, and exported sea sand inland by a canal. Both had attracted visitors of means, and although such people usually stayed put when on holiday, the germ of present-day restlessness was present. By the late 1890s, with the LSWR at Ilfracombe, Bideford, Bude and Padstow, and the GWR at Newquay, the coaching companies, especially the 'North Cornwall' concern (no relation) were carrying several thousand passengers every summer between these places. The LSWR was excursion-minded and in the 1880s was encouraging, even subsidising, coach connections along the coast to view the scenery, and from inland railheads where

7

Halwill's original 1879 passing place on the branch to Holsworthy expanded from 1886. The station suddenly awoke to much activity when the Padstow and Bude trains came in from either direction. Connecting from the 1.00 p.m. Waterloo in the evening of 22nd August 1964 was the 5.55 p.m. Okehampton to Padstow seen departing at 6.25 p.m., with 'N' Class No. 31859 and a local 'P' set. Most Bude connections, in this last summer of Waterloo services, ran separately from the bay and Standard Class 4 No. 80039 is seen there with the 6.30 p.m. for the branch. On the left Ivatt 2-6-2T No. 41249 is on the 6.30 p.m. to Torrington. (P.W. Gray)

desirable (e.g. Launceston and Holsworthy).

It is not generally realised how close the railway came to Boscastle and Tintagel, although it would have been improbable for a line to have descended to their levels, except by some fearsome gradients. The lure of the Arthurian legends was fanned in the LSWR advertising - the Southern Railway went even further and named a whole Class of engines after the Knights of the Round Table. Port Isaac was beckoned by a provision of a 'Road' station, but beaches and cliffs were nearer to Padstow at Rock, over the water, and Harlyn Bay or Trevone.

The jewels in the North Cornwall crown were undoubtedly Launceston and Wadebridge, agriculture centres, market towns and exporters of cattle, sheep and pigs. Wadebridge was also a small port which was rail-served. Bodmin, inland and already connected by the B & W R, replaced Launceston as the County Town but continued to hold the Assizes, and its attendant gaol, together with the County Asylum. A line from Boscarne Junction and Bodmin GWR to Bodmin Road, opened in 1888, could also be regarded as a potential link to the North Cornwall. Camelford town, rather declined since the 1832 Reform Act abolished its two Parliamentary seats, nevertheless contributed revenue, though the

station was some miles to the east. The line did go through Delabole (Pengelly village) and here lay the huge defile of the slate quarry, the result of joining several together in the 1830s. Hitherto slates had been carried to Port Gaverne and Port Isaac by cart. The railway soon captured this traffic and expansion followed, maintained until the 1930s. The rest of the wayside stations promoted only modest business, with the exception of the rabbit-meat trade which increased tremendously in the 1920s, especially at Tresmeer and Otterham.

As found in many rural backwaters the two World Wars suddenly brought a lot of Government business to some unknown places. Thus Tower Hill, so quiet in the early 1920s that its loop was removed, burst into life again in 1943, with facilities restored, to handle ammunition trains in a new siding. Otterham yard up on the summit and exposed to the Atlantic gales, hummed with activity following the opening of an airfield on Davidstow Moor to the south. Such activity was relatively short-lived, an artificial rise in fortune. Motor transport on the roads, not a real menace to rail in this part of the country until the 1950s, nevertheless established itself from the 1920s. Particularly the bus companies but the Southern Railway, by virtue of legislation in 1928, was ena-

bled to buy into the local Companies and so gain some control. It was surprising the Southern Railway gave as much attention to the Devon and Cornwall lines as it did. One good reason was that a line stretching for 250 miles could generate revenue by distance alone. Worthwhile then to accentuate the less populated end for holiday traffic. So attention came in the form of, firstly, publicity for the resorts and comfortable corridor coaching stock. Secondly most of the track was relaid in the 1930s and well in time for the increasingly heavy trains that did come, reaching a peak in 1939 (and again in the 1950s). One detects the hand of Sir Herbert Walker, the General Manager of the SR, preoccupied as he was with electrification of London routes at that time. After the contortion of traffic patterns in World War Two, when the lengthy 'Atlantic Coast Express' trains gave way to troop specials (even longer on many occasions!), there were great expectations for holidaymakers in 1946. The introduction of the 'West Country' Class 4-6-2 engines in 1945 seemed to underline the restoration of trains especially for North Cornwall and Bude. The names given to these Pacifics included 'Launceston', 'Wadebridge' and 'Padstow'. 'Camelford', even 'Rough Tor' came later. Travel on the 'Atlantic Coast' already famous since 1925 (although its predecessor the 'North Cornwall & Bude Express' started in 1907) again became the means of reaching Tintagel and Boscastle, the delights of Port Isaac, St. Enodoc and Polzeath, and down to Padstow. John Betjeman was devoted to this part of the County and the 'North Cornwall' is reflected in one of his poems. The ACE, nonstop at times from Exeter to Halwill, and missing out the wayside stations, became more 'express' and enjoyed a restaurant car all the way to Padstow.

The winter months resulted in thinner receipts, depending on just local travel apart from the daily through coaches to London. The North Cornwall, though, provided a valuable communication into Wadebridge, Launceston, up to Okehampton, the shops and theatres in Exeter, even to Bideford over the lately-built Halwill to Torrington branch. Passengers were induced to go to Plymouth, via Okehampton, a lengthy detour compared with changing on to the GWR at Launceston. Both ways fell prey to the buses as they went more directly, not only the National Omnibuses, but smaller concerns such as Blakes of Delabole, which ran almost daily into Plymouth. The Royal Blue long distance coaches expended their services after 1950 and certainly shared the cream of the summer months by terminating at Bude and Polzeath.

In 1950, following nationalisation of the Southern Railway (1948) the commercial and civil engineering functions passed to the Western Region of the new British Railways. The SR

pattern of train services was maintained, passenger and goods, fed through Salisbury from Waterloo and Nine Elms, connected to the Midlands by the old Somerset & Dorset Joint Line via Templecombe, and serviced by the yards and engine shed at Exmouth Junction. It might seem to be lasting for ever - the 'Woolworth' 2-6-0s plodding the length of the North Cornwall, shunting wagons at Halwill; the tang of tarpaulins, dust and straw in the goods yards, or the signalman/ porter calling out "Ot'tram" as the T9 and its train drew in from Tresmeer in the dusk of a winter evening.

But the railway was secretly bleeding. Successive management changes and direction under nationalisation, rising costs against falling revenues, and misguided (as it turned out) understanding by the staff that they were providing a 'service' to the public, was leading to the Beeching era in the early 1960s. The feeding of trunk lines by branches and secondary lines was not part of the philosophy of the British Railways of the 1960s. When the 'Report' was published in 1963, sure enough, the North Cornwall was shown to be superfluous. BR put up its proposals for closure in 1964.

Road transport in the shape of the private car, the heavy lorry (but not yet the long distance 'juggernaut') and, to a lesser extent the bus, were already drawing off traffic from rail. The North Cornwall line meandering through Ashwater and St Kew Highway, with steam-hauled trains taking two hours to cover the sixty miles Okehampton-Padstow already seemed

an anachronism. Even the introduction of diesel railcars in 1965 did little to enhance the 'run down' atmosphere posed by rusty sidings and disheartened staff. The Western Region had full control from 1963. The severance of the SR's Devon and Cornwall network from Waterloo in September 1964 upset a long tradition. Henceforth Paddington became the London-traveller's destination, though it is fair to say there occurred some remarkable timesaving to Bude and Launceston by reason of the faster Paddington-Exeter trains.

At this time - 1964 - the freight service was already slated for withdrawal. BR needed no approval to curtail or close down this operation. All goods trains ceased to run from 7 September 1964 despite appeals from local authorities. Launceston and Wadebridge were retained as railheads; they were otherwise connected than to the North Cornwall.

A stay of execution for the duration of the summer of 1966 only prolonged the inevitable date of passenger closure which duly took place on and from 3 October that Autumn. The younger enthusiasts gave what cheer they could to the final day's services. The older generation sadly bought last tickets and thronged the trains. As always on these occasions, the last extinguishment of lamps, the locking of gates and doors and the final replacement of the single-line tokens in their machines, underlined the awful melancholy of those railway closedowns of the Beeching years.

Padstow station nearly ready in March 1899 with gravelling taking place in yard and platform. The new road from the top of the town is curving down (right) but the large hotel has yet to be constructed. The 'bluff' behind the awning was removed after a few years and the platform extended almost to the stops. (R.I.C.)

Chapter One
THE LSWR IN WEST DEVON AND NORTH CORNWALL

The Devon and Cornwall Railway's terminus at Holsworthy in 1882. The station was laid out as future passing place on a through route to Bude or Wadebridge, but in the event the line was extended to the former in 1898. Beyer Peacock 4-4-0T No. 320 with 4- or 6-wheel coaches is flanked by her driver and fireman, whilst the Station Master is surrounded by various staff and townsfolk. (Mrs. G. Kendall)

The London & South Western Railway might well have arrived in Truro and Falmouth in the 1840s, such was the ambition, though at the time it was no nearer than Salisbury and Dorchester. Two projects were floated in 1845: one from Exeter via Okehampton, Launceston and Bodmin and the other, the nascent Cornwall Railway extending from the authorised South Devon Railway at Plymouth, via Liskeard to Falmouth. Neither came to pass in 1845, but the Cornwall Railway Bill succeeded in 1846. It was at this juncture that the Bodmin and Wadebridge was acquired by the LSWR directors, without Parliamentary sanction. The Cornwall and Devon Central Railway, as it was called, had been surveyed by the LSWR's engineer, Joseph Locke, though use of the B & WR in its existing form would have presented quite a problem. It was, however, significant that the Cornwall Railway could be required to lay an additional rail to their broad gauge (7'0¼") to Falmouth if a narrow gauge should join it at Truro. Another LSWR foothold, if minor, was gained at Plymouth when that Company subscribed to the Sutton Harbour improvement works.

Building railways in Cornwall proved difficult. (The Cornwall Railway needed 42 viaducts en route to Falmouth). The proposed 'central route' would not have been an exception. The LSWR was behind a new Launceston, Bodmin and Wadebridge Junction Railway proposal in 1864. This involved a 630-yard tunnel between the Kensey and Inny valleys near Pipers Pool and a route through Camelford to join the B & WR's Wenford Branch. Turning itself into the 'Central Cornwall Railway' the following year, there was an eye on Falmouth again. Access to Truro would be via the B & W's Ruthernbridge Branch. Acts of Parliament were obtained in 1864 and 1865, but it ran into trouble with the latent agreement with the GWR over territorial expansions and was abandoned in 1871.

The region traversed eventually by the North Cornwall Railway had not escaped previous speculation. As far back as 1836 a dubious 'Launceston & Victoria Railway' was aimed at Tremoutha Haven in St Gennys Parish on the North Coast. A 'Plymouth and North Cornwall Railway' would have followed a circuitous route through Five Lanes, Davidstow (with a 946-yard tunnel) to Delabole and Rock, opposite Padstow. After the demise of the LB & WJR two further lines were enabled by legislation in 1873: the Bodmin & Wadebridge & Delabole Railway via Wenford, and the Cornwall Mineral & Bodmin & Wadebridge Junction via Ruthernbridge. Both failed to materialise.

In 1860 the LSWR was at Exeter. After a foray with the Bristol & Exeter Railway, it succeeded in leasing the Exeter & Crediton Railway, linking to it through Exeter St.Davids by narrow gauge rail from 1 February 1862. This Crediton line and a lease in 1862 of the North Devon Railway to Barnstaple provided a springboard for fresh incursions into West Devon, Plymouth and Cornwall. An Okehampton Railway Company obtained its Act in 1862 to build from Coleford near Yeoford, through North Tawton to that town.

By an Act dated 29 June 1865 the Okehampton Railway, now renamed the 'Devon & Cornwall Railway' was enabled to build from Sampford Courtenay to Bude. Another Act in 1867 would have made a line to Torrington, and Bude, via Hatherleigh. Yet again in 1873 an extensive proposal to go all the way to Wadebridge was contained in an Act signed on 7th July. Of several authorised lines under the Act was one from Meldon Junction, west of Okehampton, to Holsworthy. This was the limb from which sprang the North Cornwall Railway extensions of the 1890's. Another proposed Wadebridge line from Holsworthy, via North Tamerton (with a branch thence to Bude), Camelford, to Wenford Bridge was never built.

The nominally independent Devon & Cornwall Company's immediate role in the 1870s was to front the LSWR's attack on Plymouth, Stonehouse and Devonport. By way of a Lidford (sic) extension and a junction with the South Devon Railway's branch through Tavistock to Marsh Mills, South Western trains would enter the 'Three Towns' on mixed gauge rails in 1876. An important agreement in April 1874 empowered the LSWR to work the D & CR, to purchase lines as they were built, also to decide what would be built. Thus the Holsworthy Branch, opened on 20 January 1879, was the only survivor of the 1873 authorization.

Construction and Opening Okehampton, Meldon Junction and Holsworthy

The main line to Plymouth branched off from the North Devon line at Coleford Junction, west of Yeoford. On the opening to North Tawton in 1865 a single line ran next to the ND from Yeoford to Coleford, continuing on to 'Okehampton Road' (later Sampford Courtenay) in January 1867. Okehampton itself was reached in 1871, the public train service starting on 3 October. Already, as has been noted, an extension to Lidford was authorised in 1863 but not until 1869 did contractor R.T. Relf start work beyond Okehampton. Meanwhile the temporary terminus was laid out as a through 2-platformed station in anticipation. The site had to be excavated and embanked leaving little room for expansion. A goods yard was established on the down side, quarrying provided stone for the new extension westward. The LSWR used large boulders in the sub-formations of their track. In 1879 a bay platform was es-

tablished on the south side of the Down platform for the new Holsworthy trains.

The single line to Lidford was opened on 12 October 1874, under Devon & Cornwall Railway auspices. With running powers and a narrow gauge rail laid, the LSWR (working the D & CR) could enter Plymouth, though it was not until 17 May 1876 when the first South Western train arrived there. Following this opening, doubling from Coleford Junction was undertaken reaching Okehampton on 9th January 1879, also the portion thence to Meldon Viaduct (east end) the same day.

The massive viaduct, yet rather spindly in appearance when viewed from afar, was constructed (1873/4) of Hughes wrought iron girders on piers of cast iron cylinders set in granite blocks. There was subsequent movement in these cylinders at the embanked ends and remedial walling was put in. Major General Hutchinson inspected the original viaduct in 1874, and again the widening in September 1879.

It seemed the second structure (for the Up line) was welcomed by all parties as it was interlaced with the first. It may be remembered that the Tay Bridge at Dundee, a structure not entirely dissimilar to Meldon, later collapsed in a gale on 28 December 1879. The leg struts were connected into enlarged bases and steel was used this time. At the top the piers were connected with the originals, with cross-bracing 18'0" below the carrying girders. Wheel timbers were placed directly above each girder and the top deck planked in from side to side. Major General Hutchinson ordered a test load of moving engines (at speed) and deflections of only 3/10" were found. The final structure was of 6 spans of

85'6" and they were between 120 and 140 feet above ground. After a period of six weeks while the new structure served as the single line (from a temporary signal box at the east end), the double line became available as from 1 November 1879. At present Meldon Viaduct is a 'listed' structure, though the rails now end at the Quarry.

In the meantime a junction on the single line at Meldon was formed for the new Holsworthy Branch at the 200 MP (to be). Relf, following completion of the Lidford extension, took up the Holsworthy contract starting in August 1875. Extensive embankments had to be raised to carry the line across Bowerland on reversing 15-chain curves. It then climbed around the top of Thorndon Down and south of Venn Down before reaching Ashbury, the site of the only intermediate station to Beaworthy. The road from Bratton Clovelly to Ashbury village and North Lew occupied a gated level crossing at Venndown Gate. The long embankment thence to Broadbury can still be seen today from the adjacent road. Beyond Ashbury the line snaked on a falling gradient on 30 and 40 chain curves past Patchacott and Madworthy hamlets before emerging below Henderbarrow in sight of Beaworthy, or Halwill Junction as it eventually became. Another long embankment curved, then straightening for a mile brought the line into Beaworthy (209 3/4MP). Here the railway was 600' above sea level having dropped 300 since Meldon.

Beaworthy was equipped with a simple layout - crossing loop, two platforms, 3 sidings and a signal box - similar to Ashbury and Dunsland Cross the other two stations. Holsworthy, the terminus, was more substantial. It had two platforms, again in anticipation of a future ex-

Okehampton's station buildings have survived many years of closure, but not the LSWR's 1870s pattern signal box on the Down side, which was demolished after the opening of the new one on the Up side in 1935. The Station Master, in frock coat, his clerks and serged-uniformed platform staff pose for posterity in the period up to 1914. Spiers & Pond held the general contract to run the LSWR's refreshment rooms for many years. (Author's collection).

Meldon Viaduct on 3rd June 1959 showing 'T9' No. 30726 with three Bulleid coaches crossing towards Okehampton, the latter forming the Plymouth portion of the 'ACE' and for attachment to the 8.30 a.m. Padstow to Exeter and Waterloo. The Down side of the viaduct shows the steelwork of the second line of 1879, which followed the original wrought iron structure of 1871. (S.C. Nash)

tension to Bude (not to come for 19 years!) and a handsome station house with a side office and a large goods shed. Earthworks between Beaworthy and Holsworthy were considerable below Dunsland Cross and an 8-span stone-built viaduct was necessary just east of Holsworthy. The total length of this branch was 17 miles and 64 chains.

The new line was ready in January 1879. Colonel Yolland RE of the Railway Inspectorate travelled over it on the 5th. He stated in his report that he could recommend opening subject to certain omissions being rectified. He said the rails used were 75 lb to the yard (double headed) and laid in cast iron chairs on Memel sleepers, averaging 2'8" centres. Interestingly the points were steel, only just being adopted in the 1870s. Turntables had been installed at Okehampton and Holsworthy. There were two level crossings - at Venn and Beaworthy. There were signal boxes at all four stations, each with 10 levers and the method of 'Absolute' Block by signal and telegraph was in force. Train Staff and Ticket was provided on only two sections: Meldon Junction to Beaworthy and Beaworthy to

Holsworthy. (Trains were crossing at Ashbury in 1880, so it must be assumed that four Staff sections had then been introduced). Signalling was still somewhat primitive in the late 1870s, although locking frames and block telegraph working were now accepted for new passenger lines. Colonel Yolland had found only disc signals at the facing points. Semaphore should be erected, he said, so that drivers could see signals as far away as possible.

Beaworthy was renamed Halwill & Beaworthy in July 1879. It later became Halwill Junction in March 1887, and Halwill (for Beaworthy) in 1923. Although agriculture had entered a depression in the late 1870s after a succession of wet summers and a growing importation of North American corn, the railway was looked at as an encouragement for the future. Local landowners - Lord Stanhope, Lord Clinton and Mr W.J. Harris (of Halwill Manor) actually gave land for it. Many farmers were their tenants.

Opening day was 20 January 1879 and Holsworthy was bedecked with festoons of evergreens and coloured streamers, not forgetting a triumphal arch in Chapel Street. The Directors

of the LSWR and D & CR arrived at 11.45am in a saloon attached to the first down train. After an address by the Rail Committee Chairman, Dr.Ash, a procession formed up and paraded through the town to the accompaniment of the Launceston, Bideford and Royal Marines Light Infantry bands. To a luncheon given in the Edgington Marquee were invited Lord and Lady Stanhope, two MPs, the Mayors of seven Devon towns, the Sheriff of Devon and the Chief Constable of Devon. R.H. Dutton, the LSWR Chairman said ".... that the bracken, heather and gorse would disappear, and that agriculture would improve everywhere".

In due course the railway did assist, though not for arable farming as cattle rearing for beef increased in the late 1890s supplying dealers to the east with store cattle and for slaughtering for meat. Holsworthy itself gained a measurable prosperity through this, and a sizeable community subsequently grew in the vicinity of Halwill Junction. The service in 1880 was five down trains (one, a 'mixed' goods and passenger - 9.10am from Okehampton), and two 'mixed' and three passenger up trains.

Chapter Two
THE CONSTRUCTION OF THE NORTH CORNWALL RAILWAY

That the LSWR would back a route toward Launceston and Wadebridge seemed unquestionable - though going onto Truro, as the NCR promoters had in mind, would obviously antagonize the GWR. Perhaps the choice of a Padstow terminus underlined this. In 1881 to the accompaniment of church bells and the sound of the local band a committee of Padstonians emerged from their meeting room offering to contribute to funds toward a survey of a line from Halwill to Padstow. Within a few months committees were set up at Wadebridge, Camelford and Launceston. Messrs Galbraith and Church (the LSWR's Consulting Engineers) were engaged to find a suitable route. There seemed to be no argument about bringing a line down the Carey Valley from Halwill to Launceston, but the Launceston committee had designs on a station up in the town. They were told it would have to be in a tunnel in that case - the line emerging at Penygillam! Their desire for a route through Holloway Cross (Polyphant) and the Inny Valley to Davidstow was also turned down. The Padstow committee thought up an inland route from Wadebridge, via St Issey, but as an extensive 1,000 yard tunnel at Tregella would be needed, the waterside route by the Camel was adhered to. It seems that the consultants, encouraged by the LSWR, were looking for an uncomplicated route with a ruling gradient of 1 in 73 and curves not generally less than 30 chains radius, and without long tunnels and viaducts.

Launceston had lost the Cornish Assizes to Bodmin in 1838 and the ancient Borough (with two seats in Parliament until 1832) was declining. Politics had played a strong part in bringing the broad gauge branch from Plymouth and Tavistock into the town in 1865. Local landowners, including the Dukes of Bedford and Northumberland were won over to the railway cause. Such a roundabout route to Exeter and London, and the necessity to transship goods between the narrow and broad gauges at Lidford (sic) (possible from 1876) naturally irritated Launcestonians. A request for a narrow gauge rail from Lidford (sic) to Launceston was made to the GWR, but turned down. Hence the prospect of a narrow gauge line from Halwill

was very encouraging. The Liberal Party cause was strong in North Cornwall. It stemmed from the Methodist Church (not then unified, but in various sects such as Wesleyans, Bible Christians and the 'Bryanites'). While Launceston was in the 'pocket' of the Duke of Northumberland until 1885 and usually returned a Conservative member, a Liberal invariably sat for 'Cornwall North'. Launceston, Camelford and Wadebridge were (and are) the political centres. A North Cornwall Railway would connect them nicely, and an extension to Truro, soon to become a 'City', and County Town (vice Bodmin) even better.

Camelford was isolated and less important since it lost its two members of Parliament in 1832. The population numbers stayed the same for years, but its market and shops, and position on the main road to Wadebridge kept it fairly prosperous. Also it had its share of benefactors, like the Duke of Bedford (its town hall), and James Smith (a school).

Wadebridge (and Egloshayle) grew up around the medieval 14-arch bridge over the Camel. Coastal shipping could reach the quay, which was served by

The A30 Launceston to Okehampton road passed under the single line to Ashbury where 'T9' No. 30313 rounds the 15-chain reverse curves with the 5.51 p.m. Okehampton on 12th May 1961. The front two-coach 'P' Set is for Padstow, and the rear set for Bude. Meldon Junction is in the distance (left) below the commanding height of Yes Tor (2,030 ft.). (S.C. Nash)

The station master's accommodation at Ashbury lay beyond the porch and the booking office, etc. at this end of the large single-storey premises provided by the Devon & Cornwall Railway (LSWR) in 1879. Halwill & Beaworthy and Dunsland Cross were similar. Through the gate (left) stands the Southern Railway warehouse let to the West Devon & North Cornwall Farmers Ltd. Long before this date (16th March 1966) the goods shed ceased to handle sundry goods and wagon loads of fertilizers, etc. no longer arrived after freight services were withdrawn from 7th September 1964. (A.E.West)

the B & WR. Again, the market drew numerous farmers into the town, and regular imports of coal and merchandise enabled Wadebridge's population to rise considerably in the 19th century. There were several foundries and manufactories as well, supplying local needs.

Padstow presented quite a different scene. Intensely proud, its fierce fishing and seagoing population dated from a borough period in the 16th century. Strangely the port was in better communication with Canada than perhaps London, through its connection with Nova Scotia and Prince Edward Island and it was an emigrant port in the 1840s and 50s to those colonies. Along the North Coast of Cornwall, Padstow offered the only reasonably accessible harbour, though potentially dangerous due to the Doom Bar across the mouth of the Camel. At the time of promotion in 1882, the fishing was a local endeavour, but by the opening of the NCR in 1899 the scene was changing. Brixham men had been ex-

ploiting the North Coast, though taking their catches elsewhere. In the mid-1890s, however, the East Coast of England sailing trawlers had appeared. Already fish was being carted to the Wadebridge railhead (via GWR) and in 1899 the LSWR started express services from Padstow. The extensive works started by the Padstow Harbour Commissioners, then taken over and largely financed by the LSWR will be described.

Apart from the final 5 miles to Padstow which hugged the south side of the wide Camel estuary, the chosen route for the North Cornwall Railway commenced and ended in sylvan valleys, in reality almost half in such surrounds. The remainder traversed the almost treeless uplands above the 300-ft contour from Egloskerry to Port Isaac Road. It would there skirt the northern edge of Bodmin Moor, not closely, except where an outlier extends into Otterham and Davidstow Parishes, reaching 1,000 ft above sea level at Hendraburnick. Just below

here trains in the future crawled over the line's 860 ft summit at Otterham. Yet only 3 miles away to the NW the surging Atlantic Ocean spends itself against the cliffs at Boscastle. The Moor with its two prominent tors, Brown Willy (1,375') and Roughtor (1,312') lies only a few miles to the east. Its granite mass and peaty bogs contrast with the Upper Devonian rock of which Delabole slate quarry is an outcrop, with possibilities of mineral extraction such as copper, lead etc. The land is quite different again from Halwill, through Launceston to Egloskerry where the Middle Culm Measures project from West Devon. Here the NCR would share the Carey and Kensey valleys draining into the Tamar at Launceston. The countryside was given over to grassland, hence cattle raising, thereby contributing importantly to the LSWR's and SR's coffers in due course. In the 1880's farms existed at near-subsistence levels, oats and barley grown to feed livestock. Sea sand obtainable from the Camel estuary, and Bude, was spread onto fields as a dressing. It was considered that the NCR might carry 65,000 tons a year producing a revenue of £5,000. From Bude, a canal opened in 1823 distributed sand almost as far as Launceston and the B & WR was built largely for this purpose. Wheat was grown in the area below Port Isaac at this time, but increasing imports of North American grain into Britain discouraged farmers from this crop.

Leaving aside the possibilities of extending to Newquay and Truro (a distinct option in the early 1890's) what other prospects were there of actually opening a railway across the apparently unpromising and thinly populated countryside between the four principal towns? Delabole slate quarry, for one, with its 1880's production of about 1,400 tons a year, but estimated to rise to 20,000. At that time lead and silver mining adventuring occurred in the St Teath area, even for manganese ore near Launceston. Then there was the potential tourist and holiday trade which, in the end, would become the seasonal mainstay of the North Cornwall line. Already the coach companies were feeding the established rail terminals at Bideford, Holsworthy, Launceston and Newquay, and serving Bude, Boscastle and Tintagel along the coast. The attractions of Polzeath, Trevone, Harlyn Bay and Mawgan Porth also beckoned.

While the NCR's promotion materialized another scheme was launched to connect Padstow, this time to the south. The Mid-Cornwall Railway was proposed to connect St Dennis on the Cornwall Minerals Railway through St Columb. The NCR saw no objection but the Bill got no further than the House of Lords Select Committee in May 1882. One effect was to galvanize the GWR into obtaining powers to build their branch from Bodmin Road to Bodmin, and to Boscarne Junction

An early view of Ashbury, looking towards Meldon Junction, with a '460' Class 4-4-0 and a train bound for North Cornwall entering the Down loop. Passengers used the steps down from the road to cross the line, footbridges were rarely provided at rural stations. The large post and arm of the Down starting signal is noteworthy, also the duplicated Up starting signals. (E. Youldon Collection)

on the B & WR. The Padstow committee was naturally upset at the loss of the Mid-Cornwall and then having to witness future piecemeal building of the NCR. Meetings were held in 1891 and 1894 concerning Padstow's continuing isolation.

Overcoming GWR objections, the LSWR made Agreements (1/12/82 and 2/12/82) with the NCR to work its line. The Act of Parliament authorizing the North Cornwall Railway was passed and received Royal Assent on 18 August 1882 (45 & 46 Vic. cap. ccliv). It was to run from a junction with the LSWR's Holsworthy Branch at Halwill & Beaworthy to Padstow South Quay (but not including the existing Bodmin & Wadebridge as between Pendevy Bridge and Wadebridge). The authorized railways were:

Ashwater Station house is evident on the right of this early view of the Carey Valley with Ash Mill to the left. Local merchant R.A. Moon's stores lie in the centre on the hill leading to Germansweek. After closure of the line the road was straightened to its original course. (J.T.E. Spry)

	m	ch
1. Padstow South Quay to Wadebridge	5	41
2. Pendevy Bridge to Launceston	29	54
3. Spur near Pendevy Bridge towards Bodmin	-	26
4. Junction with L&SDR at Launceston	-	15
5. Launceston to a point 16 chains NW of Halwill & Beaworthy station	13	31

The authorized capital was to be £600,000 in shares and with powers to borrow £220,000. Included in the original NCR Bill was a requirement for the acquisition of the Bodmin & Wadebridge and extensive deviations were proposed for it, with a new station at Bodmin, also at Wadebridge. (In the event the LSWR did these itself). The B & WR had been held in trust by the LSWR directors since 1846, to the GWR's annoyance, so much so that the 1882 Act omitted Amalgamation clauses. Thus the LSWR Co. legally bought it in. A cash payment of £35,000 and extinguishment on an Exchequer loan of £8,000 settled the matter, sealed by Acts dated 25 January and 1 July 1886. The 1882 Agreement with the LSWR carefully outlined the conditions regarding the NCR's association with the B & WR. There were also strictures on any future connection made at Launceston with the GWR (Railway No.4).

The working Agreements with the LSWR provided for working and maintaining the line in perpetuity, retaining 55% of the gross receipts after retaining Government duty. Thus with its 45% balance the NCR was ensured income to pay dividends from the opening date. An intricate rebate payment was also agreed by the LSWR. This was based on 10% of all gross receipts from lines east of Exeter passing to Launceston and Padstow. It also included all slate traffic from Delabole. The upward limit was £12,000 per annum, although if receipts were sufficient to pay $4_{1/2}$% on the share capital and 4% on the borrowed capital the rebate would be less (or cease) but could be revived. The Agreements allowed the LSWR to purchase the whole of the 4% Debenture stock, Debenture Bonds and Preference Stocks. In the event of these agreements the construction capital was reduced to £550,000, and £183,000 borrowing powers.

The first meeting of the North Cornwall Board of Directors was held at Bodmin on 17 October 1882. A Secretary, Edward Bellamy (London) was appointed at a salary of £400 p.a. The first general meeting was held at Bodmin (Town Arms Hotel) on 26 July 1883. In the Chair was Mr. John Tremayne (who was to hold this office until his death in 1901) of Heligan, St Austell. The meeting confirmed the directors to be: J. Tremayne, the Earl of Wharncliffe, Viscount Torrington, Charles Glyn Prideaux-Brune, Lewis Charles Foster, Charles Gurney, T. Martin, Sir W.W. Onslow, C. Bainbridge Rendle (Devonport), Capt. W. Teague and J. Oag. Lord Wharncliffe, elected deputy chairman, owned estates in the Camelford and Delabole areas, he and others were to be generous in their assignment of land to the NCR. James Oag Esq. of Thorndon, Ashwater served as a director for many years until his death in 1912 and his estate was still a large shareholder in 1922. Foster (Chairman after Tremayne died in 1901) was a director of Robbins, Foster, the Liskeard Bank. On the death of Lord Torrington in 1885, Lord Halsbury (formerly Sir H.S. Giffard) was elected. The Molesworth family were represented in the 1890s by Sir Lewis William, Bart. of Pencarrow, Bodmin and last, but not least the Prideaux-Brunes, Lords of the Manor at Padstow. Charles G. Prideaux-Brune was succeeded by Colonel C.R. Prideaux-Brune in 1908. At the first meeting Messrs. W.R. Galbraith and R.T. Church were confirmed as Consulting Engineers, J.V.H. Drew of Exeter appointed Surveyor and Robbins, Foster as Bankers together with Williams, Deacon & Co (London). Solicitors were to be: Goode, Shilton & Co (St Austell), Venning & Goldsmith (Plymouth) and Burchall & Co.

It was soon realized that financing the complete line from Halwill to Padstow was out of the question. Thus a separate Launceston & Halwill Section Act was obtained, receiving Royal Assent on 28 July 1884. Financial arrangements with the LSWR had been agreed on 18 May 1883. From now on the North Cornwall Railway would be made in several sections and it is useful here to note how it was eventually capitalized, quoting the Statement of Authorized Capital 30

Table 1.		North Cornwall Railway. Financial structure			
				Expenditure	
Section of Line	Main Act	Stocks & shares	Debenture stock (£)	(As noted to 31 Dec 1900)	Commencing rebate (£)
Launceston & Halwill	28 July 1884	150,000	50,000	200,000	2,600
Launceston & Delabole	21 July 1891	187,000	62,000	249,000	4,000
Delabole & Wadebridge	27 July 1893	150,000	50,000	200,000	3,230
Padstow line	20 July 1896	88,000	nil	88,000	2,650

June 1896 and after completion to Padstow in 1899 (see table 1).

The dual Role of the NCR and LSWR while the line was under construction, and up to 1922, needs explanation. The employment of the LSWR's engineering consultants Messrs Galbraith and Church ensured the big company's practices and standards throughout the building periods. The rental and leasing arrangements meant that the LSWR managed just about everything else from payment of Parish rates to staffing. The NCR directors could only suggest, complain, dispose of surplus land, and finally receive monetary payments from the LSWR, thus fixing dividends payable to their shareholders. Their involvement with the Padstow Harbour developments was more complicated, as will be seen.

Although references are made to 'standard' NCR buildings, it was really an LSWR design evolved during the 1870s (e.g. Morthoe 1874). Similarly the goods sheds and signal boxes followed current LSWR practice as did the permanent way materials. In all other respects the LSWR (and the NCR) had to comply with the 1845 Railway Clauses and Consolidation Act, the significant 1889 Act regarding train braking and signalling, and consequent government departmental (in this period the Board of Trade) regulation. The Southern Railway Company became the sole owner and operator from 1923.

Halwill to Launceston (1st Section) 1884-86

The first issue of shares for the Launceston to Halwill Section (15,000 shares of £10 each) was advertised in 1883 and raised over the next two years without much trouble. Interest was payable at 4% on fully paid-up shares. Several local notables subscribed, including J.C. Williams (Werrington Park, Launceston), Sir Harding S. Giffard, MP for Launceston, and the Duke of Bedford. Under the agreement with LSWR, as well as the 45% portion of the gross receipts there would be £3,000 per annum from the rebate arrangements. In addition the LSWR purchased £50,000 Debentures at 2½% premium and by virtue of this appointed a Director to the NCR Board. He was Arthur Mills Esq. of Efford Down, Bude. The terms for the Engineers were set at £350 per mile, 2½% commission on all buildings and 3% on the value of measured quantities of the works. The Surveyor was to be paid at £50 per mile. These were agreed at the October 1883 meeting and a contract for the construction was sealed with Messrs Curry & Reeve & Co (revised in May 1884). The following month the first Certificates amounting to £20,270 (part cash, part shares) were issued to them to start work. The shares, and those which followed over the next two years were for 'nominees'. It was usual for a contractor to borrow on them. On the Second Section, Curry & Reeve were paid on their Certificates by means of Lloyds Bonds, an alternative borrowing source.

Construction work on the Halwill to Launceston line started with ceremony on the afternoon of Monday 20 June 1884. The Chairman, Mr. John Tremayne, and several directors arrived on the 3.29pm train to be met by Mr. W.J. Harris of Winsford, Halwill, who gave land for the construction, The Mayor of Launceston, and Messrs. Church (Consulting Engineer), Manning (of Curry & Reeve), J. Oag and Charles Gurney (directors) amongst others. Everyone walked down to the field owned by Mr Harris where the junction was to be formed. The Rector of Halwill offered prayer and Mr Tremayne cut the first sod with an 'ordinary spade' the handle of which was covered with dark blue velvet. Mr Harris, too, tried his hand with it to the ringing cheers of the assembly. Stations were to be sited at Ashwater and Tower Hill (though Boldford Bridge, nearer Launceston, had been considered).

Curry & Reeve started work and by October an engine and a good quantity of plant were to hand. The Surveyor had established 6 miles of line in the Company's possession after the first 'notices to treat' were issued in the summer. 250 workmen were employed by December 1884, but by February some very wet weather had retarded the works and masonry was particularly behindhand. A further blow fell in April 1885 when it was reported that a major outbreak of smallpox made it difficult to keep the men together. More woe befell the project as September brought floods, and the River Tamar rose an incredible 15 ft in just a few hours, bringing some anxious moments at the new Tamar overbridge site at Launceston. Curry & Reeve asked for an advance of £10,500 on the security of their plant

An Adams Class '395' 0-6-0 waits at Halwill Junction's Up platform about 1905, with a goods train for Okehampton. The nameboard shows 'Halwill & Beaworthy' although it had been renamed in 1886. No. 442 was renumbered 0442 in 1907, 3442 in the 1930s and lasted until 1957 (latterly as BR No. 30578). The class shared goods workings with the 'Jubilee' 0-4-2s until the First World War, but one of them could still be seen at Okehampton up to the 1950s, and occasionally with engineer's trains on the North Cornwall or Bude lines. (Author's collection)

Tower Hill in the nineteen-twenties after the Down Loop had been removed, leaving the Up (as seen) as a single line. The nameboard is a new SR concrete and enamel-faced example, the station appearing to have received a face lift, including Southern Railway advertizing boards. Staff cottages beyond were provided by the LSWR and they remain in-situ although the station buildings were demolished after closure in 1966. The World War Two ammunition sidings were laid down in the field visible between the houses. (R.L. Goodman collection)

and a lien on all shares. The North Cornwall board approved in June 1885. It was repaid during the autumn, the contractors had now acquired nearly 10,000 shares. By then 4 miles of track were in and the girder bridge over the GWR at Launceston was in place. As often happened, a clergyman asked for a grant to open a Navvy Mission. This time the Rev. Mr Gough received £25. Presumably uplifted, the Navvies performance produced a line of rails 9 miles from Halwill, and Galbraith had no reason to complain of progress in February 1886.

In March 1886 the station at Ashwater was complete, including the house. The iron-framing for Launceston's engine shed, and the turntable, were on site. Curry's engine 'General Don' came down into Launceston with materials in May. Ashwater platforms, yard etc. were finished and Tower Hill nearly so in April. Launceston Station was being roofed (the subcontractor here was Burt, a local builder). Bridging works below Netherbridge (222 miles) were considerable. The River Tamar was crossed by a double span of six wrought iron mainplates, and the River Kensey needed three 28'0" masonry arches. The GWR's Launceston Branch was crossed by a single girder span of 31'0" on the skew. The contractor was quickly laying the Permanent Way by April, but ballasting was behind. The LSWR loaned two 'Lion' Class 0-6-0s (Nos. 102 'Lioness' and 108 'Ruby') to assist.

Unfortunately there were casualties on the works. A boy of 13, John Thomas Veale, died of injuries received at Tower Hill. He was employed to put tip chains on the wagons and to uncouple, and was walking between the horse and wagon when he caught his foot and fell within the rails. The wheels passed over him.

The station at Ashwater was sited where the road came down from the village, half a mile to the west, by Ash Mill. A small goods yard with two sidings, one to the goods shed and the other to an end loading dock, both fed from a shunting neck. This and the passing loop with two platforms, signal box and station buildings would be the general pattern for all the minor stations on the North Cornwall line. The other intermediate station, Tower Hill, was on a straight alignment where the Carey valley broadened out in Broadwoodwidger Parish. It was situated where the road from St Giles-in-the-Heath crossed the adjacent Carey and on to Broadwood and Lifton. Facilities were similar to Ashwater. Both layouts were to be altered over the years following, and Tower Hill would lose its down loop between the Wars. There had been a gradual depopulation in rural West Devon over the years due to the agricultural depression from the 1870s, but the new railway would contribute to a quiet revival. Access to the markets for dairy products and cattle, the establishment of fertilizer, seeds, and corn stores provided the stimulant.

The site for the narrow (4'8½") gauge station at Launceston was to lay alongside the GWR terminus about 100 yards to the south. There could be no connection to the existing 7'0¼" in spite of the authorisation for such a link (Line No.4). The GWR was narrowed in 1892 and a connection was considered in 1910, but it was wartime pressures in 1943 which eventually warranted a junction. With the intention of forging westward the new line hugged the foot of the steep hill below the town and castle. At first the contractor ramped up a temporary line from the west of St Thomas's Road to carry spoil from the Priory side to earthworks at Ridgegrove. It would appear that the cutting at the Priory (towards New Mills) and the bridge to carry St Thomas's Road was undertaken by 1886. Recent finds by the Launceston Steam Railway under this ramp (near their engine shed) include a gauge rod and contractor's rail. The road overbridge was formed on a 1 in 12 gradient. This and the sharp bend into the station caused considerable criticism from the local Board of Health, so the parapet was modified.

The twin platforms with their loops were surprisingly short and not subsequently lengthened as others. The standard style of signal box of the 1880s, and a waiting shed were situated on the up platform, while a medium sized, but not 'standard' station building was erected in stone blocks and decorative quoining, with a slate roof. To cover passengers, a wide awn-

Launceston Castle dominates the town and the two railways in the valley below at Newport. In this early view the GWR station is in the foreground and the LSWR (North Cornwall Railway) station platforms and buildings beyond. Extreme left is the engine shed slightly masked by the GWR water tank - the 49'10" turntable and the goods shed. In the centre are the enlarged cattle pens, flanked by a traders' store. The prominent villa (above the brake van - right) was the Station Master's house, and the steep path to the town may be seen leading up behind the quarried faces. (R.L. Goodman collection)

ing fronted this building. The footbridge beyond the country end of the platforms was a rather steep affair, another cause for local criticism, due to its roundness.

With an eye on prospective live cattle traffic a set of pens and a side loading dock was placed against No.2 siding (it was extended in 1891). Between the pens and the down platform was a short end-loading dock. Both these sidings led directly into a long shunting neck on the down side of the single line from Tower Hill, paralleled by a second siding. Engine requirements were satisfied by a short siding with coal stage, shed, and a 50'0" turntable. More substantial was the stone goods shed with its slate roof. Two more sidings fed this area, one within the shed. Some excavation of the hillside seems to have occurred at this time (1880s) to accommodate some stores, a mill, and later a cart weighbridge. The quarry beyond pre-dated the railway, but undoubtedly stone was taken for its construction.

Just where the stopblocks stood at Launceston from 1886 is not clear. It is known that the Launceston Gas Co. was provided with a loading bank soon after, just west of St Thomas's Road Bridge. Trood, the local agricultural and seed merchant, asked for an extension into his new premises in July 1892. The LSWR provided materials and the NCR did the work at a cost of £300, probably using the contractors currently extending the line to Tresmeer. A formal agreement was concluded in 1893. The connection to these sidings was resited in 1904. Opposite, the LSWR, in due course,

built eight dwellings for its employees.

Colonel J.H. Rich RE made an inspection of this 'First Section' of the North Cornwall Railway on 15th July 1886. His train left Launceston at 9.30 am, preceded slowly by two engines to test the bridges. He noted in his subsequent report that the 13 1/2 miles were wide enough for a double line, but it would be single line signalled by Train Staff and block telegraph. The LSWR would work the line, and the permanent way was to

that Company's standard (at that time 82lb/yard double-headed steel rails, 24-foot lengths). All the 44 bridges were substantially constructed. Most were built entirely of dressed stone blocks, but some were of wrought iron rolled beams or girders. Interestingly, as a condition for public opening, Col. Rich asked the LSWR to provide a turntable at Halwill within four months, although one had been provided at Launceston. Until that time trains would have to be restricted to 25 mph and stop at all stations. He

Opening day at Launceston of the 'First Section' of the North Cornwall Railway, Tuesday 20th July 1886. The Directors' train stands in the Down platform waiting to return to Exeter. The Adams '448' Class 4-4-0 No. 488 appears to have been specially chosen for the event, although its driving wheels would not normally be regarded as suitable for local gradients. On the left is Beattie 2-4-0 No. 0195, rebuilt as a tender engine from a tank, likely to be Launceston's own motive power. Other interesting items are the pw 'pump' trolley (left) and the broad gauge GWR carriages (right). (R.C. Riley collection)

Launceston Square in the 1930s; it was well above the two railway stations in the Kensey Valley but buses were available at times. The White Hart Hotel ran its own, first a horse bus, later a motor vehicle. Private motoring was not a serious competitor until the 1950s as this scene suggests, and although the town has been expensively by-passed, there is little room in its narrow streets to linger or park. (Firth Photo)

arrival at Launceston, the engine was turned and the train left at 11.0am for Halwill. NCR directors were aboard this time, including Chairman J.C. Tremayne, and the Mayor of Launceston (Dr. Andrews) and Corporation. At each of the stations the train stopped - and at Boldford Bridge an old man fired a gun! At Halwill Mr. J. Oag declared the line open. Back to Launceston about noon, the train was met by a vast throng, and more speeches were heard. A procession formed up and, led by the Devon Volunteer Engineers Band, climbed the stiff hill to the White Hart Hotel and Central Rooms for Luncheon and still more speeches. This was not all for the day, as a 'Fancy Fayre' was staged on the Castle Green and in the evening a ball was held in a marquee and the Castle illuminated. Money raised from these events (and on the Wednesday) was used to build a new Town Hall. The direct narrow (standard) gauge to the east of the country was welcomed. It was said at the luncheon "that recently at Lydford, 160 cattle from Launceston to Cheshire had to be changed from the broad gauge to the narrow gauge, taking an hour causing great difficulty and delay."

also stipulated that rails should be moved so that the steps would not be more than 2'3" from the edges of the platforms in stations (this would appear to refer to the dimension from rail to platform wall). The home signals at Ashwater and Tower Hill should be raised so as to be seen from the signal cabins, and clocks should be provided in those cabins, said Col. Rich. The turntable at Halwill was installed (for £170) and the speed restriction removed in February 1887. The actual line of rails sanctioned for public trains ran from the junction with the Holsworthy Branch at 209m 71ch to a point under St Thomas's

Road Bridge at 223m 42ch (i.e. 13m 51ch). Under an agreement made with the LSWR on 3 March 1888 a side line at Halwill extended 17 chains from the 'junction' (in reality end-on) into the bay platform. The NCR paid £1 per annum for the use of the LSWR land.

The opening day was set for Tuesday 20 July 1886. The LSWR provided a decorated Adams '445' Class 4-4-0, No 448, for the Officers' special which left Exeter at 8.45 am. On board were Arthur Mills MP (director), C. Scotter (General Manager), Messrs Gardner (Asst. Superintendent), White (Divisional Superintendent), Fisher (Engineer), also the Mayor of Exeter. On

Curry & Reeve maintained the permanent way for the first year after opening, the LSWR paying £14,000 to the NCR towards the cost. The public train service commenced on 21 July 1886. Trains left Halwill at 10.33am, 12,25pm, 3.25pm, 4.52pm and 9.00pm; at first the Launceston line was treated as a branch off Okehampton to Holsworthy. The latter three departures connected through from the

The North Cornwall Railway entered Launceston through the Kensey Valley from the east and St. Stephen's Church stands on the skyline to the north, providing the background to Bullied Pacific No. 34030 'Watersmeet' coming through the cutting at Ridgegrove with the 11.00 a.m. Padstow to Waterloo 'ACE' on 22nd August 1964. The coaches are in two sets of BR Mark Is supplied by the Southern Region. Discernible through the smoke and steam are the ex-GWR shed (left, centre) and the 1943 inter-company spur joining the SR to the GWR (right). (P.W. Gray)

Waterloo to Plymouth/Devonport trains at 9.00am, 11.00am and 2.30pm. Upwards the local trains left at 7.50am, 10.20am, 1.50pm, 2.50pm and 6.45pm, the first four connecting to Waterloo. An additional 8.24am from Okehampton was put on from 1887, a coach attached to the goods train on the first Wednesday of each month, to serve Launceston Market. An early goods left Launceston at 5.45am with wagons for Devonport and Exeter, and another at 3.30pm to Okehampton. During the next few years Nine Elms/Launceston 'road boxes' were running overnight affording delivery of merchandise, but it was not until the turn of the century that passengers were given through coaches from and to Waterloo. Excursionists soon appeared, encouraged by the LSWR's fares offers, and the Padstow coach-and-two was arriving at Launceston at 1.40pm and departing at 4.15pm, going via Camelford. Mr. Downing, of Launceston, organised an excursion to London on 19 October 1886 at a 12/- fare.

Over the next eighty years Launceston remained a valuable source of traffic acting as a railhead to a wide area, especially to the south parishes, North Hill, Lewannick, Alternun (as far out as Bolventor) and northwards to Boyton, Yeolmbridge, North Petherwin and North Tamerton.

A dividend of 1 1/2% on Ordinary shares was paid in 1887. The rentals amounted to £868.2.4 in August, and it would rise to £2,426 (final half-year payment) based on the 45% gross receipts and the full annual rebate of £3,000 by 1896. The 'Halwill Line' remained separate until the 1913 recapitalization. As well as the Debenture stocks, valued at £50,000, the Ordinary stocks (£10) were divided into halves at 4% Preferred and a further 2% Deferred on the £150,000 capital.

Launceston to Delabole (2nd Section) 1890-93

Contemplation of the remainder of the route to Padstow followed the establishment of the '1st Section' in 1884. The existing NCR powers would expire in 1885. Negotiation began with the LSWR and all seemed well, extra time being obtained in 1885. Relations with the GWR over the Bodmin & Wadebridge, as already mentioned, caused the LSWR to tread warily. The GWR was connected to the B & WR at Boscarne Junction from 3 September 1888, with GWR running powers into Wadebridge. Agreement between the two main line companies in 1884 had delineated the areas which they might, or might not, extend. Thus the LSWR, although actually supporting the NCR did not, as might be expected, absorb the Halwill to Launceston line. In fact the NCR remained a separate company until 1922, probably (given its desire to extend to Truro in the 1890s, and even in this century) to avert strain with the GWR.

With these considerations and a realization that available local investment would be thin, the LSWR decided that another 'separate undertaking' from Launceston to Delabole should be formed. Extra time on the original Act was obtained in 1888. The LSWR came to an agreement with the NCR on 13 October 1891 to lease and work this section at an annual rental of £4,750 which would give a 3 1/2% return on the £250,000 capital construction costs. A sum of £4,000 was to be awarded as the rebate. The £187,000 Share Capital was issued, together with Debentures to cover a further £62,000 (which could be borrowed). The NCR's Liskeard Bankers agreed to take £100,000 and the contractors (Curry & Reeve) were issued (by the NCR) with Lloyds Bonds affixed to previous Engineer's Certificates, on which they could borrow. The necessary Act was obtained on 21 July 1891. Work (Railway No.2) had already started before March 1890 under original powers, material having been taken from the Priory area to the Ridgegrove bridge site in 1885.

Launceston to Tresmeer 1890-92

Curry & Reeve assembled plant at Launceston, with station works subcontracted again to Burt of Launceston. As has been seen, the line was already in place to the west of St. Thomas's Road at Launceston, serving the Gas Works. The course thereafter was to follow the Kensey Valley for nearly 6 miles to Lanzion (below Tresmeer). From there a rather tortuous route had been surveyed to climb the 400 feet to reach the main road from Statton to Wadebridge at Otterham, and pass over a summit 860 feet above sea level at Trewanion in Lesnewth Parish. The Atlantic Ocean, only a few miles to the west at this

point, is in full view. This high elevation was maintained through Melorne (Camelford).

Staking out commenced in March 1890 with surveyor Drew on the ground buying the freehold, but there was no earth moving until November. "Much delay was being caused in the acquisition of land for the Launceston and Delabole by the exorbitant demands of landowners for accommodation works ... delay ... numerous stops for compulsory possession". It is interesting to note that in 1892 Miss Gurney of Treybursye was awarded only £789.5s. by the Board of Trade's arbitration, instead of her claim for £1,998.2s.6d.

By the turn of the year a line of rails ran through two fields but, needless to say, were in a 'veritable quagmire' due to the recent rains. During the frosty month of February 1891 work was going on in 5 cuttings with 200 men. The workforce, largely itinerant navvies, fluctuated in numbers throughout the NCR's construction. A proportion of local men were employed, but the heavy earth moving was the province of the navvy. There was a shortage of 'lodgings' at this time, but many navvies built their own shanties, some housing their families. The Great Blizzard of March 1891(it was reported snow was at rooftop level in Camelford) must have had its effect. The Engineer, Baron, reported slack progress in July and, although the number of men had increased to 445, only a quarter mile of permanent way was down on works extending 9 3/4 miles. A vast pile of timber and rails was accumulating at Launceston and, with great difficulty, the contractor's engine 'General Don' was transferred by road to Splatt. The Cornish & Devon Post described the scene. 'On Monday "General Don", which had

Reputed to be the first day of passenger services from Launceston to Tresmeer on 28th July 1892. Launceston's Mayor Treleaven arrived on this train (a special) and returned with it (by now a public train) at 10.15 a.m. The engine is an Adams '395' 0-6-0 and the four-wheeled coaches date from 1876. The new 80 lb/yard steel rails in 30 ft. lengths were the LSWR's standard at the time, while the platform heights were set at 2'6", obviating the necessity for lower footboards (still required at old stations set at 1'7"). (W. Weeks)

A holiday extra train in the 1960s, hauled by 'N' Class No. 31843, climbing away from Tresmeer and crossing the high embankment at Treneglos on the way to Otterham. The embankment was substituted for a viaduct proposed here in 1893. Between the rails may be noticed the track monuments, ie reference points for the upkeep of the alignment and superelevation (or cant). Much of the work was done by the Southern Railway's Western Division to improve the latter in the 1930s. (E.S.Youldon collection)

been repainted and had its name relettered by Mr. John Hawkins of Launceston, was moved from Launceston to Splatt (Tresmeer) by road. The flanges of the wheels had been packed level by means of an iron tyre, tightened and wedged with wood and iron. A traction engine of Pearce's (Tavistock) did the hauling, steam, however, being also used by "General Don". A difficulty occurred at St. Thomas's Road from the Station Road turning, the weight of the locomotive (20 tons) forcing out the wedges, something often repeated before the end of the journey, the whole proceedings watched by a large crowd.'

It is not always clear today why sites for stations were thus chosen. The North Cornwall was showered with letters and 'memorials' from individuals and local authorities. A public road intersection obviously called the tune, and at Badharlach Bridge a Mr. Simcol was willing to give land. The station there became Egloskerry. A second station might have been called Splatt but of course Tresmeer, a mile to the south, sounded better. Two miles of land were offered on 'favourable terms if a station was fixed at Tinks House' in October 1891 and the following month a station was ordered to be built at Melorne. Neither

of these names was adopted. The former was to become Otterham ('Boscastle Road' had been suggested), some way off but in that Parish, and the latter Camelford. Camelford itself was 1 1/2 miles to the south, but roads radiated to Boscastle (4 miles) and Tintagel (5 miles). The alleged weakness, or lack of, stone resulted in all the masonry bridges being brick-arched. The mill leat aqueduct, half a mile beyond Launceston, built with stone obtained from Langdon's Quarry at Truscott, was a masonry arch supporting a cast iron trough. The line kept to the north side of the River Kensey, but crossed it four times below the steep escarpment of Red Down and Tregear at Egloskerry. Two miles of permanent way were down in September 1891. More and more men were brought in, some loaned by the LSWR, the numbers rising to 616 in March 1892. An accident occurred by blasting at Dyers Cutting (Splatt) in November when a man called Bloomfield received a blowback in the face after recharging a hole, and a G. Harvey was killed by a material fall in Red Down cutting. By April 1892 5 miles were laid.

Trouble with subcontractors forced Curry & Reeve to build Tresmeer station themselves. Nearly all the bridges

were complete thus far in May 1892, and a June opening was in prospect. However it was late July before the Board of Trade's Inspecting Officer was invited to approve the works and signalling. A train with a 'heavy luggage engine to test several wrought iron underbridges was provided for him, and his party, which left Launceston at 9.30am on 27 July.'

That evening Colonel H.A. Yorke, RE penned a long document to the BoT. The line he inspected was 7m 69ch from the 13m 55ch point at Launceston (based on the installed mileposts this appears to have been from 223m 46ch to 231m 35ch). It would be worked by Train Staff and Ticket, he wrote, with crossing places at Egloskerry and Tresmeer. New track material for the permanent way was 80lb/yd double-headed steel rails in 30 ft lengths, and laid in 40 lb chairs. He described 23 bridges with special mention of the mill leat in cast iron though 'somewhat peculiar design, it shows no sign of leakage'. There was a public level crossing at Egloskerry, hand-operated and properly interlocked. (Notice that this station was fully signalled as a passing loop, but could not be opened at this time). Tresmeer had 300-foot long platforms at 2'6" height. Special working was ob-

Currie & Reeve's navvys were working in large numbers on the construction of the line during the winter of 1892-93, reaching Otterham by December. Situated on the Bideford to Wadebridge main road on the edge of the escarpment of Wilsey Down and nearly 900 feet above sea level, this was a very exposed place. Trees were later planted to afford some shelter from the Atlantic gales. Although a goods shed was not provided, a store was eventually built, coming in very usful for the rabbit trade which burgeoned in the 1930s and 1940s. This was said to be more valuable than cattle (or even passengers!) at some stations. (L&GRP)

served by Col. Yorke at Launceston and Tresmeer. At Launceston up trains could depart from the Down platform to 'save a good deal of shunting'. This facility was abolished in later years. The signalling at Tresmeer also allowed up trains to start from the Down, although an original LSWR plan omits reference to this. The signal box was on the Down platform: 17 (1 push and pull) including 4 spare levers. As construction work was proceeding towards Otterham by then, a catchpoint was provided at the west end of Tresmeer to protect the new passenger trains. Egloskerry Signal Box frame also had 17 levers (1 push and pull). One lever locked the crossing gates, and three were spare. Once again there were strictures regarding tender-first working. As there was to be a turntable at Delabole, 12 miles further on, Col.

Yorke suggested allowing such a practice for the time being, from or to Launceston, but at a maximum speed of 25 mph. Otherwise, provided the Gas Works siding received proper stopblocks, and Egloskerry gates discs and handlamps, passenger working would commence to Tresmeer.

Opening day, without much ceremony, was Thursday 28 July 1892 to coincide with the Launceston Agriculture Society's Show. The new Station Master at Tresmeer was Mr W Stacey, lately chief booking clerk at Okehampton. A special train left Launceston with Mayor and Mrs Treleaven aboard. It returned as a normal service at 10.15am with 250 passengers 'many of them never having sat behind an engine before' as the local press put it. As stated before, Egloskerry was not yet open. The

erring subcontractor (Burt) had not been discharged, and even Tresmeer's goods shed was unfinished. Both were built of red brick (though to standard design), the only ones so treated on the NCR. Egloskerry was opened on 3 October 1892. The North Cornwall Coach Co's conveyance serving Wadebridge and Newquay was diverted to Tresmeer, via Launceston. In August there were complaints of insufficient accommodation on the coach, though a separate daily omnibus service was running to Tintagel and Boscastle. From this opening the LSWR started paying a proportional rental of £2,750, with £4,000 of the allotted rebate already imbursed to the NCR.

Launceston's layout was altered for the opening insofar as the Down loop at St Thomas's Road end was connected to the signal box and protected by signals. A ground frame, worked on the push-and-pull principle and signal box-released, now controlled the Gas Works siding. Egloskerry's up side yard was of simple design, not even having a goods shed or shunt neck, though a cattle pen was provided. Tresmeer's layout of two sidings followed the standard layout, and on the down side here. A nasty accident happened the following December when John Skinner, aged 34 (a 'travelling guard') from Exeter, was knocked off the footboard of his shunted van as it passed the goods shed stanchions. Four wagons passed over him, and he died of his injuries in Launceston Hospital. Six cottages were erected by the LSWR for its employees, to the east of the station, but there was no water supply, except by delivery churn. Another 'might have been' railway affecting the NCR was the Liskeard & Caradon's authorised extension from Sargent's corner, just south of their existing line to Kilmar Tor, to Trewint Marsh. Work started on 6 May 1884 but reached only 1½ miles, to Rushyford Gate. The avowed goal was either Camelford or Boscastle, presumably as an outlet for the mineral traffic from Caradon. In July 1884 the L & CR obtained an Act, however, to build a line from Trewint Marsh to Launceston. It would have trailed into the NCR towards Launceston close to the Priory. The South Caradon Mine closed in 1885, but as late as 1892 the L & CR requested the NCR to work its proposed Launceston line for 15% of the gross receipts.

Tresmeer to Camelford 1892
The navvies building the line were housed in an encampment at Splatt - reference has been found to a Mission Room there - but by November 1892 the Launceston Weekly News was moved to report 'Otterham Station is very exposed, no houses within one mile. Navvies with wives and children living in huts, some single men in lodgings'. Construction work was following acquisition of land in the

This engine was once owned by Currie & Reeve while they held successive contracts to build the North Cornwall Railway from Launceston to Padstow. It was named 'General Don' after purchase from the Jersey Railways, and in 1901 passed into the hands of the Weston, Clevedon and Portshead Railway where it is seen at Clevedon in 1937. (Author's Collection)

Open well before the railway came anywhere near was the Wellington Hotel at Boscastle. After 1895 Brendons (of Bude) incorporated their coach-and-four into a road/rail summer tourist route, operating with LSWR encouragement, from Ilfracombe to Newquay. Notable visitors to the Wellington were the nobility, Sir Henry Irving, the Rowntree and Cadbury families and, in World War Two, Wing Commander Guy Gibson VC. (RIC)

summer of 1892 as far as Delabole; excavations were taking place in all the cuttings during September and October and Otterham station had been started. Argument as to the naming of the next station was resolved by the Directors when Camelford (for Tintagel and Boscastle) was chosen for Melorn. Considerable diversion of the main road at Otterham station with a sharp turn at the bridge, for Hallworthy, was authorised in 1891.

An embankment instead of a proposed viaduct at Treneglos, where the Scarsick tributary flows in a deep defile northwards to the River Ottery, required extra land, purchased in May 1891. Lack of suitable stone and a hard foundation was the reason cited.

Earthworks were considerable anyway, because the line needed cuttings and embankments to claw its way round the north side of Wilsey Down on 25 and 30 chain reversing curves. This was in order to obtain a ruling gradient of 1 in 73, to climb from 550ft to 860ft, the summit of the North Cornwall Line at Trewannion a mile beyond Otterham. Overbridges, as before, were brick-arched masonry structures. These uplands on the edge of Davidstow Parish are bare of trees and exposed to whatever weather the Atlantic Ocean produces, be it blinding sunshine to gales, mist and rain. Rainfall here is the heaviest in Cornwall. The line fell slightly towards Camelford station (750ft) and briefly accompa-

nied the Camel headwater by Worthy Vale and the legendary Slaughterbridge.

The name Delabole strictly belonged to the famous slate quarry. The 1890-period hamlets were Medrose and Pengelly; the original line would have bisected both their two streets, but the deviation allowed under the 1891 Act brought the line nearer the quarry, and only Pengelly suffered some demolitions. Apparently there had been lengthy negotiations with the Slate Company to build so near to the quarry perimeter, and the latter conveyed land to the NCR, free of charge. Possession of land was taken for the deviation in mid-1892. Progress was slow, and neither Camelford or Delabole had been started by December. Concentrating east of Camelford, the number of men employed gradually increased from 602 in December to 768 in April (1893). There was trouble in June 1893 when a navvy was charged with seriously assaulting the wife of a missionary following her visit to a lodging hut. Curry & Reeve were going all out in this difficult section and by July 7 out of the 9 miles to Camelford were laid. With a gang of platelayers from the LSWR, 852 men were working, thus encouraging a Directors' request for a BoT inspection for August 1893. Otterham was nearly complete, and track laid in to Camelford with the signal and telegraph work well in hand. However when Major Marindin RE came down he noted that the line from Camelford to Delabole was 'unfinished and quite unfit for traffic'.

He arrived in a special train on Tuesday 8 August with Messrs J.B. Fisher of the NCR, and Church the

The original awning over the Up platform at Camelford's 1893 station was replaced by a more substantial version by 1900, Camelford being regarded as the railhead for Tintagel and Boscastle and thus uniquely endowed for a wayside station. No further luxuries were provided and passengers had to use the adjacent road bridge or (unofficially) the foot crossings at the platform ends, lit on their way at night by glimmering oil lamps. 31836 waits with the 11.26 am goods from Okehampton in the Down loop at Camelford on 24th August 1960. (R.A.Lumber)

Two Members of Parliament sat for Camelford before the 1832 Reform Act, and the Town Hall dates from 1805, a gift of the Duke of Bedford. There were associations with the Pitt family, but by 1893 when the North Cornwall opened its station at Melorne a mile and a half to the west, the former borough had declined. The new railway brought benefits in the shape of tourists - also foodstuffs and merchandise for local shops from London and the Midlands - and prosperity returned. (Commercial Postcard)

LSWR's Engineer. Tresmeer to Camelford was, he reported, 9 miles and 26 chains (apparently 231m. 35ch. to 240m. 61ch.). Steeper gradients resulted from the substitution of a 90ft embankment for the 110ft viaduct at Treneglos. The line needed lifting and straightening at several places, especially near this embankment. Camelford lacked its veranda and was 'unfinished'. The catchpoints at Tresmeer should be moved to Camelford, he said, and the points and crossings at the latter connected up! Otterham signal box had 13 levers (4 spare), Camelford 17 and 4 spare. Signalling was by Train Staff and Ticket, and Block Telegraph.

The new station at Otterham and Camelford again followed the LSWR's format and design. The SM's house and office buildings were on the up side at both, but Camelford, as befitted its status, received a veranda or awning. In local stone construction, the light grey colour contrasted with the red bricks used at Egloskerry and Tresmeer. Otterham was unusual for the NCR in not having a goods shed, a strange omission, though in due course its Up side yard filled out with other stores and sheds. Adequate siding lengths were laid, also at Camelford where more pointwork connected to the Down loop. Along with Delabole and St Kew Highway the pressures of working the single lines and longer holiday trains caused the LSWR to lengthen the Camelford loops in 1911.

The opening day was set for Monday 14 August 1893. The Cornish & Devon Post's headlines included 'Great Rejoicings' and it appears that the weather that day was hot. Many of the thousand people who came from far and wide sought out cool hedgerows to await the opening ceremony. An excursion train from Okehampton took up 200 passengers from Launceston alone at 9.30am. The Director's special followed, arriving at Camelford at 1.15pm. It was met by Sir William Onslow and Colonel Hawker, the latter presenting an illuminated address to Mr. Tremayne the NCR Chairman. A large marquee had been erected in a field down the road to Camelford carrying a large board saying 'Success to Agriculture'. The procession of Directors, LSWR officials and members of the Camelford Committee proceeded thence behind the Holsworthy Military and the Camelford Volunteer Bands. Long speeches followed, during which Drew, the NCR Surveyor, alluded to the acquisition of land which, he said, was not so onerous as getting accommodation works. If he had given away on the Launceston to Camelford section costs would have increased 30%. In a sports field 1,200 school children were each given a bun and a bottle of ginger beer and a medal bearing the Cornish motto 'One and All'. At the Pain's firework display later, the illuminated motto was 'Prosperity to Camelford'.

Passenger trains left Camelford at 7.20am, 9.40am, 1.10pm, 3.05pm and 5.40pm, running to Okehampton, all except the last connecting directly to Waterloo. The latter also ran on Sundays from December 1894. Downwards the 5.50am Waterloo connection arrived at 2.26pm, the 9.00am at 5.00pm, the 11.00am at 6.16pm, and the 3.00pm at 10.30pm. There was also a 9.05am from Exeter Queen St (10.19am from Okehampton) coming into Camelford at 12.18pm. The midnight goods from Exeter, limited to 25 wagons from Yeoford as it carried mails and newspapers and calves, reaching Camelford at 6.50am, commenced in December 1894, also running on Sundays. Remarkably, the overnight Nine Elms to Plymouth 'fast' goods dropped off wagons to the 5.00am Exeter, which in turn left them at Meldon Junction for the second goods for delivery at Camelford at 10.52am. Wagons for London left Camelford at 1.50pm, and there was a second goods from there at 7.25pm.

Delabole Slate Quarry Before 1893

At the time of the North Cornwall's arrival at Delabole in late 1893, the centuries-old quarry workings covered an area of 25 acres. Five individual working faces had been combined from the 1830s to create one pit, then about 400 feet deep. The Old Delabole Slate Quarry Company gradually dominated by acquiring leases and freeholds. Upwards of 500 men and boys were employed in the quarry and the flooring yard. The principal outlet for finished slates up to 1893 was Port Gaverne, just to the north of Port Isaac and five miles away. Here sailing vessels were loaded, per tide, by women. The Slate Co. would have transported their products to Rock, opposite Padstow, by a proposed narrow gauge tramway. Money for this, however, was diverted to improve the 'Slate Road' and port conditions at Port Gaverne.

Farmers carted the slate to Port Gaverne, also to Bodmin Road GWR, though to Launceston when the broad gauge branch opened in 1865. The North Cornwall Co obtained a guarantee from the Slate Co. in 1884 to send slates and bricks by standard gauge to Plymouth, Stonehouse (where they had a yard) Devonport, and also to Exeter, at a maximum rate of 6s.8d. a ton. With the opening to Launceston (NCR) in 1886 many tons were diverted thence, and the Slate Co., only too anxious to forward their products to all parts of the country, as we have seen, supplied land free at Delabole for the NCR's forthcoming route. Within the quarry premises 1'11" replaced a 3'0" gauge system from 1890. Originally worked by horses, as the sidings spread it was soon served by 0-4-0 saddle tank locomotives.

The commemorative medal issued by the North Cornwall Railway Company on the opening of its line from Tresmeer to Camelford in August 1893. (Author's Collection)

The western side of Delabole Quarry as new workings are underway not far from the railway goods yard. The church on the horizon is St. Johns C of E opened in 1860 and a latecomer in a village strongly Methodist in persuasion. (Cornwall Record Office)

route below Camelford was, again, most tortuous; three curves of 30 (lefthand), 30 (right) and 30 (left) radii and a final sweep at 50 chains around the north side of the quarry, brought the line into a straight for Delabole's platforms. The gradients, not so severe here, nevertheless fell at 1 in 74 round this last curve. Achieving this required continuous cuttings and embankments.

Col. Hutchinson RE arrived to inspect the work (he had found unfinished the previous August), on 17 October 1893. The length to be inspected was 2m 29ch from Camelford (exclusive) to Delabole. The latterday mileage system appears to place this between 240m 61ch and 243m 10ch. The embankment at Delabole was 66 feet high and four overbridges, (Camelford Station and Delabole Barton) were brick-arched masonry as before. There was one section: Camelford to Delabole worked by Train Staff and Ticket and with Absolute Block Telegraph. Delabole signal box had 17 levers with 4 spare. Col. Hutchinson required the protective catchpoint to be placed at Delabole (work was continuing towards Port Isaac Road) and he had no objection to Up trains starting from Delabole's Down platforms, provided No. 12 points (trailing from the yard) received locking appliances and a starting signal was provided.

Opening day was declared for Wednesday 18 October 1893. A public train left Launceston at 11.20am, two

Camelford to Delabole 1892-3

A large embankment at Delabole (Medrose), on to the very edge of the quarry, still required 2,000 cubic yards of fill in September 1893. The Contrac-

tors had run short of rail chairs, thus 50 chains of route and half Delabole's yard remained to be done. The turntable had not arrived from the makers, though it had been promised. The

The industrial face of Delabole in LSWR days showing in the background the cableways (steam powered), slate splitting sheds and a raft of wagons for loading. The lamp room, with oil barrels within, shares the Down platform with the Station Master's house; the rear side has the wash house and WC (left) in his open courtyards, and the Gentlemen's' WC court opening on to the platform. (Cornwall Record Office)

The Wharncliffe Hotel in Tevena village (Tintagel) was named after the 1st Earl, a land-owner in the area and Deputy Chairman of the North Cornwall Railway. The Fry family established their own hotel here and developed a valuable transport business to Camelford in conjunction with the LSWR. (Commercial Postcard)

engines hauling 11 coaches. This was followed by the Directors' train ('two very handsome saloons and carriages, and several 1st Class carriages') and a lot of noise was created at Delabole by the letting off of fog signals. The celebrations that day were extensive and a general holiday was declared. A procession of the local committee, quarrymen and 'all Male Adults of the villages', headed by the Delabole Brass Band, marched from Lower Pengelly to a field near the new station. A free luncheon was provided for them (but for the women and children, a free tea in the afternoon). For the Directors, on the arrival of their train at 1.00pm, there was an address by the Chairman (Mr Edward Allen) of the Old Delabole Slate Company, a short visit to the quarry, and luncheon in the Co-

operative Hall. For the enjoyment of all, the Plymouth Royal Marines Band played during the afternoon, while Athletic Sports took place. A Grand Concert at 6pm (2/-, 1/- and 6d) and fireworks at 8.30pm completed the day's jollifications. The North Cornwall Railway train service terminated here for nearly two years. Although the line to Port Isaac Road was inspected on 1 August 1894 the LSWR, working the NCR, would not open it.

Delabole was provided with a comparatively large goods yard in anticipation of the increased slate traffic. In addition to the engine shed and turntable siding, another served the cattle pen and goods shed, both joining and running northward into a long shunting neck. As at Camelford crossovers joined the down loop in

both directions. In due course more sidings and a loading bank were added on the south east side as the slate trade grew in volume.

Speeds were still limited at first to 25 mph from Launceston to Tresmeer, and 20mph thence to Delabole. In the summer of 1894 the seed of future holiday expresses was sown when the connection from the 1.00pm Waterloo, the 6.00pm from Okehampton, called only at Launceston, Tresmeer and Camelford, with a Delabole arrival at 7.55pm. An 11.45am from Delabole provided a similar up service. The North Cornwall Coach service started running via Camelford to Newquay on 2 July 1894.

The LSWR authorised installation of Train Tablet signalling in early 1894 the whole way from Meldon Junction to Delabole (and to Holsworthy), but it was some years before conversion from Staff and Ticket was completed. There was expenditure on cottages for its employees at Tower Hill, Egloskerry and Otterham. At a cost of £9.12s.0d. shrubs were planted at Otterham, Camelford and Delabole.

In November 1893 250 Delabole quarrymen and friends took a train to Launceston on a Saturday afternoon, returning at a late hour. As well as the awe-inspiring castle, they were surprised at the size of the shopping area at Launceston. Launceston traders, however, were complaining that the cheap fare from Delabole was 2s. 5d. while from more distant Holsworthy and Tavistock it was only 2s.0d.

The rental and rebate of this '2nd Section' was superseded from 26 July 1894. The existing arrangement was dropped in favour of a 999-year Lease by the LSWR at £8,750 annually, pay-

Below Port Isaac Road the North Cornwall Railway descended from the high ground, through a tunnel at Trelill, towards the Allen Valley in the south. Near Trewarne, south of Port Isaac Road, on the afternoon of 12th July 1961, passed the 1.00pm Padstow to Okehampton 'Perishables'. Behind U1 Class No. 31902 were a Maunsell 3rd Open, a local 'P' Set, the returning newspaper van (for Clapham Junction) and a 'Vanfit' for the overnight 'Tavvy' goods to Nine Elms. The U1s stayed only one summer - their substitution for the last of the T9s not popular with local enginemen. (R.C.Riley)

Although a 'standard' type of LSWR building the otherwise rather dour appearance was softened by overhanging eaves at Port Isaac Road (and St. Kew). The 1880s style of signal box again denotes the LSWR influences and the SR produced an enamel nameboard, but the date is 5th May 1966. Diesel railcars (this one is single car No. W55026 on the 1045 Halwill to Wadebridge) introduced by British Railways would not be able to save the line from closure the following October. (R.A. Lumber)

able half-yearly. 3½% was paid on the Deferred and Ordinary Shares of the 'Launceston & Delabole' until the 1913 re-arrangements.

Delabole to Wadebridge (3rd Section) 1893-95

The NCR Act of 27 July 1891 included extra time for all unfinished works, and excluded the Pendevy eastern spur toward Bodmin. For this '3rd Section' agreement was concluded with the LSWR for working and finance, by respective Acts of 1 May and 27 July 1893. The St Kew tunnel (Trelill) could be constructed as for a single line instead of double (nearly all the NCR overbridges were for double line, but many fewer under the railway). The rebate for this Section was to be up to £3,250 annually from the LSWR, payable half-yearly. The ordinary share capital of £150,000 was confirmed. In the event over half of this was issued to the Contractors (Curry & Reeve again) in the form of Lloyds Bonds payable to their nominees, the rest taken up locally. £50,000 could be borrowed and the LSWR took £45,000 of this as 3½% Debentures ('Wadebridge Guaranteed'). It would appear that for this Section the LSWR applied the 1882 arrangement for work, i.e. for 55% of gross receipts, the NCR receiving the balance. In after years 3% was paid on the ordinary shares. A further Act (17 August 1894) permitted a 2m 23ch deviation north of Wadebridge, in Egloshayle Parish. This put the line on the west side of the River Allen through Treworder (252 miles).

Extension to Truro?

A Parliamentary Bill was prepared in 1893 to authorise a line from Padstow to Truro. Four 'Railways' were proposed:- No.1 from a trailing junction at Padstow station, via St Merryn, St Eval and Mawgan to a new station at Newquay. No.2 from Newquay to a terminus south of Truro City, and a spur at Padstow for direct running to Newquay from Wadebridge. Railway No.3 was to be a spur from the north of Truro to the GWR existing line and station. Nos.3 & 4, together, allowed

a line from the NCR's terminus, around the south side of Truro to Penwithers Junction. The LSWR would not support it, and the preamble of the Bill was not proved by the House of Commons Committee and, even though the House reversed this, it was not proceeded with. The Chairman of the NCR, J.C. Tremayne, however, met the GWR Chairman, Greirson, in November 1894 to ask for assistance. The NCR proposal had been strongly supported by Falmouth Town Council, the Newquay Local Board, St Agnes interests, and the Truro Merchants Association. The GWR was not forthcoming, either. Further LSWR, or NCR, ambitions toward Truro seemed to end here and Waterloo passengers, such as there

were, completed their journey to Newquay by horse coach.

Delabole to Port Isaac Road 1894

Before work continued beyond Delabole toward Wadebridge on this Third Section of the North Cornwall Railway the site of Port Isaac Road station was settled on a contrived level stretch at Reddiford on the Trewarne Estate. St Teath villagers asked for their station at Trekee, or better still at Treroosal, only a mile to the west, but were told that the gradients were not right. Only 210 men were working between Delabole and Port Isaac Road in November 1893. The amount of earth working to be done, though not heavy, was continuous as the upper end of the route followed the east side of the high ground facing the coast. The curvature was not as sinuous as further east, except for a complete half circle traversed (at 30 chains radius) between Trekee and Reddiford. Over all this distance the gradient was formed at 1 in 73, falling from a height of 650' to 400' above sea level. With 790 men employed in June 1894, and Port Isaac Road nearly ready, the line was sufficiently advanced for the Railway Inspector to visit in August 1894.

About to depart from St.Kew Highway for Wadebridge early this century is a 'K10' 4-4-0, No.341, with a train consisting of 1880s low arc-roofed bogie non-corridors lead by a 6-wheel luggage brake. 341 was built at Nine Elms in 1901 and is equipped with Drummond's cross-tube firebox, later removed. (R.L. Goodman collection)

Major Yorke was appointed to view 4m 10chs (243m 10ch to 247m 20ch). He counted 5 overbridges of stone (brick faced arches) and 10 underbridges. Port Isaac Road signal box had 13 levers, four of them spare. Once again, without a turntable at Port Isaac Road, engines would have to run tender first in one direction. Therefore, Major Yorke ordered a 20mph restriction for all trains. Neither could goods trains be brought to a stand on the steep gradients west of Delabole. The safety trap points were to be moved to Port Isaac Road. However this subsection was to remain unused by public trains for another 11 months, the LSWR declining to open it. The now-authorised Electric Tablet signalling system was installed imediately.

From Egloshayle a line of B & WR trucks may be seen (centre) on the siding leading from the tidal bridge over the Treguddick brook (left). The Molesworth Exchange (later the Town Hall) appears new placing the date in the late 1880s.

The North Cornwall Railway made a junction with the Bodmin and Wadebridge line (right) from June 1895 and a signal box was provided. It lasted until 3rd February 1907 when a separate line was formed into Wadebridge. The upper storey is an LSWR 1860s type of construction probably from a superseded block post elsewhere. The ground part was converted to a pw hut. (L.T. George collection)

Port Isaac Road to Wadebridge Junction

A fairly easy alignment was possible over the three miles from Port Isaac Road to St Kew Highway, including a rare straight near Trequite, with the gradient but 1 in 110. An early start was made on the tunnel at Trelill where a ridge of high ground to the south of Port Isaac Road had to be breached. A heading of 100 yards was achieved in January 1894, but progress proved to be very slow due to the hard rock and a drill was brought in during May; the bore was just about through in June. Of the 350 yards 108 were full size by August 1894. The navvies were now working below Port Isaac Road, about 600 in that month, but down to 575 in November.

Having taken a high position on the west side of the Allen Valley, and still to west of the Delabole to St Kew Road, it was necessary to drop from the 400' contour to near sea level at Wadebridge. The surveyors pegged out the line (as deviated) to enter the Allen Valley at Lemail, after the tunnel at Trelill and the site of St Kew Highway station on the Camelford to Wadebridge road. Earthworks were particularly heavy (a high embankment at Hingham Mill) and more hard rock was encountered as the line steadily dropped to river level.

In November 1894 the tunnel was full size (though single bore) and three quarters of a mile of permanent way had been laid on the south side. 513 men were on the works in February 1895 and the first piles were being driven into the bed of the River Camel. This and the Allen were to be bridged, also the adjacent Wadebridge to Bodmin road at Sladesbridge. In March two miles of permanent way were down and by April only 1 3/4 miles remained to be laid. The following month the girders for the river bridges were in place and the tunnel lined throughout. The number of men had dropped to 430. A decision had been made early in the year to make a junction, and not form a side line parallel to the B & WR for the last half mile into Wadebridge.

A junction with the reconstructed Bodmin and Wadebridge line was made therefore, at 0m 78ch (zero at Wadebridge Quay) or at what was to be 253m 15ch on the North Cornwall. A new signal box named 'Wadebridge Junction' was placed in the 'V' of the junction. A siding laid in for construction works trailed from the up side into the NCR line, its pointwork unconnected to the box, though secured.

The NCR asked the Board of Trade in November 1894 for the Delabole - Port Isaac Road section to be opened, but was told that the LSWR would not until the line was completed to Wadebridge. The works were completed by the end of May 1895 and the Government Inspector, Col. Yorke, arrived at Delabole on the 28th instant. According to the 'West Briton' two heavy engines, one fitted with inspection seats on the front, had been prepared for him. After traversing the unopened section to Port Isaac Road labourers with flares preceded this train at walking pace through Trelill tunnel. The first day ended at St Kew Highway. Next day the inspection train started at Wadebridge. The two engines (40 tons each) and two coaches were run up and down over the two iron river bridges at Pendevy.

Following this, Col. Yorke reported only on the 5m 76ch between Port Isaac Road (exclusive) and Wadebridge Junction (apparently covering 247m 20ch and 253m 17ch). The sharpest curve was 20ch, that taking the line across the embankment to the Junction. Trelill tunnel was lined throughout, had recesses, and there were 10 overbridges and 12 underbridges. The Camel bridge was of wrought iron girders and masonry abutments. St Kew's platforms were 3'0" (cf Tresmeer's 2'6") with 'accommodation and amenities for both sexes'. St Kew Highway signal box contained 16 levers with three spare. Wadebridge Junction had 14 levers, all in use, though the diagram shows 16 in 1905. The turntable at Wadebridge not being ready, only tank engines were to be used from here to Delabole. The Electric Tablet system was to be used for signalling on this single line. Col. Yorke was not pleased with the situation at Wadebridge station. The single platform was altogether insufficient for the additional trains from the North Cornwall line; the serious attention of the LSWR was called for and remedial measures to be made at an early date. (The LSWR was quite unrepentant! In a letter to the BoT in October 1895 it said the station was 'quite sufficient'). Additionally no goods train Col.Yorke declared, should be brought to a stand outside St Kew's up home signal. The LSWR questioned this too, offering to use two brake vans on goods trains. Col. Yorke replied it would mean two brakesmen, but if the LSWR was confident that would obviate all risks of runaways towards Wadebridge then it was acceptable. The Board of Trade was never happy about this junction and was pleased to approve its abolition in 1907, when two separate lines were laid into Wadebridge. Provision of two brake vans, with a guard in each, except where a 20-ton van could be substituted, was ordered by the LSWR and a limit of 20 loaded wagons imposed on all up trains. The contractor's siding (retained as a runaway?) at the junction was removed by the LSWR, however, at the BoT's request. Looking ahead a little, Wadebridge station was reconstructed in time for the Padstow opening in March 1899. However, the LSWR provided a new two-road engine shed and 50ft turntable in 1895 on reclaimed ground to the north of the station.

Wadebridge Opening 1895

The LSWR lost no time in starting

12.37pm. All repaired to the Molesworth Arms Hotel for lunch. Later in the day, what was to be the very first 'through' coach arrived at 6.00pm. Hired by Mr Chapman, the London builder, a saloon arrived with a party of 23 to go to Padstow (taken thence on a fleet of horse brakes by Messrs Pope & Son). The initial passenger service was: 7.00am, 9.18am, 10.20am, 1.15pm, 2.36pm and 6.05pm from Wadebridge. The 5.50am train from Waterloo connected into Wadebridge at 2.32pm, the 9.00am at 5.22pm, the 11.00am at 5.59pm and the 1.00pm at 8.36pm. The Exeter 1.00am mail and goods was extended to Wadebridge as was the 5.30am goods from Exeter (Queen Street). Stopping goods trains left at 12.46pm and 4.55pm, thus putting Wadebridge into the 'road box' system, as well as opening up direct narrow (standard) gauge access for cattle, fish, coal and

was presented with an address by Henry Symons, Chairman of the local 'Demonstration Committee'. It was Wednesday 12 June before the Official Opening from Delabole to Wadebridge took place, delayed to coincide with the Royal Cornwall Show at the latter, held at Trevanyon Road. The directors' special of LSWR saloons came through Launceston at 9.35am, picking up Mr and Mrs Tremayne and Colonel Byng. There were ten ordinary coaches as well, possibly bogies and, if so, a formidable load for the 'special and large' engine. It arrived at Wadebridge's single platform at 11.10am. Once everybody had gathered together the inevitable address was read by the acting secretary of the Wadebridge Representative Council. As well as the NCR directors, that Company's Secretary (Price) London Agent (Birchall), Solicitor (Venning), Surveyor (Drew) and Auditor (Hare)

Wadebridge as a terminus in 1895 showing the original box, another example of an LSWR 1860s upper structure, brought in this time in 1888, following the complete remodelling of the original B&WR layout. At first only GWR trains from Bodmin used the station, but this view includes the new 1895 engine shed (right). Access to this was from the turntable only, near the Class '460' 4-4-0 (centre). A run-round loop (with vehicle) is flanked to its right by the access siding to the quay. The station was remodelled again in 1899 for the Padstow extension. (NRM)

trains. On Friday 31 May several trucks with 50 cattle were taken up to Delabole for attachment to the 2.00pm goods. They had been bought by Mr. Pearce (Camelford) for sale at Chichester Market - a foretaste of what was to come on the North Cornwall! Saturday 1 June saw the 7.00am passenger train away from Wadebridge surrounded by a large crowd. Meanwhile the first down train, starting from Launceston at 8.23am, included Mr Oag, an NCR director. The second, from Okehampton, took Mr Tremayne (the Chairman), Mrs Tremayne and others, arriving at Wadebridge at

merchandise with the rest of Britain. Manual transfer of goods had been necessary through the broad gauge break at Bodmin Road up to 1892. The following Monday was the Whitsun Bank Holiday and many took to riding in the new train service to Wadebridge. Back at Otterham a special from Exeter and Plymouth, organised by Mr Rundle Brendon, the Bude coaching proprietor, set down 500 excursionists for conveyance to Boscastle and Tintagel. To celebrate at Port Isaac village, field and water sports were held. Sir William Onslow, Bart. of Hengar and an NCR director,

were present, together with Major Hext, Mark Symons etc. of the North Cornwall Coach Company. The Exeter District Superintendent of the LSWR (Vallance), the District Engineer (Fisher) and Crouch, their Resident Engineer on the works, were joined by many notables. However the Mayor of Truro arrived somewhat late, his train (presumably from Bodmin Road) having been delayed. After the ceremony and speeches the party proceeded to the Town Hall, headed by the Royal Marines (Plymouth) Band, for refreshment.

The 1886 Wadebridge Station, then a terminus from Bodmin and Bodmin Road, was enlarged in 1899 on the opening of the Padstow extension. In this c1910 view the advertising signs for coffee, etc. show how these proprietary goods became widely available after the railway arrived. (L.T.George Collection)

The Bodmin & Wadebridge Railway Reconstruction and a new Terminus at Wadebridge 1888

Opened in 1834 the primitive sand railway from the quay at Wadebridge to Bodmin, and its mineral branches to Wenford and Ruthernbridge was, as we have seen, acquired by the LSWR in 1846. The latter operated it at arm's length, supplying materials, including engines, by sea through Wadebridge. Track was relaid in places (there were 6' stone sleepers, and 'T' section rails) in 1866 and 1879. The passenger service to Bodmin, such as it was, was suspended from 1 November 1886. The arrival of the GWR at Boscarne Junction, by a standard gauge branch from Bodmin Road/Bodmin, and with running powers by agreement with the LSWR (5 June 1886), found the B & WR's Wadebridge terminus totally inadequate to receive its trains. A new station building, and platform 230ft in length, was placed 12ch to the east of the old B & WR premises. It was provided by the LSWR under an agreement with the GWR, which was to share the running expenses (the GWR retained its own booking office here until 1915). The NCR's partnership in this 1886 agreement remained muted until 1895. In 1899 the LSWR tried, unsuccessfully, to charge the NCR a proportion of the re-signalling costs. A single line to Boscarne Junction was instituted, ready for use from 3 September 1888. Alignment improvements to the B & WR (undertaken by Curry & Reeve in 1894/5) included a totally new terminus at Bodmin. So, only the GWR was operating passenger and mixed trains into Wadebridge until 1895. Even more unusually, its local system from Bodmin Road, standard gauge from the start, was an enclave in a broad gauge area until conversion of the Cornwall Railway in 1892. LSWR services from Boscarne Junction into its own Bodmin terminus did not reopen until 1 November 1895.

New Layout at Wadebridge

As related elsewhere, efforts by the NCR in the early 'nineties' to extend to Truro were thwarted and instead a separate Act obtained in August 1896 confirmed Padstow as the terminus. Meanwhile the LSWR overcame its coolness to the BoT's strictures on Wadebridge station, and further reconstruction work, in view of the Padstow extension, was taken in hand. It included Molesworth Street Level Crossing, a new junction with the quay sidings, virtual doubling between there and the east end of Wadebridge, a new island platform with loop, and two signal boxes. The total LSWR (ex B & WR) line involved extended from Wadebridge Junction 253m 15ch to the 1888 terminal stopblocks (at 253m 77ch), thence over a 10-chain conversion of the B & WR's quay siding to an end-on junction with the new Padstow line at 254m 7ch. The two signal boxes and the new layout were brought into operation on 12 March 1899, in time for the Padstow opening on the 27th.

The island platform, 315 ft long, faced the converted 1888 loop, and on its north side received an Up loop for Bodmin trains. The whole Up side layout into the sand dock and engine depot needed realignment for these works. The terminal stopblock disappeared under a realignment of the Down 'main' and points leading to the new Up 'main' and Up loop, also allowing for westward lengthening of the Down platform. The B & WR engine and carriage shed sidings and the weighbridge loop were removed. A double line now existed to 253m 79ch from a point opposite a new East signal box at 253m 59ch. The sharply curved eastern exit from the old platform was straightened and then eased to a flatter 30 chain radius and longer leads provided to the goods shed, to a total of 460 feet. The island platform was equipped with a waiting room and verandah, and a period LSWR wooden footbridge to the down side. The 1888 'Wadebridge Signal Box' at the Bodmin end of the terminus platform was demolished.

Both the East and West signal boxes were constructed in stone with the LSWR's central 'pillar' style of the mid-nineties. Wadebridge West box (254m 4ch) was situated at Molesworth Street Crossing, thus lengthy rodding runs were necessary to work the west end of the station but shorter to the lead points and trap points at the quay.

Colonel Yorke inspected the Wadebridge station work in May 1899, two months after the Padstow opening. It seems that the Molesworth Street Crossing was still exercising his mind, as he delayed submitting his Padstow report on the latter until 29 April. The East signal box held 29 levers (1 push and pull) and two spare, the signalman here operated the adjacent occupation crossing to the river by a gate lock. The West box had 20 levers and three spare, and a wheel to operate Molesworth Street gates. After describing the new platforms, the boxes and the conversion of the B & WR quay line, he yet again referred to Molesworth Street. As this crossing disturbed Wadebridge citizens for many years, it is worth recounting the story in more detail.

The level crossing taking the North Cornwall's Padstow extension across Molesworth Street, Wadebridge, was under construction early in 1899. The imposition of fences and gates was unpopular with the Wadebridge citizenry and Col. Yorke, the BoT Inspecting Officer for railways, held a special meeting to discuss their grievances. (A. Fairclough Collection)

Wadebridge Quay in the 1880s, then owned by the LSWR after the legalities of 1886 confirmed its purchase of the B & WR in 1846. It had opened in 1834 and the siding emerging from between the houses (left centre) curved sharpy to each side of the two docks and to the river frontage (right). The two sheerlegs cranes were for loading granite blocks from wagon to dockside, thence to ships' holds. The terraces in Eddystone Road (centre-right) echo the use of De Lank granite for the lighthouse, moreover for some of London's bridges and smaller products were still being sent (by rail) up to the 1960s. (R.I.C.)

Molesworth Street Level Crossing

While only intermittent traffic passed on down to the quayside at Wadebridge and shunting was minimal, in B & WR days the obstruction of Molesworth Street mattered little. Neither gates nor fences were provided. Under the 1882 proposals the line might have stopped short of it by 80 yards, a Padstow line circumventing Wadebridge to the south. Once it was realised that the 1890s route would really project over the crossing, there was great concern from the inhabitants. The newly-created County Council made representations, and an Inquiry was held in the Molesworth Hall on 20 March 1894, under the chairmanship of Major C.S. Hutchinson RE. Interestingly the proposed line was referred to as the 'Launceston to Truro'. On market days, it was said, 45 vehicles, 42 horses and cattle, and 476 footpersons crossed in one hour. In the event, the normal lie of the gates was to be against road traffic, though a footbridge was provided. In practice road traffic was given a fair chance in view of the few trains (about one an hour each way) to and from Padstow. Shunting was a different matter! The Urban District Council complained in 1904 about 'prolonged shunting' but Col. Yorke in his report on the Wadebridge alterations of 1899 was adamant that road traffic preference against rail was 'rarely allowed'. He had been confronted by Council and Wadebridge UDC officers on his inspection of the Padstow extension in March, not only regarding Molesworth Street, but in connection with the Commissioner's Road several hundred yards to the west, the crossing at Harbour Lane (blocked) and 'encroachments' on

Eddystone Road. Again, in 1908, the UDC complained that the gates were 'closed 15 minutes at a time'. An appeal to the BoT was met with the blank reply that it (the BoT) 'does not appear to have any statutory authority in the matter' and that the 1863 Railway Clauses Act did not apply. The crossing was an obstruction, of course, and with the advent of the motor age matters got worse. It was additionally the main road from North to West Cornwall, later designated the A39 Trunk Road from Taunton to Fraddon.

Wadebridge Junction to Wadebridge Widening Works 1907

The single line from Wadebridge Junction to Wadebridge Station was proving inadequate for the ten or so North Cornwall passenger and goods trains each way, and a new Rail Motor service (1 June 1906) on the Bodmin Branch. There seems to have been a last-minute arrangement for a junction rather than two separate lines into Wadebridge, the Board of Trade having been unhappy about this since 1895, situated as it was at the foot of the long gradient from Delabole. The provision of two lines was covered by transferred powers from the NCR's original 1882 Act, and confirmed by LSWR Acts in 1883 and 1891 for the B & WR deviations.

Widening work commenced in 1906 to take two single lines in a width of 30ft. The overbridge at 253m 47ch (No 145A) was already built for double track (but at only 26ft). The east end of Wadebridge was remodelled so that the new single line (for North Cornwall) was aligned with the up platform. A scissors crossover was laid in below Guineaport (253m 62ch) thereby permitting trains from Bodmin and

North Cornwall to use the Down platform or to arrive in the Up loop, also to depart from the Up platform or Up Loop platform. New works were also undertaken at Wadebridge west end for the Rail Motors (a berthing siding) and provision for trains to depart for Padstow from Up Loop. Wadebridge West Signal Box frame was modified to suit.

Major Pringle RE inspected them in June 1907. He reported that a new single line 'about 65 chains' ran from the now separated junction (at 253m 15ch) to Wadebridge. The East Signal box frame was extended to hold 43 levers, including two spare. Tablet working was now in operation from here to St Kew Highway and Boscarne Junction. The rails used were second-hand, hard steel, 82 lb/yard. Wadebridge Junction had been 'taken away' and the temporary connection (i.e. the original contractor's siding) removed. (It appears, however, that the LSWR had actually connected its points to the frame as late as 1905). Major Pringle was worried by the curvature, and asked for speed checks to be made for the exchange of Tablets. The 65 chains actually extended to the revised junction with the NCR's Padstow extension at 254m 10ch. Wadebridge West Signal Box (254m 4ch) had not figured in Col. Yorke's May 1899 Report (though Molesworth Street Crossing was scrutinized). The new 'Rail Motor' facilities resulted in the West Box frame now holding 27 levers and two spare, and its operation was now approved.

Wadebridge to Padstow

Deliberations in 1894 over extending to Truro rather held up action regarding the 1882 objective, Padstow. Time to construct that far, under the 1882 Act, had long run out with piecemeal arrangements only just attaining Wadebridge in 1895. The intermediate portion from the west of Wadebridge Junction to Wadebridge Quay being LSWR property, the fourth section would commence just beyond the quay at 254m 7ch.

In December 1895 the Delabole to Wadebridge section was still in the Capital account. £2,529 had been received in revenue and of the rebate from LSWR for the six months since opening, also £3,692 for the 1st section and £4,229 for the 2nd. The 1st Section ordinary shareholders were receiving 4% in 1895, for the other Sections it was 3 1/2%.

The enabling Act to extend to Padstow received Royal Assent on 20 July 1896, the remaining £88,000 under authorised capital allocated. There were preferential shares this time. The NCR directors, however, asked Padstow citizens to guarantee £3,000. C.G. Prideaux-Brune put up £1,000, even so the first £1,000 was met by Foster's Bank. The LSWR promised the remaining £1,750 of the yearly rebate and agreed to work it for an annual rental of £2,650, again on a 999 year

The steamer 'Dunraven' brought merchandise from Bristol to Wadebridge Quay, some of it loaded to rail for Bodmin, but sea-borne trade declined after the North Cornwall arrived in 1895. The Padstow Harbour Commissioners built a 218-foot wharf and siding, leasing the embankment and path on the right to the LSWR after the latter sought to acquire the whole river frontage in the 1870s. (R.I.C.)

Believed to be a Forester's parade in Eddystone Road, Wadebridge about 1914, with the gates across the railway (folding against themselves) in Molesworth Street. The Padstow extension curves away under the original wooden footbridge, while the nearer points lead into the sharp curves to the Quay. The LSWR's facing point protective blocks, the ground signal (right) and the trap points just inside the gate were worked by the rodding (boxed in) from Wadebridge West box. (R.I.C.)

lease. The 'Padstow Leased Line Stock' was taken up by County backers, the Bolitho family, Michael Williams (a director), Coode (solicitor) and Grylls & Co Ltd (bankers). The latter also held £20,000 of the Wadebridge Guaranteed stock as nominees of Curry & Reeves. The North Cornwall Co had sealed Lloyds Bonds to the latter, which were now cancelled.

Once the Padstow extension Act was passed. The North Cornwall Co. could choose their main contractor. Curry & Reeve were once again appointed, from December 1896, piling starting straight away for a temporary bridge at Little Petherick. Acquiring the land proved rather complicated. Only 2 1/2 miles were in possession in April 1897, and negotiations were

started with the Duchy of Cornwall over the foreshore of the Camel. Then there was the proposed embankment at Wadebridge carrying the line from the quay area across the flats, together with a footpath to Polgammon Point. twelve owners were involved and it was well into 1898 before the last piece of land was obtained. Discussions were held in May 1897 between the BoT's Harbour Department, the Padstow Harbour Commissioners, and the North Cornwall Co. regarding the establishment of a new quay at Padstow. The hillsides behind run steeply to the shore, divided by seven valleys or creeks. The widest creek to cross was Little Petherick. Here a 200 yard embankment faced with massive concrete blocks was linked to the Dennis Hill side by a long viaduct, all on a 20 chain curve. The 1882 submission proposed an opening bridge 30ft wide, and ten arches of 30ft. By 1896 larger vessels were no longer trading to the Sea Mills inside the creek, and that site had been acquired earlier by the NCR, presumably to safeguard its situation. Other than crossing the creeks, room for the line was found by shelving into the hillside, but with several deep cuttings. Heaviest were at Ball Hill, and Dennis right outside Padstow, with its 25 chain reverse curves. About halfway to Padstow it crossed the frontage of the Camel Quarries, with access allowed to the beach by a path under No. 149 bridge. There was just one overbridge, at Whitehouse, taking a narrow way down from Tregunna.

The North Cornwall Coach Company played a leading part in the development of the North Cornwall Railway's route to Padstow. Starting in Launceston in 1886, its coaches successively served the advancing railheads until the Wadebridge opening in 1895. Even then the onward stage route to Newquay was maintained and this NCCC coach is seen at the Red Lion St. Columb Major, about 1905. (R.I.C.)

The iron viaduct at Little Petherick, Padstow, in 1899. Three pairs of N-trussed girders supported wrought iron cross members and rail bearers, the latter carrying the sleepers of lightly ballasted track. Curry and Reeves' platelayers are completing this ballasting while carpenters (right) are finishing the walkways. (J. Ruff collection)

In this view from Denis Hill, the train leaving Little Petherick viaduct in Padstow appears to include an inspection car at the rear. The line was inspected by Major Yorke on 20th March 1899 which may confirm its presence, but the viaduct was also tested for deflections by a train of four engines and three coaches. (R.I.C.)

Progress was slowing by April 1897, for labour was scarce. The number of men gradually rose but only 294 were on the books in November. By then material from the cuttings was forthcoming by then for the embankments at Dennis and Wadebridge. The station house at Padstow, followed by the buildings, were under way at the turn of the year. In February 1898 ironwork was being delivered by barge for the Petherick viaduct, from Wadebridge Quay, with the first cylinders sunk in March. The contractors were J.H. & N. Bell of London, erection was by subcontractors Eastwood, Swingler & Co of Derby. The 133ft spans of pairs of 'N' truss wrought iron girders weighed 350 tons each. They rested on pairs of 8ft diameter cast iron cylinders which had to be driven through 53ft of mud before reaching solid rock. They were then filled with concrete. The abutments were masonry and stood 16 ft above high water, and 30ft above the mud. Men arrived from completion of the Bude extension in August - 300 were on the books in September. There was optimism for an early opening with $3\tfrac{1}{2}$ miles of permanent way down, Padstow station (but not the goods shed) complete and the last of the bridge cylinders in. Early in January 1899 rails were across Molesworth Street and the signal box completed. It was all too slow for the North Cornwall directors, however, who complained that the 'Engineers had stated they thought the position of affairs very discreditable to the Contractors.'

To accommodate the line between Eddystone Road and the quay sidings, the latter needed remodelling. The inner siding was shifted 15ft northwards, which sharpened the leads into four existing B & WR sidings, and a dividing fence was erected for security. To improve the Harbour Lane entrance, a corner of land was also purchased next to the Temperance Hotel. Eddystone Road was fenced off which caused local complaints that it had been 'encroached upon'. This short link was acquired by the NCR from the LSWR under authorisation in 1898, apparently from 254m 7ch to 254m 10ch.

To accommodate Padstow Station, the site of the old Higher Shipbuilding Yard was purchased, filled in, and the hillside cut back to form a level site. Two private roads, one rising to New Street (Station Road), and one towards the Inner Harbour were built. A small harbour, remnants of the yard, a dock wall and a shed formed the nucleus of the fishing port which was to come. A larger area of land (and foreshore) was not entirely used at first. The station consisted of a single platform 320ft long, served by the running line ending at stopblocks (259m 44ch), and a run-round loop. A standard North Cornwall Railway Station Master's house and offices, but with a fairly short awning, was all Padstow merited, possibly as the

On 5th May 1964 'West Country' Class No. 34033 'Chard' crosses Little Petherick viaduct at Padstow with two coaches of the 'ACE'. The wrought iron supporting cylinders of the viaduct were driven 53 feet through mud to reach solid rock under this creek leading to Sea Mills. The original 1882 plans included a bridge with an opening span for access to Tregaskes' quay there. (S.C. Nash)

end of February 1899 and Major Yorke was invited to inspect the new line on 20 March. The permanent way was second-hand 80lb rail (79lb worn). Even as late as this, one solid wooden treenail in three was used (the other two were iron spikes driven through hollow trenails). No doubt the LSWR was trying to save equipping the line with Electric Tablet signalling and, indirectly, as they were contributing heavily to the constructional costs. A train of four engines (and three coaches) was employed to run up and down over Little Petherick Viaduct to test deflection. The latter was 'very modest'. The only station was Padstow; all complete with 3ft high platforms. The signal box there had 13 levers (including three push and pull) and five spare. The inspector recommended that the line could be opened subject to:

(1) A turntable installed at Padstow and until such time, tank engines to be used,

(2) A footbridge for the Harbour Commissioners' road at Wadebridge,

(3) The signal wires to be cased.

A rider stated that speed should not exceed 20 mph until the line was thoroughly consolidated. In the event the turntable was provided, and the footbridge in due course. The length of line inspected was 5m 37ch (i.e. 254m 7 ch at Molesworth Street, to 259m 44ch the stop blocks at the end of the platform at Padstow). As noted the NCR acquired the first three chains at Wadebridge from the LSWR in 1898. The 1882 authorised length was 5m 41ch (i.e. from 254m 10ch to 259m

grand concept was a terminus at Truro, even in 1899, with nothing greater like Bude or Ilfracombe. All walling was in stone including signal box, station goods shed and cattle dock. The goods yard was equally unpretentious, no better than the wayside stations, but the goods shed was in the large (No.1) LSWR style, with side windows. More emphasis was placed on serving the PHC's Inner Harbour, and a new fish quay where two long sidings (see later) were laid down. No engine shed or turntable seemed to have been con-

templated by the LSWR (Wadebridge was nearby), but the Inspecting Officer thought otherwise.

The Metropole Hotel which looms above Padstow station opened its doors in May 1901. At first called the 'South Western' it was built by the Cory family of shipowning and colliery owning fame, at a cost £12,000. As a reminder of their Padstow origins, it remained in the family until sold to Trust Houses in 1936.

The bridges, station and permanent way were in a fit enough state by the

Padstow about 1902 before development of the fish quays, but showing the new 'South Western' Hotel. In the centre are the fish sidings, one lined with watering points for van washing. The 02 0-4-4T hauling the North Cornwall line train in the platform was unlikely to have worked it beyond Wadebridge. The stock appears to be a six-wheel first, a low arc-roofed 30ft. bogie brake and a pair of 41ft bogie carriages of 1890s vintage. The open fish wagon on the right is one of a small fleet converted from carriage underframes (some were new) and equipped with vacuum brake for use in specials, or as tails on passenger trains. (G. Reeve collection)

Padstow from the east end about 1908 with the fish trade building up well, judging by the piles of boxes and barrels. The isolated shed was known as the Bigwood store. In the platform is a steam railcar, and a rake of 1870s bogie passenger coaches is in the first siding, with bogie brake and box wagons. The fish train consists of round-ended open wagons and is headed by a '460' Class 4-4-0. Under the canopy of the fish shed are more 4 and 6 wheel vans, but a nearby row of grounded coach bodies appears to be early accommodation for the fish traders. (R.I.C.)

The deep cutting blasted out of the rock at Ball Hill (257m. 60ch). Removal of spoil was entirely by hand, and no evidence of the use of a 'steam navvy' (as on the contemporary Bude extension) has been found. The high construction costs of the Padstow extension is reflected in this cutting, that at Denis Hill and the expense of Little Petherick Viaduct. (R.I.C.)

other Directors, Drew the Surveyor and Messrs. Coode and Venning (Solicitors). For the LSWR, there were Chairman Col. The Hon. W. Campbell, Owens (General Manager), Andrews (Chief Engineer), Dugald Drummond (Locomotive Superintendent), Vallance (Exeter District Superintendent), Jacomb-Hood (District Engineer) and several other Officers.

Overnight light snow fell at Padstow, though it had largely disappeared by morning. Well wrapped up on the platform were local dignitaries including Messrs. J. Hicks JP, G.A. Hellyar CC for Padstow, F. Bray Chairman of Padstow UDC, James Nicholls, F. Sluman, and representatives from the parishes of Padstow, St Merryn, St Issey, St Eval, Little Petherick, and no less than six local sea Captains. Joining them was the Lord of the Manor, C.G. Prideaux-Brune, who had backed the North Cornwall's entry to Padstow so admirably, and it was Miss Prideaux-Brune who declared the new section open after the train pulled in at 12.30pm. It steamed slowly ahead and cut a tape which crossed the line, while the Padstow Artillery and Delabole Brass bands played 'See The Conquering Hero Comes'. A royal salute of 21 rounds were fired from the big guns on the quay. Mr. Hicks read an illuminated address to the directors - in the waiting room where it was doubtless warmer! In a marquee nearby luncheon was served for about 60, provided by Spiers & Pond at the behest of the NCR directors, followed by toasts and speeches. The special train left Padstow late in the afternoon.

After that two specials were run to Wadebridge and back. The first carried 600 children, who on their return were each given a Cornish Pasty. The second was for adults, about 500 in all. At Padstow the new RNLI Lifeboat was demonstrated and open for viewing, a free meat tea was provided in the Institute for over a thousand locals, and more salvoes of artillery were fired by

51ch), but extended further towards the South Quay by arrangement with the PHC. For accountancy purposes the Quay Line was treated as a separate branch from a junction at 259m 28ch to 259m 54ch - actually the gate to the PHC's siding.

Padstow - The Completion of the North Cornwall Railway

The opening ceremony was truly auspicious judging by the number of local and railway persons present. On Thursday 23 March the director's special left Exeter at 9.30am, called at Launceston at 11.00am and reached Wadebridge at 12.10pm. The latter station was decorated for the occasion. On board were Messrs J.C. Tremayne (the NCR Chairman's son), L.C. Foster, C.G. Prideaux-Brune and three

At least 30 East Coast sailing trawlers are moored off Padstow in this pre-1914 scene. The turntable (foreground) is on its original site with two vacuum braked (or piped) cattle wagons in the stub siding. The Bigwood store lies to the left. (R.I.C.)

The directors' special had just arrived at Padstow at 12.30 p.m. on 23rd March 1899. No record has emerged of the engine, which appears to be an Adams 4-4-0, but the train consists of LSWR 46 ft. First, Directors' Saloon, 1877 Directors' Saloon No. 9, 47 ft. 6 in. 'Eagle' Saloon and a 30 ft. Brake. Notice the ribbon ready for cutting by Miss Prideaux-Brune. (R.I.C.)

Delabole and Launceston to Meldon Junction where it connected with the Plymouth-Nine Elms overnight goods. £600 was authorised for further moorings in 1903 showing that both companies were more involved with the increasing number of East Coast vessels now using the port.

By 1908 facilities were inadequate, and the existing jetty would shelter only a dozen trawlers. In 1909 the PHC sought powers to lengthen the short NCR quay to 780ft. The estimated cost of this (then known as the West Quay), the extension of the fish shed, and sidings alterations was £20,000 to be met by a Board of Trade grant, the NCR guaranteeing £3,000 and the LSWR £10,350. The PHC could issue Bonds on the strength of an Act of Parliament obtained in 1910. The LSWR extended the fish shed, on its own account, at a cost of £503. Work was in full swing in 1911. The PHC's contractor took infilling rock from behind the goods shed and from the river bed. The construction of the dock wall was taken over about 1910 by the

Gunner Philp. Unfortunately the Lifeboat 'James Stevens' was lost on 11 April 1900 and eight Padstow lifeboatmen were drowned.

Public services started four days later on Monday 27 March. Passenger trains left at 6.50, 8.54, 10.20am, 1.04, 2.10, 5.40 and 8.12pm (all except the last two, connected to London and the 8.12 terminated at Launceston). Downward the arrivals were at 9.31am (mixed from Wadebridge) 10.55am, 12.44pm, 2.45pm, (off the 5.50am Waterloo). 5.07pm (9.15am Waterloo), 6.20pm (11.00am Waterloo) and 8.43pm (1.00pm Waterloo). No Sunday services were provided. A local goods, apart from the mixed train, ran in the afternoon from Wadebridge, and the special fish train to Exeter has already been mentioned.

It was a cold morning on 23rd March 1899. Light snow had fallen overnight, but a warm welcome awaits the special train at Padstow. An illuminated address is ready for presentation, bunting applied - and the word 'Gentlemen' subsequently erased by the prudent photographer. Over on the right is the stock ready for use on the public specials to Wadebridge later in the day, together with an 02 0-4-4T. Train services started on 27th March. The white post is the 259½ milepost, but notice that the fish shed had not then been constructed. (R.I.C.)

Padstow Harbour Developments

The Padstow Harbour Commissioners (PHC) were set up by an Act of Parliament in 1844. 24 were elected by parish ratepayers, and one each appointed by the Duchy of Cornwall, the Prideaux-Brune estate and HM Customs & Excise. As Lords of the Manor, the Prideaux-Brunes leased the Inner Harbour to the Commissioners, which was used initially by Curry & Reeve to import some materials. One of the first sidings was laid from here towards Wadebridge, as we have seen the NCR's new property ended just short of the South Quay. It is worth noting that the Commissioners' writ extended to Polbrock Bridge, upstream from Wadebridge, and so adjoined the LSWR again at the old B & WR quay. In 1897 the LSWR sought to obtain the freehold frontage of this Quay at Wadebridge, thus relations with the PHC here were not as friendly as at Padstow. The 1899 terminus was laid

out on the site of the Higher Shipbuilding yard, with parts incorporated into the river frontage.

Already in the 1890s Brixham and East Coast trawlers were fishing off Padstow, attracted by the herring shoals in the autumn. The arrival of the NCR in 1899 immediately opened up Padstow to all parts of Britain, and the LSWR was already approaching Lowestoft owners and buyers in 1900. The NCR itself was providing extra buoys that year and was lent £3,394 by the LSWR (at 3% interest) to fund the new fish shed, dock wall and extra sidings. From 1899 the LSWR put on a 3.30pm fast goods train calling only at Wadebridge, Camelford,

LSWR who used three quarter ton concrete blocks brought by rail from Exmouth Junction. A steam crane was employed on a temporary track to lift these blocks in and move material for the wall foundations. The top was coped with granite blocks and the wall protected by vertical and horizontal timbers. The West Quay was largely completed in 1912.

The 1910 powers also provided for a massive new jetty 800ft long and 40 ft wide, to parallel the West Quay. At the seaward end piers and a gate would close the gap thus forming a wet dock, the cost estimated at £40,000. Agreement between the NCR, LSWR, and PHC was reached in August 1911

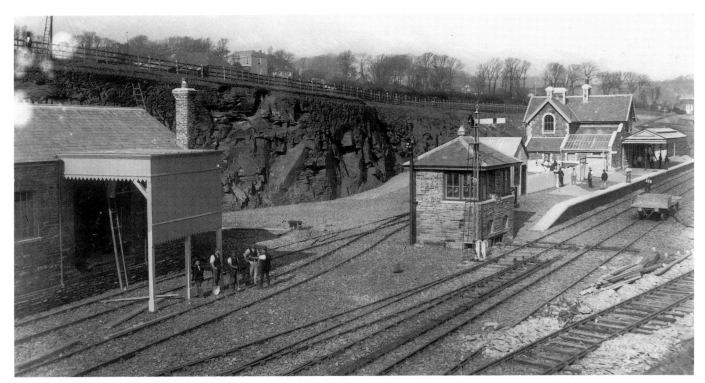

This view may have been taken earlier in March 1899 Padstow's signal box had been open for use from the 12th. The contractor's trolleys (or 'lorries') stand in the loop and a gang of platelayers is being directed by their ganger, while the goods shed is getting finishing touches. Excavation of hard rock was necessary to site the yard and shed. The terminus did not appear to warrant a sizeable building as at Bude (1898); the standard building does have a glazed over courtyard and a platform awning is provided. (R.I.C.)

and a Provisional Order in 1912 enabled the PHC to sell or lease these undertakings. The LSWR took further Bonds up to £30,000 and in 1916 leased, and virtually ran, the port from then until 1966. Looking forward, these Bonds (then amounting to £86,000) were renegotiated in the latter year, the PHC to commence repaying this debt to British Railways (the successor to the LSWR) and forthwith to run Padstow themselves.

In the event the gate arrangement was not formed and the dock remained (and remains) tidal. The tenders for the new jetty were let in December 1912, together with a further extension of the West Quay. 2½ acres of foreshore were acquired by the LSWR and NCR and the existing short jetty demolished. Work continued into World War One and was probably completed in 1915, though some was still going on in 1920. The jetty was formed by two mass-concrete walls, strengthened by embedded rails, sited in rock foundations, 40ft wide carrying two sidings on grouted rubble infilling and a gravelled surface. The depth of water at ordinary neap tide was 12 to 13ft, and on completion would hold 60 trawlers between it and the West Quay. The jetty was referred to as the 'Railway Pier'.

The West Quay was again extended, 160ft in 1928, at a cost of £13,000. Yet more works by the Southern Railway in the 1930s saw the completion of a 'bull-nose' and breakwater at the extremity of the Railway Pier, and a breakwater protruding from the North Quay. The latter was 360ft long and constructed of concrete reinforced by old rails. These works were largely fi-

nanced by Government grants (under the Public Works Facilities Act 1930) to alleviate unemployment, the total cost thought to be about £40,000. It should be noted here that the 'West Quay' is now referred to locally as the 'Inner Dock Wall' and the long 'Railway Jetty' as the 'Outer Dock Wall'.

Alterations to sidings, building work, ancillary services and rail services are described later. Before World War One the Government of the day wanted to improve the Cornish Fisheries and the LSWR, mindful to the revenue from high value fish carrying, could see the advantage of developing Padstow. The new General Manager,

Herbert Walker and the Chairman, Sir Hugh Drummond, paid a visit to Padstow in July 1912 and the LSWR's ultimate controlling interest in the port stems from then. The North Cornwall Company retained only a minor interest financially, though it was the landowner. The fortunes of the fish trade varied. In the 1910 season 1,735 tons were landed, increasing to 3,074 tons in 1911. Even in the First World War, when a large number of trawlers served as minesweepers, many of the remaining East Coast vessels fished out of Padstow summer and winter. In the post war years the LSWR and SR still carried sizeable loadings -

Between the masts of the two Lowestoft-registered sailing trawlers (left) the new 800 foot jetty can be seen under construction. The date would seem to be about 1909. (R.I.C.)

Padstow-registered steam trawler 'Apple' moored to the West Quay in the late 1920s. Steam coal was largely railborne, in the type of 12-ton wagons on the quayside. (Author's Collection)

1,747 tons in the 1931 season, with 70 boats working. By this time the trawlers were steam-powered thus requiring coal supplies, most of it by rail. Right up to 1938 the tonnage increased annually and, even in World War Two, fish trains were run on occasion. By the 1950s, however, the fishing had declined and only one or two East Coast vessels used the port, not helped by the destruction by fire in 1950 of the ice factory. The closure of the freight facilities at Padstow in 1964, and British Railways operations generally in 1966/7, sealed its fate. Or would have done. The role of the Commissioner's responsibilities changed dramatically in the following years, but this is not part of the railway story. Visitors to Padstow today can observe the new works subsequently undertaken, though the fish shed still stands as a memorial to the hectic dealing and loading that went on in advance of a fish special, timed to steam away from Padstow about 4.30pm of a winter's evening in the 1930s.

The Final Years 1900 to 1922

After the Padstow opening in 1899 the North Cornwall Railway Company settled down to a background existence as a satellite of the LSWR. The Board of Directors sat almost monthly in the first decade of this century, often at the South Western Hotel at Padstow. The Annual General Meetings took place there, as well, but as the shareholders were receiving regular dividends derived from the LSWR rentals, little dissent occurred. The Padstow Harbour Works were in full swing from 1910 and with the LSWR paying for most of them, the Company was even more satisfied!

Following the death in 1901 of John Tremayne, who had been Chairman since 1883, L.C. Foster was elected in his place. Tremayne owned estates in the Wadebridge area and had been an active and influential promoter of the Company's interests. His seat was at Croan, in Egloshayle Parish, and the family was related to that of Sir Trehawke H. Kekewich of Peamore, Exeter, who was elected to the Board in 1901. Lewis Charles Foster (1844 - 1923) was a partner in Robbins, Foster & Bolitho, bankers at Liskeard, also known as the East Cornwall Bank. He was Chairman of the Liskeard & Caradon Railway, County Councillor, J.P. and a Deputy Lieutenant of the County. The Earl of Wharncliffe had been Deputy Chairman for many years. His estates in

Tintagel and Delabole etc. were disposed of before 1914. On his death in 1899 his son (the 2nd Earl) was elected in his place, but in 1913 Col. the Hon. C.C.G. Byng became the Deputy. The Williams family of Scorrier, Redruth, who had large interests in mining and smelting in West Cornwall and South Wales, later turned to banking. In 1905 the Liskeard bank (then Bolitho, Coode, Foster & Grylls - 'Consolidated Bank') was taken over by Barclay & Co. This bank, as we have seen, had backed the North Cornwall Company for many years. Michael Williams (1839 - 1907) was elected a Director in 1893. He had inherited estates in Davidstowe, Minster and Lesnewth (and a share in the East Cornwall Bank) subsequently making his home at Halwill Barton, Delabole. Bankers, again, the Bolitho family of Penzance, were large stockholders in the North Cornwall Railway Co until 1922.

During the lifetime of the North Cornwall Railway, the Molesworth and the Onslow family interests were represented by Sir Lewis of Pencarrow, Bodmin and Sir William of Hengar, St Tudy. The Molesworths were great benefactors of Wadebridge, while the Onslows - Sir William was a director from 1883 until 1899 - both gave land for the construction. Last, but not least, the Prideaux-Brunes of Padstow had pressed for the railway to extend there for many years, though it was 1899 before the family could look out from Prideaux Place and see steam rising from the new terminus in the town. Charles Glyn Prideaux-Brune was a Director from 1883 until his death in 1907. He was succeeded by his son Col. Charles Robert and, appropriately, he was the last Chairman in 1922.

Prideaux Place, the seat of the Prideaux-Brune family, is the scene of a ceremony in this Edwardian photograph. C.G. Prideaux-Brune, a Director of the North Cornwall Railway Company until his death in 1908, was succeeded by his son Col. C.R. Prideaux-Brune until the end of the Company in 1923. (Author's Collection)

38

Padstow about 1920. The new jetty is complete (but the 'bull nose' is yet to come) and one of the two sidings holds a line of LSWR ventilated fish vans, a bogie guards van and an open fish wagon. The West Quay is almost complete (centre) while the original Padstow Harbour Commissioners' South Quay, with its siding, is in the foreground. Bray and Parken's store is behind the masts and the lower road winds with the sidings toward station area (right centre). The white ice factory stands out in the distance, worked by electricity as was all the lighting on the LSWR/PHC quays at this time. (R.I.C.)

On the Devon side James Oag of Thorndon, near Ashwater, was for long a Director (1883 until his death in 1912), as well as C. Bainbridge Rendle of Devonport, also a Director of the Delabole Slate Co., and Lord Halsbury figured largely in the affairs of the NCR Co. The latter, as Sir Hardinge Stanley Giffard, sat as MP for Launceston from 1877 until becoming Baron Hardinge in 1885 to hold office as Lord Chancellor. With a seat at Pendruccombe House, Launceston, he was Constable of the Castle. A Director from 1885, following the death of Lord Torrington, and further created the Earl of Halsbury in 1898, he continued as such until his death in 1921.

The LSWR appointed Arthur Mills MP as their Director on the NCR Board and, on his death in 1899, F.J. Macauley and Sir F.C. Scotter (LSWR General Manager 1866 - 1898, thereafter a SWR Director).

In August 1912 there was a suggestion that the LSWR might absorb the North Cornwall Co. or, at least, offer a reorganisation of the financial stockholding and existing rentals and rebates. The new General Manager, Herbert Walker, wrote to the NCR in October setting out the LSWR's proposals:

(a) A fixed rental of £25,250 per annum, paid half-yearly in place of the exist-ing rentals and rebates.
(b) Payment of Delabole to Wadebridge Section arrears of interest (£5,035).
(c) Payment of the £3,000 invested in the Padstow Harbour works.
(d) Necessary Parliamentary powers for consolidation of stocks.

As far as (d) was concerned, the existing issued capital (£574,000) and the Debentures (Launceston/Delabole 3 1/2% = £62,000, Launceston/Halwill and Delabole/Wadebridge £50,000 each) would be converted to 'North Cornwall Line Stock' revalued at £801,000, the rental income paying about 3 1/2% on the capital. Acceptance by the NCR shareholders came in 1913, agreement in April and ratification by an LSWR Act of 15 August.

Under the amalgamation powers for the new Southern Railway Company in 1922 the NCR would be absorbed by the LSWR in the first place. In the final count, at an extraordinary meeting held on 17 November 1922, the LSWR was already seen to be the largest shareholder (£130,308). Other large holdings were by the Curry interests (from the contracting years), the Oags and Bolitho interests, Colonel Prideaux-Brune, and the Eastern Telegraph Co. These, and minor shareholders received equivalent LSWR stocks totalling £161,309. The North Cornwall Railway Company was for-mally wound up at the last meeting at Finsbury Court, London on 6 March 1923. The four remaining Directors, L.C. Foster, H.D. Foster, Col. Prideaux-Brune and Sir T.H. Kekewich were compensated for loss of office, and the Secretary (E.C. Price) received a £250 testimonial.

Quotations by the SR, post-1923, recognised an 'actual' mileage from Waterloo, quoted in the timetables. The Engineer's Department employed the 'milepost' mileage for obvious reasons - bridges for example - and these are used in this book. The slacks in mileage on the North Cornwall were about 8 to 12 chains, so that the stopblock at Padstow 259m 55ch was seen locally as 259m 44ch.

The assets of the NCR comprised the land and permanent way, all structures and the stations. Not all buildings were the Company's, the staff cottages and the signalling system were LSWR for instance. The North Cornwall began on the boundary with the LSWR (17 chains beyond Halwill Junction station) and ended similarly short of Wadebridge Junction. The double line (as from 1907) to Wadebridge, and through to Molesworth Street was LSWR. From the latter point to Padstow South Quay (but possibly not all sidings on the other quays) comprised the Padstow extension.

Egloskerry station opened two months late in October 1892 - the buildings had not been completed. Unusually for the North Cornwall this station, and Tresmeer, was built in red brick although the outer walling was in familiar dressed stone. Certain NCR stations acquired slate cladding on the upper storey as protection from driving rain. Prominent here, and at all stations, was the oil lamp room (centre) necessary for the attention to the numerous signal, platform, station and domestic illumination. (Andrew Muckley)

Chapter Three
THE LINE DESCRIBED

On the last day of steam, 1st January 1965, Class 4 4-6-0 No. 75025 is by the turntable in Okehampton depot, probably to work the 12.10 p.m. to Bude and return therefrom at 2.40 p.m. The Plymouth - Brighton train was already diesel hauled ('Warship' No. D815) though steam heating from a boiler in the engine is noticeable! (P.W. Gray)

Domesday Borough, Charter Town (James I - 1623), a cattle market and with a military presence from the proximity to the Dartmoor training areas, Okehampton loomed large in railway developments. The station was well above the town to the south, a half mile steep climb for some, but horse and (later) motor buses served other users. Most local trains had portions for Bude and Padstow dividing and attaching further west at Halwill. The two-platform layout with a departure (only) bay on the Down side was restrictive, entailing carriage stock movement conflicting with shunting the goods yard. A fifteen-lever signal box was formerly situated on the Down platform. A rudimentary locomotive establishment was sited on the Up side to accommodate the Holsworthy tanks, but in 1894 proper facilities were provided with a 50ft turntable and one road engine shed. Further sidings were required by the end of the 1880s for increased traffic. To accommodate the Army an extensive two-sided loading bank served by three sidings was constructed by 1909 on the Up side to the

west. As there was simply no room for long shunting necks, most moves from both sides required occupation of the running lines in the platforms. The underbridge at the west end was widened about 1886 to improve the exit from the bay, with provision for a limited 'neck' for shunting the goods yard. The rising cattle traffic in the 1880s

resulted in a landing with pens beyond the goods shed. Enlargement of the goods yard with three long sidings meant more quarrying out - and building up an embankment. The goods shed itself was a large country LSWR type, in local brown stone masonry.

The 1871 station building on the Up side originally comprised a large Sta-

A diesel railcar train waits in the North Cornwall Bay at Okehampton, probably in 1965. (R.K. Blencowe)

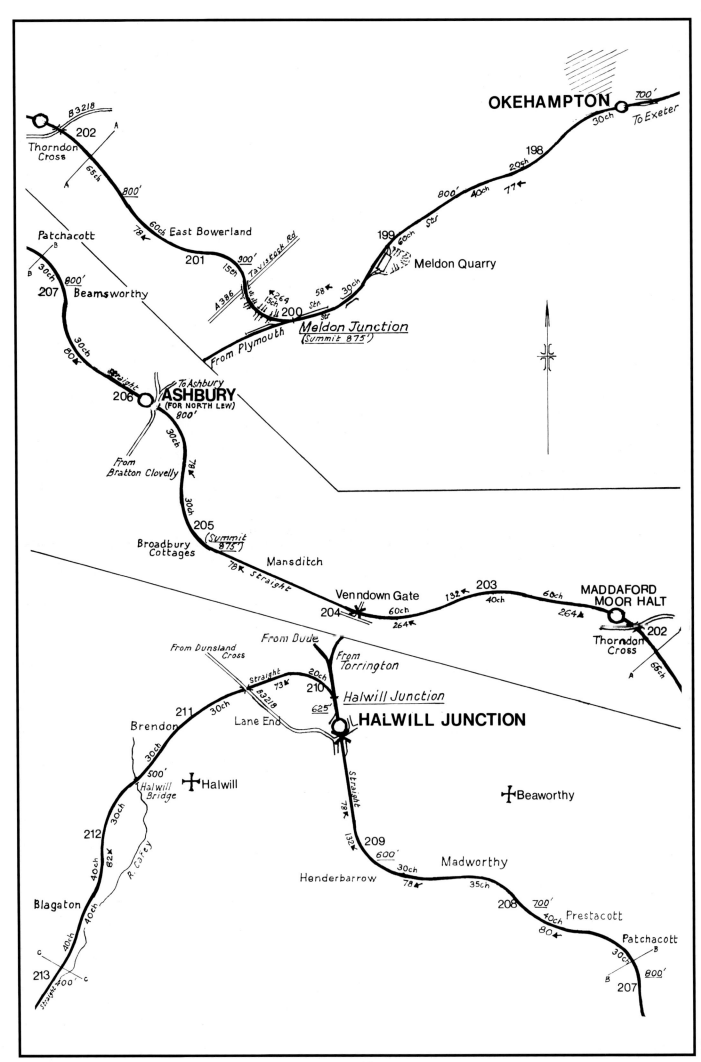

In the Military sidings at the country end of Okehampton is Drummond 'T9' No. 30719 in its last summer, 1960. (R.K. Blencowe)

tion Master's house and single storey offices to the side. A large awning was provided - it can be rather wet at times in Okehampton! A waiting room was provided on the down platform, and toilets in due course.

The SR undertook rebuilding and resignalling in the 1930s. A new signal box was erected on the Up side, opened on 12 May 1935, and Up side offices, a refreshment room (all in brick), together with a steel-framed awning over the platform. Some alterations to the layout took place in 1935 and 1939. Okehampton was at full

stretch in World War Two, especially from 1943 when the US Army built up for the Normandy Invasion. There were yet more changes after the war. On its cramped ledge to the east of the station, the locomotive depot was completely revised. The new 'West Country' Class 4-6-2s needed a longer turntable, so a new 70ft replacement was sited at one end, with a nest of three sidings between it and the engine shed. S15 4-6-0s working to Meldon Quarry could also now turn at Okehampton. At the height of the holiday season, however, the depot was

hard-put to service engines in this restricted site.

The turn around of passenger trains was usually done by train engines, but a shunter/carriage pilot engine pottered about Okehampton most of the day. At one time '495' 0-6-0s or a K10 4-4-0, but in the last years a Drummond '700' Class (30691 for instance) filled this role. It could also push a snow plough shield kept here for clearing the way around Dartmoor. Certain North Cornwall goods trains also started and terminated at Okehampton, so there were invariably 'N' Class 2-6-0s shunting as well. Over the years the siding accommodation increased to a capacity holding of over a hundred wagons. In addition to the box and open ordinary wagons, occasional empty ballast wagons for Meldon, army lorries and guns on flats, cattle wagons (for loading and transit), petrol and tar wagons were dealt with here. After the demise of Meldon Junction sidings in the 1920s, which had handled a lot of the Plymouth and Cornwall exchange traffic, Okehampton took on this role. Yeoford's sidings were enlarged in the Second World War, thus some goods trains now passed Okehampton, en route there (or to Crediton) to the Western sorting yards at Exmouth Junction.

Okehampton and Meldon Junction
From a level stretch in the platforms at Okehampton, the Plymouth main

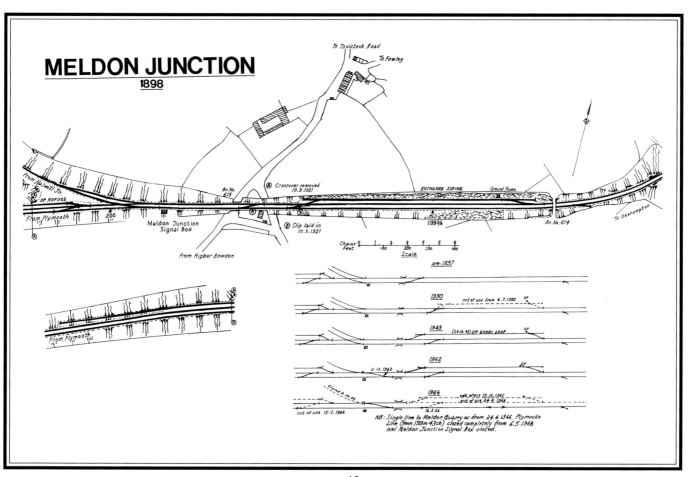

line climbed 2½ miles at 1 in 77 to Meldon Quarry signal box, at 199m 22ch. The large quarry on the Down side, originated by the LSWR in 1882, had little to do with operations on the North Cornwall apart from such ballast as it required. However, some passenger trains did call at the tiny staff halt (199m 41ch), one being the Saturday afternoon working to and from Launceston. A special coach was taken by an Okehampton engine to and from Okehampton for the quarry staff. The Viaduct was difficult to maintain, but after repairs in the 1960s, the heavier axle-weight rebuilt 'West Country' Class were permitted to run to Plymouth. From 24 April 1966 the Up line was taken out of use and a single line instituted between Quarry signal box and Meldon Junction signal box.

Meldon Junction

The original layout of the junction at Meldon, where the Holsworthy branch turned off in 1879, comprised facing and trailing points in the double line converging to single towards Ashbury. It was more than just a simple junction. After 1897 there were two sidings on the Up side, one on each side. On the Plymouth end lay the 'refuge'

latterly holding 30 wagons. On the viaduct side was a new 'exchange', and here sorting of wagons for the Plymouth line and North Cornwall/Bude took place. At 900ft above sea level and on the weather side of Dartmoor these operations must have been onerous, especially on dark winters' nights. No lighting in that period, just handlamps and pinpoints from the ground signals. The exchange siding was connected originally only to the Down line at the west or signal box end. The east end joined the Up and was controlled by a ground frame released from the box. The gradient here fell sharply at 1 in 58 towards the viaduct, so great care was necessary to avoid mis-shunts, and runaway wagons. The early morning Devonport to Launceston goods would set back over the ground frame points into the exchange. Brakes were pinned down and sprags applied to wheels to arrest wagons, while the engine went on down to Okehampton to deliver, collect and turn. On return, brake vans were left on the Down (many goods ran with two individual guards and vans, and a travelling shunter). The Launceston goods could draw directly out onto the Down line and set back on to the brake vans. Plymouth line goods would also leave

wagons (secured as above) for collection by Halwill-bound trains. Until 1966 there were two trailing crossovers as well, each side of the junction points. They, and their ground signals, were operated by 'push-pull' levers. The gradual disuse of Meldon exchange siding in favour of Okehampton and Halwill caused its final abolition in July 1930 including the ground frame, although it was not removed.

Meldon Junction signal box (199m 78ch) was rather a squat edifice of the LSWR's 1870s pattern. The signalling was concentrated at first, with no fewer than three bracketed junction signals in the Down direction:- distants at 816 yards, outer homes at 144 yards and inner homes at 17 yards. 26 levers in the frame controlled them, those towards Bridestowe and Ashbury, as well as the pointwork and locking. At first the Ashbury single line was protected by a Staff, but from the 1890s a Tablet system was introduced (Tyers No.3) to the new block post at Maddaford Loop, but in BR days a returnable Token was substituted (to Ashbury). A 10mph restriction was imposed for exchange of Tablets. 200 yards towards Ashbury the Up and Down lines converged to single line. An interesting altercation between the

The Up line from the Junction Box over the Viaduct to Meldon Quarry Signal Box had been taken out of use when this view from the front of a diesel railcar was taken on 5th March 1966 with the signal and facing crossover set for Ashbury. The direct facing points with a 'diamond' crossing on the Up (Plymouth) line had been removed from 12th December 1962. Numerous changes were made to Meldon Junction's layout over the years reflecting its use (subsequently declining) as an exchange point for North Cornwall/Plymouth wagons in earlier years, the lever frame holding 26 levers, all in use. (R.A. Lumber)

Board of Trade and the LSWR occurred in 1897. The latter laid in a trailing runaway point in the Down line leading to Ashbury. Major Marindin did not like it at all. Nothing like it had ever been sanctioned before and it would be a danger to branch and main line, he said. The LSWR, under pressure, removed it in 1898. For Up trains Regulation 5 (first from Maddaford Loop and then from Ashbury) i.e. flagged signals to inform Up line drivers that Meldon Junction could not be assumed to be clear, with no protection from overrunning the Home signal. The previously mentioned down inner Homes at Meldon were subsequently removed due to the lack of overrun length to the junction points.

The exchange siding was reactivated from 24 October 1943 but as an Up goods loop. The eastern end was still ground frame operated. This wartime providence appears to be associated with the new ASD yard at Halwill for ammunition trains. A new facing crossover came into use 2 December 1962 and henceforward North Cornwall down trains used this to gain the single line (the direct lead and diamond crossing being removed). Most connections and the goods loop were recovered in 1966 with the singling over the viaduct. The end of Meldon Junction and signal box in relation to the North Cornwall came on 30 October following withdrawal of passenger trains on the 3rd. To complete the story here, after withdrawal of services between Okehampton-Tavistock North-Bere Alston on 6 May 1968, a temporary stop block was placed on the single line at 199m 43ch (at the east end of the viaduct). In the 1970s a shunting neck was reopened over part of the viaduct (199m 48ch) to better serve the ballast trains in Meldon Quarry. This has since been removed.

Meldon Junction to Ashbury and Halwill Junction

Leaving Meldon Junction a double reverse curve of 15 chains on a high embankment here (at 900 feet above sea level) set the line in a westerly direction. On this exposed plateau there are not many trees of size and hedges rise high to shelter livestock in numerous small fields. Two miles from the Junction lay Maddaford Moor Halt (202m 14ch). The sub-title 'For Thorndon Cross' originally referred to a proposed health resort. The Southern Railway was induced to open this halt on 27 July 1926. Development of bungalows continued into the 1930s, but no resort. Maddaford Moor survived, quite well used, until closure in 1966. The oil lamp by the waiting shed was placed there by train guards as required.

Until 3 May 1919 a Down passing loop existed on the future site of Maddaford Moor Halt. Opened in 1899 it was fully signalled for passenger trains and controlled from a box centrally situated at 202m 28ch. Exceptionally long at over 1,000 feet and suitable for a 50 wagon, or 12 coach train, the LSWR's requirement appeared to stem from increased traffic to Halwill Junction, now the North Cornwall was fully open. Not wishing to go to the expense of doubling, provision of this loop broke the long six-mile section from Meldon to Ashbury. The reason for closure is not known. Every train was required to slow to 10 mph to exchange Tablets and it was not equipped to be bypassed by switching out. In the event the box and loop were kept in-situ until 1921.

Situated on a gently falling gradient of 1 in 260 and in a shallow dip between the summit at Meldon and the next station on the line, Ashbury, it was relatively safe from runaways.

Maddaford Moor Halt opened on 27th July 1926 on the site of a passing loop and signal box which existed from 1899 to 1919. Thorndon Cross was to be developed as a health resort; little came of it, though numerous bungalows were built on the site. (Lens of Sutton)

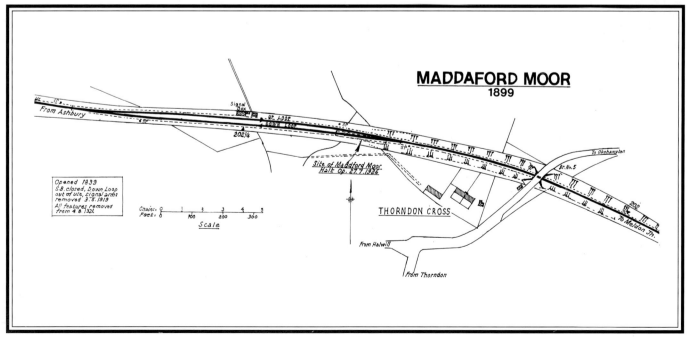

A mile and a half further on came Venn Gates Crossing. Protected by distant and home signals, it was not, however, a block post; the gateman received bell signals and acknowledged them, set his signals, but then only closed, and reopened, his gates by hand. The line then climbed, now on an embankment, to another summit at the 205 mp. From here down to Halwill the gradient fell at 1 in 78/80 for five miles and was the scene of a spectacular runaway in February 1905, described elsewhere in this book. Just one mile down lay Ashbury Station. Not very near Ashbury (the population was only 54 in the 1920s), or its sub-title 'for North Lew' (682) nevertheless it served a wide area including Germansweek and Bratton Clovelly. It should be remembered from this distance in time that rural roads were unmetalled, atrocious in bad weather, and public conveyance almost nil. The arrival of the railway as a quick transit to market, or town, was truly welcomed. Although it meant a long walk

Ashbury (for North Lew) offered one passenger on 16th May 1964 as the single coach and van of the 3.13 p.m. Bude drew in behind No. 31849. Both parishes lay to the north of the station, several miles away and, by this time, only the occasional wagon of coal or fertilizer was shunted into the sidings. The poster on the left advertized the passenger closure proposals. (R.A. Lumber)

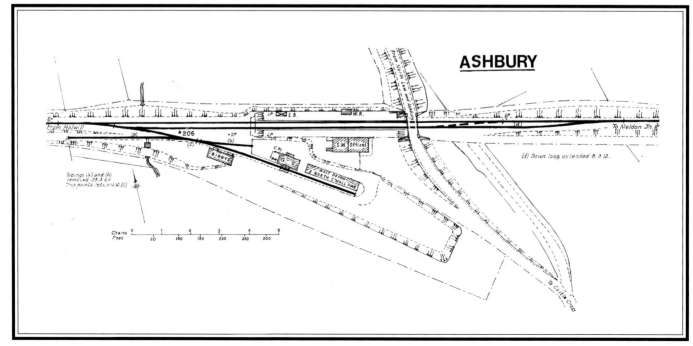

Messrs. S.R. Hawkins and H. Smallacombe were running Ashbury station in its last year 1966. The 1879 signal box, much rebuilt and renovated over the years, latterly served as a ticket office as well. (A.E. West)

to a station for many people places like Ashbury could attract quite a few customers, certainly up to the 1930s.

The 1879 Ashbury (205m 75ch) hardly altered until closure in 1966. On the Down platform lay a bungalow-style station master's house and offices. There was no footbridge on these wayside stations passengers using the road bridge at the east end, but there was a barrow crossing at rail level. Another squat signal box on the up platform dated from the opening. It was always manned by shift signalmen as traffic warranted their full time presence (though a ticket office was later opened at the box end). Longer goods trains in this century necessitated lengthening the Down loop (it is believed from 1912) and the equivalent wagon limit was raised to 34. The lever frame held twelve for the simple crossing loops and access to the goods siding (push/pull operation again). Flanking this siding were a goods shed and a cattle pen. In due course an agricultural store was established by the West Devon & North Cornwall Farmers Ltd and an SR concrete unit store used by Messrs Bibby. This yard, on the down side, could be shunted by running onto the single line towards Halwill, but the original non-returnable Tablet had to be taken out and carried through as the Down starting signal was well inside the loop. In World War Two, Ashbury could be open 24 hours a day with Halwill handling numerous ammunition trains through 1943/44. The provision of a returnable Key Token to Halwill from this date was much more helpful.

Ashbury was the vital part of this line between Meldon Junction and Halwill with its passing loop. The evening goods trains from Halwill loaded heavily and needed a good clear run towards Meldon on the four mile climb at 1 in 78. The sight and sound of a 'Woolworth' 2-6-0 charging up through Ashbury (hardly slowing for the Tablet) with 40 wagons on is not easily forgotten, the echoing bark from its chimney carrying back over the darkening winter-landscape on the way up to Venn. On a summer Saturday, too, there was much activity from holiday trains (none stopped) and light engine movements to cope with their various divisions at Halwill or Okehampton. The passing loop was retained in the diesel era, when many others lost them, and Ashbury remained a typical LSWR rural station of the 1880s period, retaining even its oil lamps to the end.

From Ashbury the single line dropped steeply and sinuously by way of Patchacott and Madworthy. Quite extensive views could be obtained from this side of the plateau across Hatherleigh, and further to Exmoor. Eventually Halwill could be seen in the distance, though there was a 1/4 mile climb on a rare straight, just before the Junction, for Down trains.

Halwill Junction (209m 60ch)

Along the Holsworthy Branch of 1879 a site for a station was chosen about half way between Halwill and Beaworthy, both 'churchtowns' as termed in Devon, but in reality mere hamlets. The road from Okehampton to Dunsland Cross had been improved in the 19th century and the mail coach from Holsworthy and Stratton used it in due course, though earlier it followed the Hatherleigh Road to North Tawton and Exeter. This later road paralleled the Holsworthy Branch for most of the way and was thus rather *too* convenient for the bus substitution on closure in 1966.

As with many rural junctions, Halwill could be deceptively quiet for parts of the day, perhaps only the Bude branch tank doing some shunting in the yard between turns. Quite suddenly arrivals from all quarters brought forth much activity. Dividing and attaching coaches, exchanging wagons (especially around 5 pm), even the Torrington line contributing its quota. This latecomer, the North Devon and Cornwall Junction Light Railway (an independent concern until 1947 but worked by the SR) complicated the Halwill layout from its opening on 27 July 1925. It represented the last vestige of railway expansion. Despite dismissive remarks to the contrary, a fair-sized tonnage passed from it into Halwill over its 40 year life.

Halwill on 19th June 1926 with '460' Class No. 0471 on the 10.00 a.m. Okehampton to Padstow and Bude. In the bay (centre) is Drummond 'M7' No. 35, an 0-4-4T which came to work on the Bude branch in the mid-twenties. Another '460' No. 0473 from Barnstaple shed, is waiting in the yard to return with a train over the newly-opened Torrington Light Railway. (H.C. Casserley)

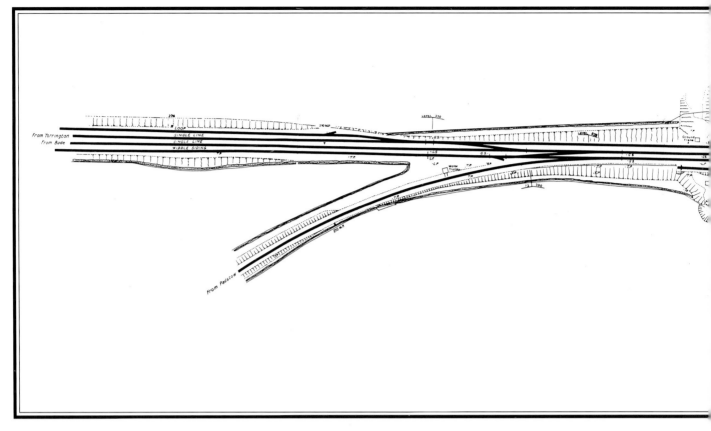

Although no plan has survived, it is likely that Halwill resembled Ashbury in 1879 as a simple crossing place - two loops and a goods siding. All three wayside stations to Holsworthy received the single storey station buildings on the Down side, signal box and waiting shed on the Up platform. This was to change in 1886 when Halwill's layout needed to cope with Launceston trains as well. The South Western Co. allowed the North Cornwall 17ch 'mileage' which stretched from their land boundary to the centre of the station - a by-line as it were. The latter paralleled the Holsworthy Branch and joined the Down platform loop. New facing crossovers were provided between

both lines and the existing loops. A bay was put in behind the Down platform, enough only for a tank engine and three six-wheel coaches. Slip points enabled this bay to be used for Holsworthy and Launceston trains in both directions. Extra sidings and a turntable were added to the yard. It is probable that the loops were extended at this time at the Ashbury end, then extending two tracks across the level crossing.

The signal box had to be enlarged; it appears to have been the existing structure raised much higher to accommodate a larger lever frame and to give a commanding view of the 1/4 mile long layout. The levers now numbered 38. Trains from Holsworthy and

Launceston could draw right up to Inner Home signals or be kept at the Outer Homes. With Staff and Ticket working, every yard of track inside station limits (i.e. the home and starting signals) was valuable. Even so, the tails of goods trains would often be well down the gradient towards Ashwater. Twice there were runaways through mis-shunts and failure to pin down wagon brakes. It was always necessary to do a lot of shunting in Halwill's loops as goods trains exchanged wagons from and to the branches. A long 'middle' siding (costing the LSWR £846) was laid in, paralleling the Holsworthy line, in 1894. Now a goods could be safely berthed inside the signals, though it is doubtful if it was used as much as it should. The Tablet system (with interlocking of starting signals) may not have been introduced at Halwill until the early 1900s, probably at the same time as the Up inner homes (26/27/29) were removed. No 26 and 27 were for North Cornwall arrivals, and slotted to the outers, 29 for Holsworthy trains. Henceforward the Bay would handle only Down departures, and it was lengthened at the inner end, to take an engine and three bogie coaches. The signalling remained unaltered until the Torrington line opened in 1925. Even then changes were only marginal, as the latter was self-contained and worked by ground frames. In 1934 wholesale replacement of ground signals took place and signal arm heights changed. The 'main' aspects were now for the North Cornwall line (the lower placed arms for

A destructive crash in February 1905 at Halwill Junction. A goods train coming down from Ashbury became parted, the rear portion crashing into the front near the crossing gates. A pig-sty (right) was demolished and the wagons spread-eagled right (and left, out of the picture). In the distance is the Junction Hotel, but notice the wicker-basket for the rabbit trade (lower right). (Author's collection)

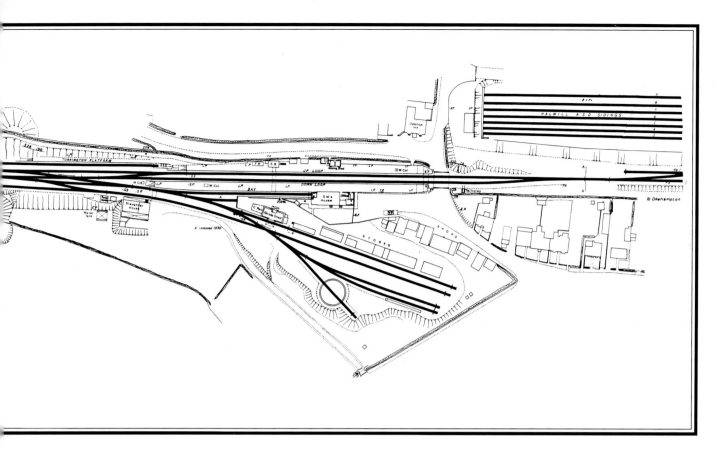

the Bude Branch) on the Down main and Branch starting signals. Further signalling and layout alterations at the Ashbury end came in 1943 under wartime pressures.

Halwill's main platforms were gradually lengthened over the years. The Down considerably so in 1886, to match the new Bay, the Ashbury ends as noted, and the Up on the Torrington line opening in 1925. The latter ex-

tension fed a little pathway round to the Torrington platform. While their extension was constructed in local stone, the Torrington was made of mass concrete. Seven coaches could now be accommodated in the platforms, adequate for local traffic. The holiday trains in the 1930s were increasing in length to twelve coaches at times, troop trains even reached 16 in the Second World War and later pi-

geon specials to Bude frequently numbered the same, as bogie vans. From the 1900s local train were usually in combination to and from Okehampton, with engine and Padstow train proceeding after detaching or attaching a Bude portion in the Halwill platforms.

Halwill goods yard was primarily for local traffic. Although some remarshalling occurred there, much wagon sorting took place out on the

The signalman's view of Halwill Junction was improved by the elevation of the original 1879 box, probably in 1886 on the opening to Launceston. The 1925 extension (to the left) housed the new Torrington line apparatus as well as Tablet machines to Hole, Dunsland Cross, Ashwater and Ashbury. On 28th August 1960 the 1.00 p.m. from Padstow is arriving with a Brake Composite, through to Waterloo, and a local set for Okehampton. The Set from the 2.01 p.m. Bude has been drawn back to await attachment. Drinking water for Dunsland Cross is likely to be the contents of the churns. (R.A. Lumber)

Halwill Junction was renamed Halwill for Beaworthy by the Southern Railway in 1923, though it continued to be referred to as the 'Junction' and to this day the village road sign says it is! The 1879 station building and SM's house (at the far end), also the platform lighting, have an electric supply in 1963. The telegraph post carried the bell code and Tablet system wires, the single-needle telegraph and the telephone circuit wires - vitally important ancillaries. They were maintained by Linemen and mates based at Okehampton, Launceston and Wadebridge. (P. Paye)

running lines, especially between 5 and 6pm when the up Bude and Wadebridge goods were in the loops. The final layout afforded four holding sidings for coal, agricultural traffic and cattle wagons. A fifth siding served the 50ft turntable and a small coal stage. A cattle pen was situated on the dock behind the Down platform (the direct end-loading siding here was removed in 1930). Cattle wagons were cleaned on the end of No 4 siding which was extended in 1912. Further along the goods shed siding, two more cattle pens were provided in the 1900s to cope with the expanding business. Farther on, national and local seed and fertilizer merchants established themselves in storehouses. Latterly Silcocks, the West Devon and North Cornwall Farmers, and Thomas Oke & Sons conducted business here. Halwill being one of the main sources of cattle traffic, a market was opened a hundred yards or so down the road towards Halwill village. However, it was dead stock, slaughtered ex-market, which eventually dominated. A wooden slaughterhouse was built and a siding extended to it, at a date unknown but probably prior to 1900. From 1904 a direct connection was put from the North Cornwall side (No 15 points) and the siding lengthened to the west. In 1932 652 wagons arrived with livestock for slaughter, but 272 wagons of live cattle went to eastern destinations like Banbury and Sevenoaks. 22855 sheep were slaughtered that

year. A much larger brick building and long platform replaced the old one in 1938. It was closed under wartime conditions but reopened as the tonnage of meat increased tremendously. Insulated vans, used in the 1920s and 1930s and forwarded by overnight goods services via Exeter, gave way to demountable containers in the 1950s. The containers were rated as passenger traffic and were attached to the two afternoon 'perishable' trains from Bude and Padstow. Most went to Smithfield, roaded from Nine Elms, though certain traffic was for the Midlands, via Templecombe. Apart from meat, there were tremendous quantities of eggs, 100,000 daily, it is said (a very delicate commodity) along with 'day-old' chicks and butter/eggs.

Such merchandise as ordered locally was handled in the stone-built goods shed. It was medium sized, but unlike Holsworthy, received only a stanchioned 'port' over the siding. No crane was provided but the SR leased out a cart weighbridge in the station approach.

The growth of Halwill Junction as a railway centre in West Devon is reflected by the following establishment: Post Office ('Beaworthy'), police station, bank, public house ('The Junction Hotel'), a chapel (Baptist), a small cottage hospital, garage, cattle market, an egg packing station and some shops. The combined population of Halwill and Beaworthy was just over 600 in 1931 and grew perceptibly while

other West Devon parishes declined. Since 1966 the name 'Halwill Junction' has survived as the road signs declare, even though the site of the railway has been covered by a housing estate.

Although the area of the station grew, the original station master's house and offices remained unaltered. Houses built for railway employees by the LSWR were situated to the south of the goods yard. On the Up platform stood the enlarged signal box and the waiting room was rebuilt in 1905. The Permanent Way Inspector used an office on this side, and there was a small goods store. Water supplies for Halwill were maintained by a large tank and electric pump on the top of the cutting (down side) - very necessary for the two water columns on the platform, the slaughterhouse and the cattle wagon washdown. Even Holsworthy was supplied in drought periods (in a converted engine tender) and some of the Torrington line stations could also run dry.

Suddenly in 1943 Halwill entered the forward logistic planning for the invasion of France. The US Army, building up its ammunition supply, distributed it around the Devon countryside and extra yards for wagonloads were laid down at Tower Hill and Whitstone (on the Bude Branch). On the Ashbury and Up side at Halwill a large area of ground was levelled. The SR put down eight sidings capable of holding no less than 220 wagons. The outer siding faced a hard standing for lorries of the Supply Service, often driven by coloured US troops. It is estimated that 35,000 tons were handled at these railheads, as well as Launceston, the yard here opening on 26 September 1943. After 'D' Day, 6 June 1944, only 4,000 tons of ammunition had still to be forwarded to the beach heads in Normandy. Operationally, a long loop siding (No1) holding engine and 60 wagons was opened from 26 September 1943 paralleling the line towards Ashbury. At that end a connection to the single, protected by a spur, was controlled by a new ground frame 'C'. Trains could be 'shut in' by restoring the Halwill - Ashbury Token to an auxiliary machine at this end. At the station end the loop (and spur) were slotted into Halwill's main signalling, and entry here indicated by a ringed-arm (30) bracketed to the Up starting signal. 'N' Class 2-6-0s handled these trains, and one of these, No.1833 was to be the cause of a spectacular rescue. On the 16 June 1944 1833 left Halwill's Up platform, gathering speed to rush the bank to Ashbury. Unfortunately the facing points to the new loop were left open, but the spur points at the far end closed. In spite of braking, the engine crashed through the stop blocks and nose-dived into the Beaworthy road. It was no problem to crane out the tender, but the engine's recovery was much more serious. A ship's hawser was obtained and two engines normally prohibited beyond Meldon, a S15 4-6-0 and a USA 'S160' 2-8-0 (probably No. 2356), plus another 'N' together tried to pull her out. The second attempt also failed (the 2-8-0 suffered a buckled beam). On the third attempt a greased plate was laid under 1833's wheels and no less than three 'N' Class and two N15s (including No.453) managed to do it. The 4-6-0s and the 2-8-0 were specially authorised to cross Meldon Viaduct.

Halwill Junction to Ashwater

From Halwill Junction, 600ft above sea level, a way was found to join the head of Carey River valley. From the junction at 209m 71ch a sharp 20ch curve took the line in a SW direction, along a straight under the Dunsland road at Lane End, and then over a series of 30ch reverses to join the infant river at Blagadon. Beyond the stone arch over the river at 213m 8ch there is little sign now of a siding which existed between 1919 and 1920. This faced Down trains and was worked by a 2 lever ground frame released by the Tablet. Paid for by the Pitwood Association Ltd. (a consortium of Monmouthshire and South Wales Colliery owners), it could hold ten wagons and, as the title suggests, exported pit props, wood chocks etc. It is said to have been fed by an overhead cableway, and worked by Belgian refugees. The wagons were sent to Yeoford to join wagonloads from the North Devon Line to South Wales.

Below this point the valley sides begin to steepen, but there is still room for the 28ft width of the North Cornwall Railway. All overbridges to Wadebridge, and abutments of some underbridges, were built for this double line requirement if necessary. The ruling gradient of 1 in 73 and curves generally no sharper than 30 chains, adopted as a standard for the NCR, continued down to Ashwater. Early in December 1893 the rear of an Up goods train (21 loaded cattle wagons, a meat van and the brake van) managed to run away backwards from Halwill. It had been left on the curve at the Junction and had, apparently, been nudged during shunting operations. The emergency bells rang to Ashwater, and further. Fortunately the line was clear. The runaways reached Tilleshow Woods, about seven miles away, in about eight minutes. Thankfully they came to a halt on a slight rise of 1 in 220 and no harm was done. In the aftermath (and there had been a previous runaway in 1887) the rules were tightened. If a goods train was left outside the Up Home signal it had to have two brake vans, or an engine, at the Ashwater end. The 1894 long siding ('Middle') at Halwill was part of this new protection.

Ashwater (214m 67ch)

Down the hill from Ashwater, with its pleasant green and church, lay the North Cornwall station, in the vicinity of Ash Mill. Five miles from Halwill, the mileage was 214m 67ch from Waterloo. It was approached from that direction by a 40 chain curve, under Bridge No.14 spanning a deep cutting, and into a straight on a 1 in 330 falling gradient. The platform would take only seven coaches, but the Up loop (lengthened from 18 October 1936) was suitable for 35 wagons or a twelve coach train. Before this date, a lengthy up goods, or cattle train, would have to shunt its tail into the yard. Ashwater's yard could be quite busy at times; cattle forwarding was heavy before 1914 and again in the next war.

The Ashwater signalman exchanges single line Tablets with the crew of No. 34066 'Spitfire' passing through on the 11.00 a.m. Padstow to Waterloo on 11th September 1964. This engine was involved in the Lewisham disaster of 1956, but is seen here in the quiet valley of the Carey where it begins to narrow towards the south. (R.A. Lumber)

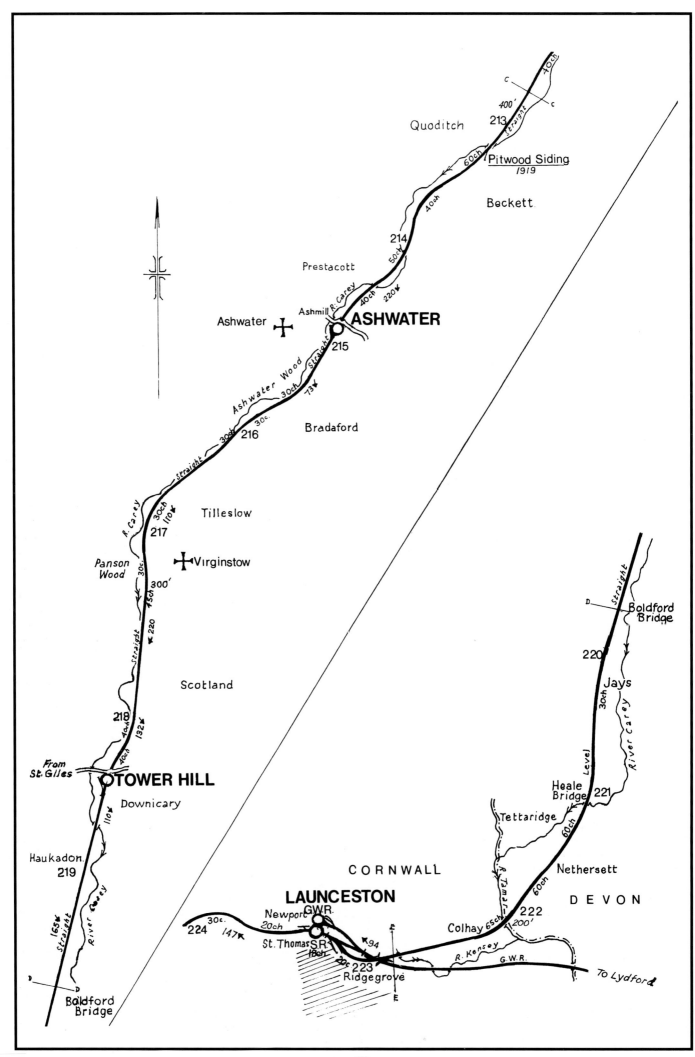

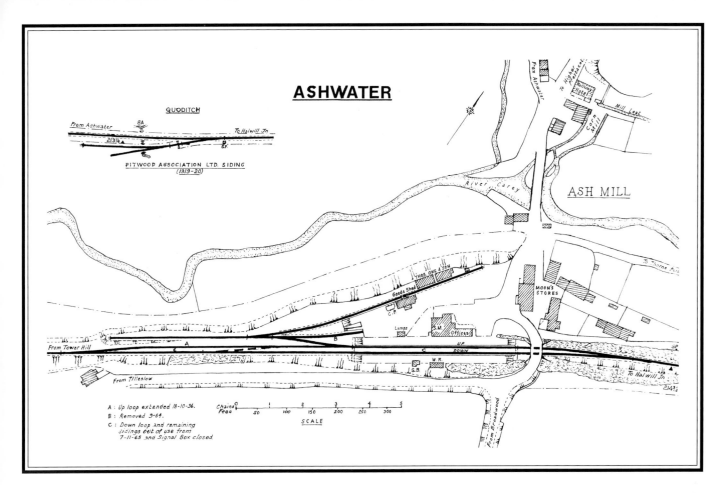

ASHWATER

As in other stations, the SR built and leased a fertiliser, seed and agriculture store to a local firm, Thomas Oke & Sons of Holsworthy. The majority of business, however, was conducted by R.H. Moon & Sons, who ran an extensive store on the other side of the road at Ash Mill, for all manner of merchandise including coal. A small iron goods shed flanked the outer siding, the inner one ending in a side and ending loading dock. Quantities of timber on offer at Ashwater brought forward an extension of the loading dock in 1909. In the 1930s, Mr. Harry Spry sent pig carcasses to Smithfield Market, in London. They were brought by horse and cart from Prestacott Farm and loaded into a reserved van left in the platform by the 11.35am Up goods train from Wadebridge while the engine shunted the yard. Ashwater was a destination for roadstone from Wilminstone, a common material seen in Devon yards. Local farmers carried it further, under contract to the County Council. The rabbit trade was conducted locally by a Mr. Dymond, who forwarded tremendous quantities over the years - this happened at most NCR stations, as we shall see. The standard type of station building evolved by the LSWR in the West was repeated all the way down to Padstow. Ashwater was built of local brown stone, including a large station master's house with station offices adjacent and situated on the Up side. The SM's houses were quite commodious

comprising three bedrooms, parlour, kitchen, WC and wash-house. Within this block was the ladies' waiting room (and WC) opening to the booking hall/waiting room. The latter, the booking office, staff room/or parcels office and SM's offices were in the single storey extension. On the other side of the house adjacent to the enclosed SM's courtyard was the gentlemen's toilets. There were siting variations down the line (with Camelford and Padstow equipped with awnings) but room dimensions, door and window placings

were essentially similar. A LSWR signal box of their 1880's design with extensive glazing stood on the Down platform. It had eleven levers, all in use. The last SM was Mr. J.H. Lashbrook in 1926, when control passed to Launceston.

Alas, apart from seed, fertiliser and basic slag traffic, goods business declined and the goods yard closed with others from 7 September 1964. The station was reduced to an unstaffed halt on 7 November 1965 and all points were clipped and padlocked. The sig-

Ashwater goods shed was constructed, unusually, of corrugated iron sheeting, conforming with the LSWR's No. 1 pattern. Although closed eighteen months earlier, coal and fertilizers were still being imported by Messrs. Oke and, Moons, by road. (A.E. West)

The signal box at Ashwater on the Down platform was of the fully glazed pattern adopted by the LSWR in the 1880s. 'N' Class 2-6-0 No.31845 arriving with the Up afternoon goods from Wadebridge in the 1960s. (R.K. Blencowe)

The dressed stonework of overbridge, station buildings and platform walls at Tower Hill is apparent on this damp day in the 1950s. The new 1943 signal box was sited across the booking office frontage (centre). The Carey Valley widens considerably here, and the alignment through the station and toward Launceston started a rare straight reaching over two miles in length. (R.L. Goodman collection)

nal box was closed, leaving the former Up loop as a Single line.

Ashwater to Tower Hill

Below Ashwater the line kept to the east side of the Carey. In places, due to the steep side of the valley, it was shelved into the lower hillside to maintain the 30 chain radii. The valley is well wooded through Ashwater to Tilleshow (216 miles) but widens out at Virginstow (217 miles) and the curvature was less severe, including a long straight towards Tower Hill. The levels fall from the 600 foot at Halwill to the 300 foot contour at Tower Hill, with gradients easing from the initial 1 in 73 to 1 in 110. Ashwater and Tower Hill served Broadwoodwidger and Virginstowe villages to the east and St Giles-in-the-Heath to the west. In 1921 the population of Ashwater parish was 659. The combined number in the latter parishes was 1,105 which shows the low density in this part of

West Devon for many years. In earlier times people walked to Ashwater or Tower Hill, and farmers would use a pony and trap. Dressed stone seemed to be available in quantity for this first section, but many of the cattle creeps were simply rows of old rails, and two waybeams laid across stone abutments. In due course these (and Meldon Viaduct) would cause the prohibition of heavier engines. Where the line skirted the river, careful watch had to be kept for scouring, as water levels and volume could rise rapidly. In one wet winter, early on, slips were recorded within this section of the line.

Tower Hill (218m 35ch)

Approached down a steep road from the east side, and situated near the road bridge over the Carey leading to St Giles up a long hill to the west, Tower Hill was named after an adjacent farm. The stone-built station was identical to Ashwater, and the origi-

nal goods yard layout, with the passing loops laid out on a straight. The first signal box stood on the Down platform, again in the roomy 1880s style. After the 1914-18 War the crossing facilities were abolished. From 15 June 1920 the Down loop was taken out of use, and the signal box closed, thus creating a seven-mile section from Ashwater to Launceston. An amber light was displayed, thereafter, on the former Down distant signal as a marker for the approach to Tower Hill. At first the signal box levers were retained, but later on a ground frame was substituted, released by the Section Tablet, to operate and lock the siding points on the push/pull principle.

The last stationmaster was Mr. Dolby. From 1928 control came under Launceston. Tower Hill slept on through the thirties, the goods yard moderately busy with incoming coal and agriculture products, and the occasional cattle wagon for loading. The station house was occupied by one of the porters, while at the back of the yard were terraced houses (of LSWR origin) for the permanent way men. The end of the goods shed siding was shortened in 1933.

All this was to change in 1943 and at Tower Hill two sidings and hard standing for lorries were laid down on the up side to serve U.S. ammunition dumps in the surrounding countryside. This gated yard trailed into the shunting neck which was lengthened considerably. As a preliminary, the Down loop was restored, longer by 150 yards than pre-1920, at the Launceston end. A signal box was established in the booking hall, protruding several feet on to the Up platform. All this was brought into use on 28 March 1943 and the following month points leading from the goods yard were moved 150 yards towards Launceston and connected to the new signal frame. There were now sixteen levers (two spare). With provision for holding a 40 wagon train (and engine and van) in the loops, and another 40 in the shunt neck, Tower Hill could handle the thousands of tons of material railed into this end of Devon. By August 1944 most of the ammunition had gone to Normandy. The yard was removed in the 1950s but the long crossing loop retained. It would prove most useful as a passing place in postwar summers when the North Cornwall holiday trains multiplied. None ever called at Tower Hill, and this rural corner of Devon lapsed into quietude again until closure in 1966, lit by oil lamps to the end. Services were withdrawn in February 1964, and the goods yard was lifted in 1965. Again the Down loop was placed out of use and the signal box closed, this time

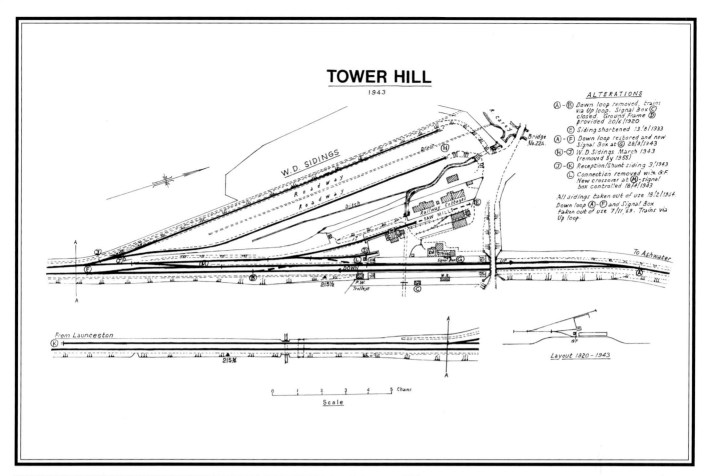

TOWER HILL
1943

ALTERATIONS

Ⓐ-Ⓑ *Down loop removed, trains via Up loop. Signal Box Ⓒ closed. Ground Frame Ⓓ provided 20/6/1920*
Ⓔ *Siding shortened 13.8/1933*
Ⓐ-Ⓕ *Down loop restored and new Signal Box at Ⓖ 28/3/1943*
Ⓗ-Ⓚ *W.D Sidings March 1943 (removed by 1955)*
Ⓙ-Ⓚ *Reception/Shunt siding 3/1943*
Ⓛ *Connection removed with G.F. New crossover at Ⓜ signal box controlled 18/4/1943*

All sidings taken out of use 18/2/1964.
Down loop Ⓐ-Ⓕ and Signal Box taken out of use 7/11/69. Trains via Up loop.

Layout 1920 - 1943

Scale

On Saturday 11th July 1964, in the last year of steam on the North Cornwall and through coaches from Waterloo, 'N' Class No. 31859 brings a Waterloo to Padstow train into Launceston. The signalman walks around to pick up the Tower Hill Tablet, and hand the Egloskerry Tablet to the driver. (R.A. Lumber)

on 7 November 1965. Thus, with Ashwater signal box closure, a 12½ mile single line Section was created for the remaining diesel car trains from Halwill to Launceston. Tower Hill is the only station to have been demolished on the NCR since closure.

Tower Hill to Launceston

The valley widens below Tower Hill and the NCR engineers were able to project their line almost straight for about two miles towards Jay's Farm (220m 20ch) on a reasonable gradient of 1 in 165. However, the Carey meandering through the meadows needed bridging twice more, at Hawkadon and at Heale. Here, a minor public road into Lifton and the river shared the two 15ft wrought iron spans taking the railway round a long 60ch curve towards Launceston. The town surmounted by its spectacular Norman Castle is clearly in view here. The Carey goes off to join the Tamar three quarters of a mile to the north, but the NCR skirted the hillside at Nethercott and then, supported on a shallow embankment beyond, headed towards the Tamar to cross the county boundary into Cornwall.

Crossing the Tamar by a double span wrought iron girder bridge on ma-

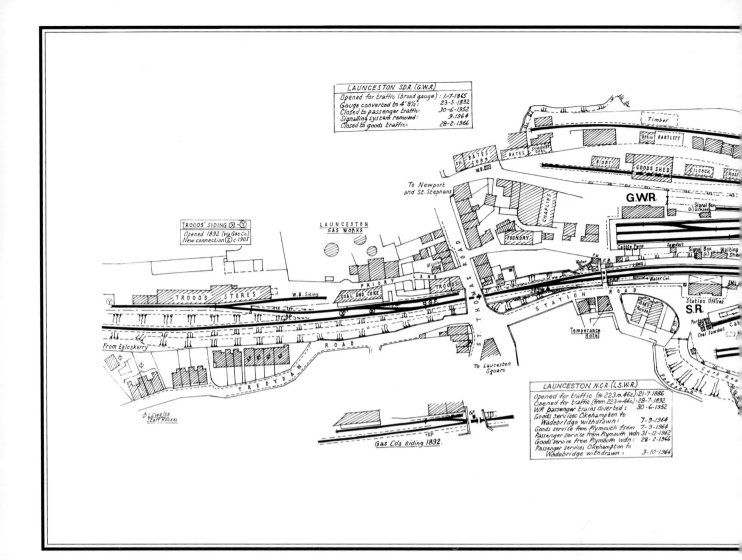

sonry piers at 222m 9ch, the North Cornwall's profile here 'bottomed out' at 200 ft above sea level, then initially rose at 1 in 94 towards Launceston.

For the next fourteen miles engines of Down trains would work against the collar to climb 600ft to the Otterham summit. Past Colhay Farm the line made straight for its first crossing of the River Kensey (over a three arch masonry viaduct), then curving right crossed the GWR by a 31ft skew span of wrought iron lattice girders. At this point it came to the base of the hill-side below Launceston, passed under the steep Ridgegrove Lane, and a few hundred yards on came to the eastern end of Launceston goods yard.

Launceston (223m 34ch)

Launceston stood as the 'gateway to Cornwall' for centuries. While rail travel was in the ascendancy the title waned, the GWR line over the Royal Albert Bridge at Saltash taking over. The rise of motoring in the 1920s re-established Launceston's 'gateway', though the town is now by-passed by the sheer volume of traffic, too much for the narrow streets, the tortuous turns, and the Southgate arch. Down the hill from the town for just over 100 years the GWR, the LSWR, the SR and then BR, trains served the town. It grew considerably on the south side and in the Newport area, where the station lay. It attracted a tourist element to view its magnificently sited Norman castle, the richly decorated Church of St. Mary Magdalene and some fine Georgian houses. The main attractions of Launceston were the

Built in local dressed stone with Portland stone quoining, Launceston station was larger than the minor stations. The Station Master lived across the road, thus leaving only (left to right) booking office and hall, waiting rooms, WCs, and parcels office to be accommodated, as seen here in 1966. The front awning and decorative cross beams had disappeared by this time. (R.L. Goodman)

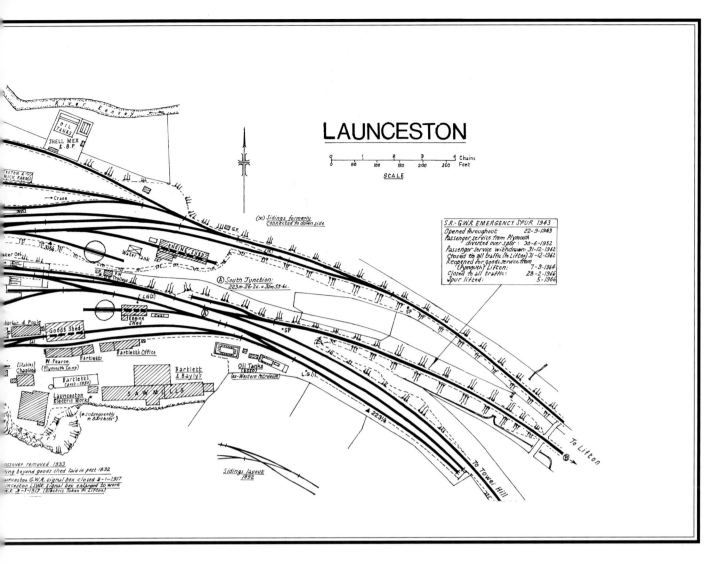

LAUNCESTON

SCALE

S.R.-G.W.R. EMERGENCY SPUR 1943
Opened throughout   22-9-1943
Passenger service from Plymouth
    diverted over spur : 30-6-1952
Passenger service withdrawn: 31-12-1962
Closed to all traffic (to Lifton) 31-12-1962
Reopened for goods service from
    (Plymouth) Lifton: 7-9-1964
Closed to all traffic: 28-2-1966
Spur lifted: 5-1966

Markets, both Pannier (in the Square) and the important Cattle and Sheep Auctions, latterly at Race Hill. Although both well away from the railway and down a very steep hill, this did not deter country people in a former age used to walking. The Station Master (only one, as we shall see) actively canvassed for business for both, though this loyalty must have been strained! His station was the railhead for many miles around, from Boyton and North Petherwin to the north and to Lewannick, Lezant and North Hill in the south, but for many years it was the lifeline to the numerous traders and manufactures in the town.

Following the opening of the GWR in 1865 and the LSWR in 1886, the stations at the bottom of the steep hills leading down from Launceston Town and St Stephens village were simply referred to as the 'Great Western' and the 'South Western'. By earlier agreement, but under wartime circumstances, on 10th August 1915 most of the traffic work on the two stations was amalgamated, thereafter known as 'LSW & GW Joint' (SR & GW Joint after 1922). The Station Master was always an LSW/SR appointment, but his staff remained either Company's servants (as they were then termed). The GW passenger guards

wore that company's uniform and buttons for instance, but the shunting staff were in LSWR uniforms, and worked in both yards - only their brass buttons showed the joint status. Between 31 December 1916 and 3 January 1917 the GWR signalmen were transferred to the rear of an enlarged LSWR box, working a separate frame and the Electric Staff instrument to and from Lifton. The single-needle tel-

egraph to Lifton was put into the LSWR booking office. Under war conditions again, the two Launceston systems were joined by a spur giving direct running for Up SR and Down GWR trains. From 19 September 1943 the GWR completed its signalling arrangements (the SR the previous 30 May) and the spur was ready. It was completed for munition trains, but not at that time for intercompany transfers.

The footbridge at the country end of Launceston's platforms drew early criticism over its steep stairway. The supporting abutments are about all that remain of the station today. (R.L. Goodman)

57

Launceston's Station Master Walter Greenslade with his SR and GWR joint staff in 1937. Front row: Hugh Godbear, signalman; Horace Martin, shunter; Harry Bishops, porter; Fred Manning, goods clerk; Francis Parkhouse, goods clerks; Walter Greenslade; Claude Sowdon, booking clerks; Monty Phillips, booking clerk with 'Tiny'; Sidney Mitchell, parcels clerk; Charlie Bradford, goods checker; Wesley Sleep, porter. Back row: Jim Walters, District Inspector; Oscar Kitts, GWR passenger guard; Sidney Webber, GWR passenger guard; Jack Osborne, parcels porter; Harry Nelder, signalman; Fred Coombe, porter; Dick Parkhouse, goods porter; Jack Endacott, Clerk (Chaplins); Albert Vodden, goods guard; Bill Manning, relief signalman; Ted Andrews, goods checker; Fred Wright, porter; Jack Chilcott, goods guard; Mr. Passmore, W.H. Smith & Sons Manager; Mr. Palk, District Cattle Inspector. (R.L. Goodman collection, courtesy C. Barrett)

The spur did achieve continuous use, however, from 30 June 1952. After nationalisation in 1948, the GWR station was suffixed 'North' and the SR 'South' (1 January 1952). Not lasting another six months, the 'North' station was closed to passengers and the local WR Plymouth trains diverted into the Southern station. The Western side remained open for goods traffic, including the engine facilities, and was still fully signalled.

The Great Western station was established in a side lane off the main road through Newport, opening on 1 July 1865. Although it appeared to be a typical GWR bywater for almost 100 years, this belied the fact that its goods business outstripped the LSW/SR in volume. The large goods shed was served by road boxes from Paddington and Plymouth and there was considerable traffic in cattle feeds, fertilizers etc. This, in spite of the Broad Gauge (until 1892) and the shorter LSW route to Exeter and London from 1886.

The North Cornwall (LSWR) station platforms were on a slightly higher level and situated on the south of the GWR terminus. Access was from the main road, but just up the hill off St Thomas Road. Station Road sloped away to the buildings on the Down side, with the goods yard entrance opposite on the right. The sharp rise formed by St Thomas Hill Bridge was a hard test for horses hauling the station buses and cartage vehicles further up into town, several hundred feet above. An easier gradient than the St Thomas Hill was earlier found by a road skirting the west side of the Castle. No less steep was St Stephens Hill to the north, later relieved by

Roydon Road further east. In the 1920s the White Hart Hotel had its exclusive horse bus to the station, lesser folk using J.B. Smith's bus. Soon, motor buses were substituted by Truscott, then by the Western National's town service from 1938. Chaplins, the LSWR and SR cartage agent, had changed to lorries by the mid-1930s though Mr. Gynn, agent, for some of the London wholesale houses, still used horse and cart until 1948.

The single storey building was unlike the usual NCR (LSWR) design. The Station Master lived in a large house opposite (only lately demolished) and the building was entirely devoted to offices (booking and parcels), staff room, waiting rooms and toilets. W.H. Smith & Sons ran a small bookstall on the platform side. The material used for construction was local stone with much Portland stone quoining, and Delabole slate for the steeply pitched roof. The building was backed with a generously wide cantilevered awning. The central stanchions supported the cross beams with gussets of most delicate tracery. The SM occupied a separate office at the east end. On the Up platform stood a large waiting shed again made of dressed stone, as were the platforms. The signal box of 1886 with its multiple glass panes, was almost duplicated rearwards for the additional GWR frame of 1917. Water columns on the departure ends of the platforms, a staff foot crossing at the east end, and the criticised round-arch footbridge beyond the country end ramps, completed the structures. The station was lit by gas right up to the 1960s, then briefly (the booking office and signal box) by electricity until closure.

The South Western station was the centre of attraction in the true railway age. The population in the 1930s was over 4,000 with another 1,500 in St Thomas and St Stephen parishes. News of national importance came through the telegraphs and the newspapers, and crowds would gather. Extraordinary scenes greeted two Methodists in 1902. They were returning from jail sentences at Exeter, passed on them for refusal to pay the Educational Rate. In 1914 men of the Devon Regiment left for service in India and Mesopotamia. As early as 1886 a local organised an excursion to London at a fare of 12s 0d. The Station Master and his clerks canvassed the Sunday Schools for excursions to the seaside - Paignton and Exmouth were the favourites. The local Liberal Party ran several excursions to London, South Wales and the Isle of Wight. In reverse the LSWR offered weekend ex-

Looking down on Launceston LSWR station; the GWR station is beyond. The lengthy bank of cattle pens is flanked by an end loading dock (with horse box) and a contemporary non-corridor North Cornwall local train (44 ft. guards van, 46 ft. Composite and 42 ft. Third in salmon pink and brown livery) is in the Up platform. Newport lies to the left and St. Stephen's on the hill above. (Author's collection)

A petrol storage tank was installed in the yard at Launceston in the 1920s. Western Petroleum Co. Ltd., based at Plymouth, also dispensed fuel oil, paraffin and lubricants. Notice the horsedrawn road tanker and hand pump. (R.L. Goodman collection)

cursion rates to Launceston, as well as the seaside resorts. World War Two brought evacuation trains from London. In August 1939 children and teachers arrived from Lambeth and Camberwell many going further into the surrounding villages. Some drifted back, but when the 'Blitz' started in earnest in 1940, fresh specials arrived (including one carrying 449 from Vauxhall). In 1944 a special came from Folkestone, for Kent was suffering from the V1 'Doodlebug' offensive. Launceston was filled with US Army personnel from 1943, both black and white. The former were Services of Supply men; they unloaded stores in the yard and ran the ammunition

dumps in the countryside (e.g. Tower Hill). The brown and grey clothing of German and Italian prisoners of war also became familiar, as train loads came to occupy the camps firstly at Werrington, then Pennygillam and Scarne after the Normandy Invasion.

The goods shed, suitably large, handled considerable quantities of foodstuffs and general merchandise - anything from pianos to tin baths. A 2-ton crane was installed, but most items were barrowed in and out of the wagons. The 'road box' system of delivery is described elsewhere, Launceston sharing with the lower end NCR stations an overnight delivery from Nine Elms (and Exeter and Ply-

mouth). Outside in the yard a variety of carts and motor lorries, backed up to wagons to load heavier items - coal, basic slag, fertilizers etc. Several warehouses were built for distribution of the latter, also animal feeds ('cattle cake') and seeds. On a small scale in the 1930s, this business increased considerably in the 1950s. There was Bibbys and Silcocks in the GWR yard, and Levers in the Southern. Bibbys occupied the SR Goods shed from the 1950s, and the railway sundries traffic was transferred to the GWR shed. Chamberlain and Poole distributed Lever's products over a wide area. Troods Ltd owned a private siding which will be described later. A major occupier of the yard was Bartlett & Bayley & Co the timber merchants and sawmillers. This firm's products were handled by a railway timber gang sent from Exeter with their own Inspector, for this was specialized work. Overlength trunks on bogie wagons required match wagons. During the Second World War Bartletts was supplying the SR with track keys and ferrules, and the Trebartha Estate forwarded timber for wagon planks to the LMSR at Derby. Opposite the goods shed, William Pearce's 'SW Agriculture Stores' dealt in corn and coal. The latter business passed to the Plymouth Co-operative Society in 1941.

Linked to the fortunes of the railway was the Dunheved Iron Works (1892) at Wooda, run by the Bate family, T.W. Bate later trading as M.A. Bate & Co. Not only were various farming machines and parts manufactured there, but items were brought in too,

'N' Class No. 31810 propelling wagons over the Down loop at Launceston en route to service Trood's and the Gas Works sidings beyond the bridges. Troods (later Fulfords) used rail extensively for its general builders' supplies, agricultural products and coal business, opening new premises at Newport in 1894. (Lens of Sutton)

A standard type of country waiting shed, rather larger as befitted Launceston, is flanked by the extended signal box. The newer (1916) end faced the opposite way towards the GWR's yard beyond. (R.L. Goodman)

Launceston's corrugated iron shed with its adjacent 50ft turntable, was used by an 'N' Class 2-6-0 as an overnight stable. This post-1952 view shows a Plymouth North Road train behind a WR 2-6-2T, waiting to cross via the 1943 connection to the GWR branch. (Photomatic)

Petherwin and Werrington parishes to the north) and the seasonal export of sugar beet. This was substantial in the 1940s-60s, going to Ely and Kidderminster. Coal came via Plymouth (Sutton Harbour) at first, also from Fremington Quay (via Torrington) but direct from the collieries in due course.

While railways held the premier position in land transport, certainly up to 1914 and well into the next decades, one could always expect yards such as Launceston's to be pretty busy. Not only the sundry merchandise through the goods shed and wagon loads in the yard but the movement of livestock and later fresh meat from local slaughterhouses. The driving of cattle from the other side of the town has already been mentioned. Control of these and loading them into wagons was no easy task! Beforehand, adequate numbers of wagons available was dependent on the Station Masters' local knowledge of the markets. A record number of 60 despatched in one day is known. Special empty wagons trains would be sent down from Exeter or Yeoford (or held at Tower Hill) and these could be washed at a special facility at Halwill. On Cattle Market Tuesdays the engine, probably a K10 or L11 4-4-0, would be all day marshalling wagons in and out of the cattle pens road. A railway Cattle Inspector would also be on hand as the regulations were strict. The staff at Launceston well remember the noise, smell and sweat of pushing cattle into these wagons!

Destinations for cattle before the First World War was initially Exeter, then, encouraged by the LSWR, further afield to Chichester and to the London terminal at Maiden Lane

both from within the UK and from North America. Most machinery (not only farming) was within the 9'3" maximum width allowed on rail, and binders or cultivators could be loaded sideways. The railway companies would arrange 'out of gauge' loads if requested. Even large threshing machines were transported on special 'Lowmac' wagons. This underlines the importance of side and end-loading docks at almost every station.

In 1911 the Launceston & District Electricity Supply Co Ltd opened a generating station at the back of the yard in the quarry site. The gas oil engines were supplied by rail tanker. Increased demand for motor oils in the 1920s saw the establishment close by of a base, for the Western Petroleum Co, served by its own wagons. This later passed into the hands of Esso. Other bulk commodities were roadstone (once imported by Devon County Council from its Wilminstone Quarry near Tavistock for use in North

Launceston Signal Box was constructed in the style favoured by the LSWR in the 1880s. The original structure was extended to the rear in 1916 to house the GWR signalman, locking frame, levers and Electric Token to Lifton.

The parcels van employed to carry tin can cases to the Ambrosia Creamery at Lifton managed to get derailed one afternoon after a rough shunt, which also pushed a cattle wagon over the top of the stopblocks. The logging business, beyond, was part of Bartlett's, long a user of rail facilities at Launceston. (R.L. Goodman collection)

(LNWR). Private Treaty sales followed to eastern and northern counties buyers, routed via Basingstoke, Woking, Kew and Banbury. Easingwold and Boston received specials from Launceston in later years, forwarded by Messrs. Chudleigh, Wonnacott and G. Uglow. The last one of 18 wagons was seen behind a 'Deltic' on the East Coast Main line in 1964. There was a reverse trade in calves from East Devon and Somerset. Sometimes a horse box was used for these - attached to the 10.00am from Okehampton. They might also be seen, trussed up in sacking, in the guards van on the 'ACE'.

Some livestock went locally, sheep to Halwill slaughterhouse for instance, and the Launceston Shows brought exhibition cattle on rail. The LSWR provided Prize Cattle wagons for many years, and horse boxes were very common, some even built by BR. Such vehicles were equipped to run in passenger trains. In 1946 a number of horses were sent to the Channel Islands to make up depleted stocks. They were also sent away for slaughter, a sad process and not popular with the staff, as much care was needed in placing them within the wagons. Pigs went to Harris (Sausages) Calne and to Brettell Lane, Wolverhampton. Local farmers would have preferred a local bacon factory, they said, in the 1920s. Carcases of pigs and beef were

already going to London and the Midlands before 1914. The LSWR introduced ventilated fresh meat wagons in the early 1900s. Equipped with vacuum brakes and oil axleboxes, they were suitable for fast goods, or as tail traffic on passenger trains. Strangely, there was no abattoir in Launceston until 1938, though there was some road competition even at that date. After the Second World War demountable containers were substituted. Smithfield Market in London (and up to 1945 the Midlands via the SDJR at Templecombe) received them, loaded at Launceston etc. but craned off flat wagons at Nine Elms onto lorries. The predominant breed locally was the 'Devon Red', a dual dairy/beef animal. These, and sheep, would be sent eastward for further pasturing, the latter's destination often Sevenoaks, and to stations on Romney Marsh (Kent). Allied to slaughtering were tanning and hide production (Hender's Kensey Vale tannery was over in the GW yard), gut and fats. The gut was loaded onto flat trucks for Cattewater (Plymouth). Wool shearings were railed to Bradford by R.D. Gilbard & Son, declining in later years - an early loss to road transport. Whole sheepskins were another by-product; in 1933 over 14,000 went away to places like Yeovil and Buckfastleigh.

The rabbit trade, as everywhere else on the North Cornwall, was considerable. P.H. Tonkin, Hartnell (Alternon) and G. Robinson & Sons (Cornwall) Ltd collected in the Launceston area. Hung by their back legs into crates holding 24, the rabbits were despatched to the Medway towns, also Leicester, Nottingham and Birmingham etc. via Templecombe. A consignment of rabbit meat was despatched in a refrigerated van in 1934, but the crated method persisted. Though little milk was sent from here (by LSWR) there was a steady business in eggs, again to the Midlands, and by container-full in SR days. Day-old chicks went both ways - from Launceston, and inwards from Yorkshire and East Devon.

Siding space in Launceston yard was reasonably adequate. The two long sidings toward Tower Hill were each sufficient for 30 wagons. The usual practice was for a Down goods train to be run-round in the Down loop, the engine then drew local wagons back into the sidings, the ongoing wagons left with brakes pinned down. Up goods trains were similarly left in the Up loop, the engine and local wagons drawing forward, then back through 5 and 6 points. If a whole train was assembled in the yard, to get to the Up line entailed propelling throughout the down loop towards Egloskerry, thence forward over 9 points. The two sidings in the yard each held twenty three wagons, the inner through the goods shed. A crossover beyond the shed was removed in 1933. The cattle pens held eight wagons, the dock spur three. Petrol wagons had to stand on the short length at the yard throat opposite the storage tanks.

Although the running line connection between the SR and GWR was opened in 1943, it was not used for wagon exchange in Company days. Indeed it was said that some wagons for Troods Siding arriving at the GWR station were rerouted back via Plymouth and Okehampton to the SR yard! This underlines the strict appointment of wagon mileage and adherence to recognised exchange points, not only at Launceston but at St Budeaux and Lydford. It did not apply to through munitions trains in World War Two or of course, after Nationalisation in 1948 when both yards at Launceston were available, particularly to handle the increased slag and fertilizer. Fertilizer traffic from Avonmouth came mostly via Tavistock Junction to the ex-GWR yard, some blocks of wagons going forward to Otterham etc.

Trood's siding on the west side of St Thomas Road bridge was, as we have seen, an extension of the Launceston Gas Company's original 1887 accommodation. The Gas Company retained a single siding, part of which faced a loading bank (with canopy). Outwards, coke and tar went to Plymouth. Trood appeared to use the goods yard at first, though acquiring land west of the bridge in Priory Meadows. He imported corn from Bideford, and coal from Plymouth (and S. Wales via Fremington). His new premises opened in 1892, celebrated by a 'sit down' supper for 40 at Newport House. The new store measured 120 x 30 feet and was flanked on the south side by a new gated siding extending on from the Gas Co's headshunt. An improved connection further west (costing £155) was completed in 1904. The sidings were usually serviced at 7.30am by the early down goods. The ground frame working the points and ground signals was released by Launceston box. Wagons were propelled on the Down loop, and into Troods. Empties were drawn out and left on the Single line (within the Up Home Signal) the loaded ones returned up the short ramp to inside the gate, the engine not permitted beyond it onto the weighbridge. The Gas Company's wagons were gravitated back to their loading bank, the shunter required to leave them ready and secured. Troods Ltd (later Fulfords) imported building materials (e.g. bricks from Pinhoe), sea sand from Bude or

Rock, hedging stone from Hingston Down, and timber. They were also wool buyers and sent wagonloads to Bradford until the 1920s.

The semi-terminal nature of Launceston's traffic resulted in a necessary base for servicing engines. The original shed and turntable was used right up to the 1960s but the SR and GWR fortunes became intermixed once the physical junction of 1943 was laid in. The LSWR shed was home to succeeding Beattie, Adams and Drummond engines, originally subordinate to Wadebridge. Subsequently, under Exmouth Junction, it provided overnight accommodation for Okehampton and Exeter T9s, and Maunsell 2-6-0s. 1943 initially saw two cleaners out-based from Exmouth Junction, and the start of considerable co-operation with the GWR depot from then until the end of steam. The iron-framed and corrugated-clad LSWR shed succumbed to the weather and corrosion, so that the (usual) T9 was housed over in the GWR shed. It also used the GW turntable, but needed extension ramps. Along with other sub-depots in the west, Launceston received an ex-LNWR sleeping car as a dormitory for firemen detached from Exmouth Junction. Notwithstanding the transfer of the WR Plymouth trains into the SR platforms from 1952, the 45XX 2-6-2Ts continued to use the GW shed (and were invariably turned). Two crews were based here for relieving Exmouth Junction and Okehampton men down and up the North Cornwall line. A night man was employed to clean, light up and coal engines.

Station Master and Goods Agent in the 1890s was Mr. F. Trimmer followed by Mr. J.B. Lodder, but it was George Stevens (1909 to 1925) who became the 'Joint' Station Master in 1915. Ashwater and Tower Hill came under Launceston from 1927. From 1928 Mr. Walter Greenslade was supervising over 25 traffic staff in the two stations. This included two signalmen and a porter/checker at Ashwater, and two porter/signalmen at Tower Hill (from 1943). At Launceston SR were two booking clerks, two signalmen (and a relief man), one parcels porter, two goods guards and a goods checker. On the GWR side were one booking clerk and one goods clerk, two signalmen, two passenger guards and a goods checker. Apparently employed in either station were: a shunter, two goods clerks, two porters and a goods porter. Signalman Hugh Godbeer worked Launceston (SR) box for 21 years until 1947, after previous service at Exeter, Ashbury, Tisbury, Delabole and Camelford, from 1890.

Other long-servers were Guards Vodden and Chilcott, and Messrs

Nelder, Mitchell Gerry, Wright and (1943 to 1966) C. Arthur. Succeeding SMs were: Messrs A.E. Kelland (1938 - 47), E.G. Jeffrey (1947-53) and finally Mr. A.G. Fenner until closure in 1966.

Launceston escaped the total freight services withdrawal from Okehampton to Wadebridge/Bude as from 7 September 1964. The tonnage of bulk fertilizer carried there (now confined to stores at Launceston and Otterham only) was sufficient to re-open the ex-GWR Lydford line as from that date. That branch had succumbed to closure on 29 December 1962 when the 'last trains' were caught up in a severe blizzard. The 'North' or ex-GWR yard, was, of course, connected by the wartime spur. In anticipation of re-opening from Lifton (where the Ambrosia milk traffic remained operative after September 1964), the District Engineer inspected the line in his coach, hauled by Ivatt tank 41308, in May 1964. The Electric Token signalling was still in situ, but from September the Lydford to Launceston was reduced to 'one-engine-in-steam' operation. The signalling in the ex-GWR terminus had already been recovered in 1964, and the only signals remaining were the Down (GWR) spur home and the starting from Launceston SR (15). The Ambrosia (via Lydford) traffic ceased from 28 February 1966, the fertilizer business having already passed to road transport. The final freight left Launceston on the 26th behind NBL D6311. The spur was removed in May 1966 along with the signalling frame in the box. After clipping out of use on 24 July, the points (6) and ground signals feeding the SR yard were recovered, Launceston retaining only the loop and sets of signals to operate the basic North Cornwall DMU passenger service. Trood's (Fulford's) siding had been truncated in November 1965 and the SR yard was cleared in the summer of 1966. The WR shed housed the SR engine until 1964, the SR building becoming wholly derelict. Nevertheless it serviced steam until the end of 1964 though the Class 4 4-6-0s drafted in could not use the 50ft turntable, and worked tender-first to Halwill and Okehampton.

Today the sites of the two Launceston stations show little sign of the railway; both were virtually levelled in the 1970s to provide an industrial estate, but beyond St Thomas' Road bridge the railway has returned. Not T9s, but little narrow gauge 0-4-0s. The trackbed from the end of the old station, 223m 42ch to the present terminus at Newchurches (225m 0ch), now has a 1' 11 5/8" gauge railway laid upon it. The Launceston Steam Railway was opened on Boxing Day 1983; while there is a halt near the old 224 MP the actual Launceston terminus

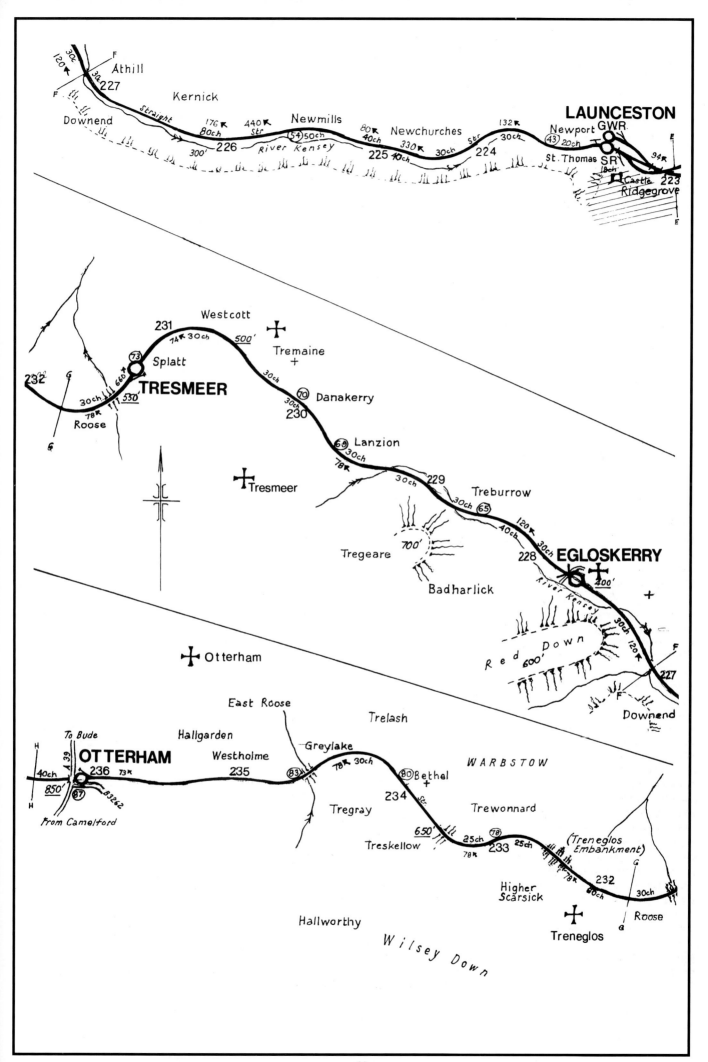

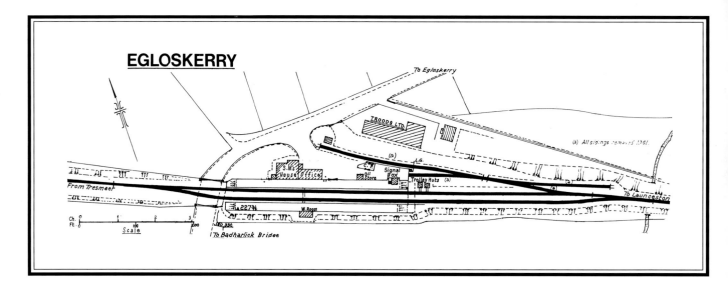

EGLOSKERRY

is to the west of St Thomas' bridge on the site of the Gas Works siding and the former cutting has been infilled. The station looks startlingly like Launceston SR at first glance, but the large awning came from Tavistock North! 'Lilian' with her North Wales slate quarries sister Hunslets, 'Covertcoat' and 'Velinheli', will remind you of the smoke and steam Launceston once knew many years ago.

Launceston to Egloskerry

The line of rails followed the Kensey River valley for the first six miles out of Launceston. After the restrictive confines of the town, the Underlane to Egloskerry on the Down side, and the mill leat aqueduct, an alignment

was found on the northern side of the river rising gently at not more than 1 in 132 until Newchurches (225 miles). As the latter became cut off from its fields, the NCR had to provide six cattle arches. From New Mills the valley narrows. The south slopes are well wooded here in contrast with the bareness of the landscape only a few miles further on. The curvature was not severe, and there were several long straights until Red Down (227 miles) was reached. Here the engineers had to ease a way through with a road on one side and the Kensey (twice crossed) on the other. Immediately beyond lay Egloskerry station.

Egloskerry (227m 58ch)

Laid out on a rising gradient of 1 in

330 and partially on a straight, Egloskerry was the only place on the North Cornwall proper, with a level crossing. The station and minor goods yard were situated a few hundred yards down the hill from the village and its ancient church of St Petroc. It served North Petherwin, to which a new road was constructed with a £250 contribution from the NCR. The loops held only twenty two wagons and a brake van, or a seven coach train and engine. This restricted length (and at Tresmeer and Launceston) meant that timings of Saturday holiday expresses needed careful regulating. For the late opening on 3 October 1892 local people were presented with a bright red brick and grey slate-hung edifice to the standard NCR layout. The level cross-

The 1892 signal box at Egloskerry held the lever frame only, after the Tablet instruments were transferred to the booking hall in September 1930. The porter signalman thereafter operated the level crossing (locked by lever) opening the gates by hand as well as pulling off the signals themselves. 'N' Class No. 31855 was calling at Egloskerry with the 1:00 p.m. from Padstow, the second vehicle being the previous night's Down newspaper van returning to Clapham Junction on 11th July 1964. (R.A. Lumber)

ing, at the Tresmeer end, was operated by a wheel in the adjacent signal box, and the gate locked by lever. Under the economics of the late 1920s control of Egloskerry was passed over to Otterham. The last Stationmaster was Mr Lashbrook.

In the profitable years the goods yard, though not equipped with a goods shed (for sundries) or a crane, nevertheless was busy enough. A cattle pen was provided on a loading dock by No 2 siding (ten wagons) with a short inner siding for end-loading. In the 1930s the SR provided one of their standard stores, which was leased by Troods Ltd of Launceston for agriculture feeds and fertilizers. Further economies occurred on 25 September 1930 when the Tablet machines and single needle telegraph instrument were taken from the signal box (on the Up platform) and placed in the booking office. Thereafter they were operated by porter-signalmen. The signal box was left with 14 levers (5 spare). The connection to the yard was operated by a push-pull lever, the associated LSWR ground signals (No 11) removed in the 1930s.

Behind the yard to the north side the LSWR provided a row of six semi-detached cottages. In 1924 two signalmen and four permanent way men lived there. No piped water supply for them, or the station, for drinking water was delivered in churns from Launceston. Egloskerry lost its goods facilities in 1961 but, with the gates, retained its loop until the general closure in October 1966.

Egloskerry to Tresmeer

Out of Egloskerry the North Cornwall line began climbing in earnest, mostly at 1 in 73 with many a reversing 30 chain curve. Still following the Kensey, beyond its north bank at first but crossing over at Treburrow by a double deck bridge, the top brick-faced stone arch took a narrow lane up to the hamlet of Tregeare. River and railway footed the north side of the 700ft Tregeardown Beacon as far as Lanzion. The Kensey Valley was left here, the NCR engineers having to plot a way round the contours in the farmlands of the Parishes of Tresmeer and Treneglos. Embankment followed cutting as the line rose to 550ft at Tresmeer station. There was a surprising momentary fall in gradient under Danakerry bridge (230m 3ch) while at Tremaine, 1/2 mile onward, commenced a series of five semi-circular curves (some at 25 chain radius) which snaked left and right for nearly five miles (almost to Otterham). It was here that a North Cornwall train was really tested - whether a T9 4-4-0 and its coaches leaning to a curve round a bare hillside shelf labouring up to Otterham, or an 'N' 2-6-0 controlling its train of loose coupled wagons on a descent towards Launceston.

Round the first of these curves a down train arrived in Tresmeer station - at Splatt where the minor road runs south from Canworthy Water to Laneast. Tresmeer village lies about a mile and a half to the south east and not very direct at that. The station served Warbstow, Fonston and Canworthy Water to the north. Warbstow is noted for its large barrow from which views of the bare North Cornish landscape are superb. The population in the 1920s was not large in these upland parishes - only 164 in Tresmeer and 332 in Warbstow - of scattered farms and wayside Methodist Chapels. The line of the Ottery River was the southern limit of Anglo-Saxon settlement. Place names were more Cornish to the south of this river, which rises near Otterham station.

Tresmeer (231m 29ch)

Of all the wayside stations of the North Cornwall, Tresmeer seemed to acquire a name out of proportion to its size! Possibly because staff there

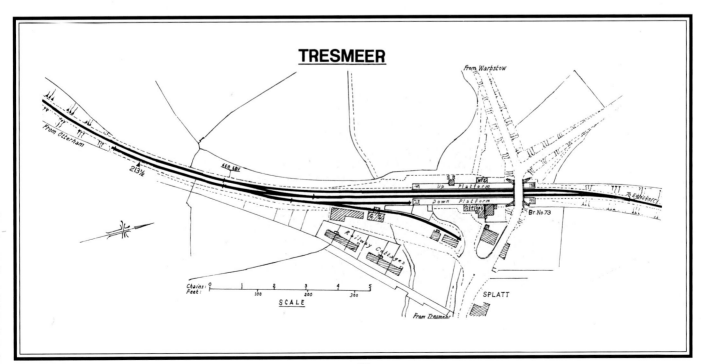

TRESMEER

The brick-built station house at Tresmeer faces the westerly evening sun on 22nd August 1964. Only a fertilizer van stands by the goods shed in the Down side yard, which would be closing the following month. (P.W. Gray)

tended to move on to higher positions on the Southern Railway. A small station like this, after all, gave all-round initial experience from signalling to accountancy. Station Masters, helped by their clerks had to be all things to all people, and were the Company's representative in any community. At Tresmeer it was farming of course. The last SM was Bert Holmes (an ex-LBSCR man); after 1927 the station came under Otterham.

This station actually faced north to south due to the gyrations of the alignment. Platforms here were on a slighter plane, actually rising 1 in 660 in the up direction, and on a straight. The loops were short - only for twenty four wagon trains - and controlled by an eighteen - lever signal box on the Up platform. Economy measures from 28 October 1930 saw the Tablet machines, telephone and single-needle telegraph moved to the booking office to be worked by porter-signalmen. The standard North Cornwall buildings were in red brick, and on the Down side, as at Launceston and Delabole. The stone-faced platforms were at the new 2'6" height of the 1890s and an extra-wide arched overbridge straddled them and the tracks at the Launceston end. At the south end of the goods yard three pairs of houses were built by the LSWR for its staff.

Tresmeer had a brick goods shed, of the minor design, but with a 40cwt crane, on the longer of the two sidings. There were cattle pens here of course and an end-loading dock. Troods opened a coal store in the first year, and Grants & Canns followed with a thriving business in general merchandise and wide distribution by horse and van, then by motor. Later, the Southern Railway built a fertilizer/seed store for lease. The Delabole Slate Co. commenced sending slates from Tresmeer in the opening month, so landing the LSWR with a bill for £71 from the Highway Board, for damage to the road. With the North Cornwall Coach Co. diverting their service to Wadebridge to start in the yard, Tresmeer was rather busy for a while. When the parishes to the north were

Of the wayside stations on the North Cornwall only Tresmeer and Delabole were on the Down side. This is Tresmeer in the 1920s and an Adams 'Jubilee'0-4-2 is arriving from Otterham with the usual two coaches and guard's brake van formation of that period. The passengers may have walked quite a long way from Tresmeer village (to the south) or Warbstow. In the distance are the lamp room, the No.2 style goods shed, Messrs Trood's store and a row of six railway staff cottages. (R.L.Goodman collection)

Tresmeer's signal box and waiting shed on the Up platform. The telegraph posts carried the numerous circuits for the signal tablet signalling, the box-to-box telephones and the station telegraphs. Before the G.P.O. telephone was commonplace, the public could send telegrams over the telegraph. It was operated by the booking clerk by key and single needle instruments. (Lens of Sutton)

in Devon, the County Council sent regular truckloads of roadstone from its own (once Hoare's) quarries at Tavistock, and some from Delank on the Wenford Branch. A permanent way man was lent on a Friday to help unload.

In the news in 1898 following an accident to a passenger train, South Western employees were subjected to an Inspector's Inquiry. 'Roller' 4-4-0 No 386 heading the 6.10pm from Okehampton was approaching at 7.49pm on 19 November, when the driver sighted a goods train in his path.

He braked heavily, but was unable (at 25 mph) to prevent a head-on collision with 'Jubilee' 0-4-2 (No 535) with the 4.50pm goods from Wadebridge, and forced it back some 15 yards. It was raining heavily, the Wadebridge driver had passed the Up home signal at danger, tried to stop, but his engine slid on the wet rails. The four passenger coaches remained on the track, hardly damaged, but six wagons on the goods were derailed. Apart from 386's driver and fireman needing hospital treatment, injuries were slight. It took some time before the Exeter

and Salisbury breakdown cranes could arrive and clear the wreckage.

Even before the railway opened west of Launceston two 'Regrators' (dealers in dairy products) were driving to the GWR terminus en route to the Plymouth Friday Market. From 1893 Messrs Parsons (Hallworthy) and Cowling (Canworthy Water) appeared to have induced the LSWR to attach box vans to the early train through Tresmeer (7.35am). These vans were taken on to Okehampton, thence Plymouth, while the Regrators (the LSWR called them 'Higglers') diverted to catch the GWR train, carrying some lighter baskets. On their return in the evening the LSWR was even more accommodating. The last train down the North Cornwall had already been cut back to Launceston in November 1894, but the railway allowed the train, with vans of empty baskets, to continue on to Tresmeer with Messrs Parsons and Cowling as the only passengers. These arrangements lasted up to 1914, but were resumed after the First World War, with the upward vans later starting at Otterham for yet more Regrators (Messrs Stacey, Marshall and Sandercock). In the 1920s the 8.00am passenger train from Launceston to Padstow detached two vans for loading in the Down loop at Otterham. The engine of the first Up passenger (8.20am Padstow) would attach them to the front of its train at Otterham

Treneglos embankment, a mile to the west of Tresmeer (observed in the distance above the engine) was reached by a continuous 30 chain curve and is the scene on 22nd August 1964. Sheep and cattle on open pasture land is typical of farming in this part of North Cornwall, but by 4 p.m. passengers on the 10.35 a.m. Waterloo to Padstow were, by now, anxious to arrive on the coast and start their holidays. The 'N' Class 2-6-0s were still employed, with the Bulleid Pacifics, on the holiday extras in this last summer of steam and through workings to and from Waterloo. (P.W. Gray)

about 9.05am and proceed to Launceston (and Okehampton). In the evening, however, the vans and train went back to Tresmeer only. In 1924 the Regrators turned to road transport all the way to Plymouth.

Needless to say the despatch of rabbits eastward was heavy here. Mr. Staddon regularly sent one hundred and forty crates a week and the Bolt Brothers of Warbstow forwarded from Tresmeer (and from Otterham). It is said the rabbit business was more valuable than the cattle. The station staff could complement their earnings by a commission of 6d per hamper, and some became quite well off! Again the Midlands was the principal destination - Holloway & Collins at Leicester, Bennett at Sheffield and Nottingham. The hampers weighed 11/4cwt, holding 'twenty couple' (ten on each bar). The vans were transferred at Templecombe to the Somerset & Dorset Joint Line, Interestingly, the price to be paid was telegraphed (by the ubiquitous single-needle instrument) to Launceston and thence phoned to the receiver.

The cattle traffic was quite considerable for this small station. At one time there was a market nearby each Friday, and there was the import of weaning calves from Axminster. Many stations, such as Tresmeer, also loaded bulls and stallions for breed and stud - difficult animals to handle! In the yard cattle feed arrived from Southampton (for Trood - sometimes five or six vans a week) also wheat in sacks from Avonmouth, Liverpool and Tilbury, Milk was never a big traffic on the NCR, but a few churns were sent from here to Launceston daily.

Alas, this activity, which local people assumed would last forever, was doomed. Tresmeer's goods yard closed on 7 September 1964, and was stripped by the end of 1965. The signal box closed on 14 November 1965 and the diesel units used the Down platform line thereafter, until they were withdrawn in October 1966.

Tresmeer to Otterham

The problem of maintaining the 1 in 73 gradient and 30 chain objective, while raising the level from 560 feet at Tresmeer to 860 at Otterham, yet not building tunnels or viaducts, was solved by going round and round the contours in this difficult landscape. Hence the four complete half circles at 25 and 30 chain radii between Tresmeer and Greylake, in Warbstow Parish, 3 1/4 miles for the 21/2 miles as the crow flies. The embankment at Treneglos (instead of the viaduct) was the largest and highest on the North Cornwall at 86 feet, and covered 300 feet across its base. The numerous cuttings, including the one just to the west, in shale and harder rock, provided the necessary fill. A criss-cross of minor, narrow, but public roads bridged the line at Treneglos, Scarsick, Trewonnard, Bethel and Greylake. A slight dip in profile at the 234 3/4 MP, a welcome respite for down trains, was followed by a series of reversing 80 chain reversing curves for the next 11/4 miles to Otterham, albeit on a steadily rising 1 in 73 gradient.

Otterham (236m 20ch)

Otterham - the most exposed station of them all at 850 feet above the sea which here is not far away to the north west. On a fine day the inland views and over the Atlantic are magnificent. The wide platforms were somewhat sheltered in their cutting situation. Some pines were sown on the Down side and a few grew up on the slope leading to the stone-built overbridge

The North Cornwall Line, rising from the 1 in 330 in the platforms to the 1 in 73 towards the 860ft. summit three quarters of a mile away, passes under the main coast road at Otterham where co-acting arms were provided for the Down starting signal aspects. This station was the main railhead for Crackington Haven, and St.Juliot (of Thomas Hardy fame) but Otterham village itself lay a mile away by footpath. The waiting shed was built in dressed Delabole stone with Portland stone quoins, as was the station main building. In this 1920s view the nameboard retains black lettering on white background in the LSWR style. (Lens of Sutton)

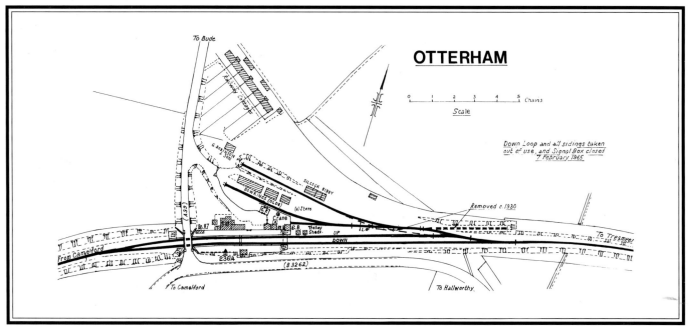

All quiet again at Otterham as the 1.00 p.m. Padstow to Okehampton leaves for Tresmeer on 22nd August 1964. It would be an hour and a half before the next train in - the 10.35 a.m. Waterloo 'ACE' to Padstow - this station attracting a fair number of passengers, mainly for Crackington Haven and St. Gennys. The agricultural feeds and fertilizer traffic was also considerable, distribution from the line of warehouses (centre) covering a wide area to the north (as far as Week St. Mary) and Cow & Gate's cheese factory at Davidstow made a lot of use of the railway, e.g. whey cream to Wincanton. (P.W. Gray)

at the western end. Otherwise there was hardly a tree of any size to be seen in the bare countryside, wide open to the fury of the ocean gales in winter. The station house may be spotted today from a car speeding by on the new A39 alignment, but sometimes impossible in the thick rain and mist!

The station was on the up side and repeated the LSWR's rural styling, in local Delabole dressed stone, with Portland stone quoins and decoration, together with the neat little waiting shed opposite. Lighting was by oil to the end. The Station Master's post was retained at Otterham, with his signalmen, thus the Tablets and telegraphs remained in the signal box during the 1930s economies. A terrace of six LSWR standard houses was built in 1894 for the P.W. men and signalmen. (The cost was then £1,312).

The station was supposed to serve Boscastle, but passengers generally used better road connections from Camelford. Otterham was the nearest station to Crackington Haven, St Gennys, St Juliot and Lesnewth to the north west. Otterham village to the north was one and a quarter miles by footpath, and scattered Davidstow lay to the south. The total population of Otterham, Lesnewth and Minster

(Boscastle) was barely 800 in the 1930s.

The 'Atlantic Coast Express' limited-stop trains called at Otterham, and up to two dozen people would be seen waiting for the morning train, having come up from the Crackington direction. The rise of the omnibus threatened Otterham's passenger traffic in the 1930, Crowells of Crackington starting a St Gennys to Launceston school bus in 1935. Previously, Secondary School children arrived up to an hour late and, subject to the various timings in and out of the summer timetable, the first up train from Otterham left about 9.30am, into Launceston at 10. Homewards it was either around 4 pm (however the 'ACE' was timed) or wait until the 6.30pm train from the town. It is not difficult to visualize that local coach operators and the private motoring expansion in the 1960s eclipsed what was left of Otterham's business.

The effect of the railway's arrival on the village of Boscastle was soon felt. It had been on the tourist map for over a century, J.W.M. Turner painted there (the harbour in a storm) and Tennyson and Sir Henry Irving (the great Victorian actor) both came. The earlier registers of the Wellington

Hotel reveal nobility, members of the Rowntree and Cadbury families - and a party of Germans (1887). Most used the coastal coach as part of a tour, but others stayed a week, some a whole season. Immediately the North Cornwall line opened to Otterham and Camelford in 1892 Boscastle's fortunes grew, as the wagonettes, brakes and a horse bus brought lesser mortals to view the glories of the cliffs and ocean. Boscastle itself changed little as it was part of the extensive Manor Estate (until 1946). Up to 1892 sailing ketches and smacks supplied coal, timber and groceries in enough quantities for the local people and the small influx in the summer. But the sea trade fell away in face of the ease of railway communication, albeit up some very steep lanes to the stations! The Boscastle merchants established themselves at Otterham station, as we shall see.

Not the least important activity at Otterham was the considerable rabbit trade. Bolt Brothers of Warbstow would send 60-80 crates (of 20 brace) a week to Manchester, Birmingham, Leeds and London in the 1930s and 1940s. Mac Fisheries was a large buyer. G. Robinson & Sons (Nottingham) also bought in at Otterham, collected by Bill Sleep from surrounding farms. There was a great exersise in weighing and labelling as the afternoon 'Perishables' approached about 4 pm. Mention has been made of the Regrators who were served by the LSWR and SR from Tresmeer, and the extension to Otterham, on Friday mornings. Two miles to the south east was Hallworthy Cattle Market. It grew considerably, drawing business to its auctions from a wide area to the north of Bodmin Moor. Originally taken on hoof, the cattle were later taken by lorry (Mason, Camelford) to Otterham. Boscastle's two annual markets once contributed lambs driven up to Otterham's pens. 'Spring' lambs, early born, fetched good prices up to June. As well as eastward, Pascoes forwarded to Truro, presumably via Wadebridge and Bodmin Road - an interesting example of the way the railways would once accept and transfer a wagon from and to any destination.

Shunting goods trains needed care, and on departure for Launceston a number of wagon brakes would be pinned down for the steep gradients dropping down to the Kensey Valley, through Egloskerry. Already recounted is the cautionary tale of the Halwill runaways. At this opposite brim of the great dip down to Launceston a similar event occurred in December 1943, only the six wagons and a bogie brake van at Otterham went much further, seventeen miles in fact, ending up at Helebridge, south of Tower Hill. The local paper stated "They set up a record speed to Launceston, covering the distance faster than any passenger train has". This happened in spite of a regulation prohibiting goods trains being stood outside the down facing points with wagons detached therefrom. The whole train should have been taken into the Down loop, run round, and propelled into the yard. The 1943 saga ended by the wagons running to and fro inside Devon, the signalmen at

Launceston having set the points into Trood's siding just in case.......

At the top of the 1 in 73 from Treskellow the gradient eased to 1 in 330 through the platforms on a 100 chain radius curve to the left hand. The loops held 33 wagons, engine and van. The long shunting neck running up on its own embankment was abandoned in the 1920s to ease the gradient into the yard. A double slip arrangement was replaced by a single connection and trap points.

In spite of the upland situation the farming was not as poor as might be expected. Cattle raising, especially the dual Devon breed for milk and beef invited a market for animal feeds and Otterham station provided a railhead for them, as well as fertilizers and seeds. The SR built quite extensive storehouses from the 1930s, leased latterly to Levers, Bibbys and Silcocks. The Boscastle merchant Browning was established quite early, the business combining with Oldes in due course. Ward & Son of Boscastle, provision and grocery merchants, distributed all round to the village stores - boxes of jam, for instance, were received overnight in the road box system from London or Plymouth (Underwoods). The general merchants also handled coal and sand from Bude or Rock (via Padstow) in 10 or 12-ton wagonloads, and quantities of lime from the kilns at Cattlewater (Plymouth). When horses were usual in city streets, hay was in demand. Hence truckloads, piled to the limit of the loading gauge, went from Otterham to Plymouth. In common with many stations in the west the bulk traffic in fertilizers and basic slag grew substantially up to the 1960s. Whole trains from Avonmouth were split for distribution to here, Camelford and Delabole etc. The slag came in lesser loads from Thomas's, Plymouth. Seed potatoes inward were balanced by potatoes despatched - and Boscastle's earlies were (and are)

much prized. No direct-loading goods shed was provided, an omission rectified by a goods store soon built on the up platform. A two and a half ton crane stood behind it on the dock and just beyond, a single cattle pen. The crane would come in useful in World War Two and later, (in 1960) when an entire farm was moved from Coates (Swindon) in 32 wagons, with a passenger coach for the farmer and his family, destined for St Clether. There were 61 head of cattle, 750 poultry, a car, tractors, farm implements, and household possessions. The two yard sidings held 20 wagons each, and a short siding served the end-loading ramp. A few miles to the south a large airfield was opened in October 1942 for the RAF, and later the RCAF. Otterham was naturally the railhead for coal, stores, bombs and building materials, but the airfield remained operational only until September 1944, closing in 1945. The buildings were later occupied by Cow & Gate for milk processing, some of its products (e.g. cheese) going away by rail, including churns of whey cream to Wincanton. Pigs fed on the separated milk reached considerable numbers and added to the volume of livestock passing through Otterham, en route to the bacon factories.

Up to the 1920s the Station Master and his staff lived in comparative isolation. Local men and their families were used to it, but the SM might well have come from an urban background and he and his family felt it more strongly. This was more common after 1923 when they were likely to arrive from the former South Eastern and Brighton companies. The newly-promoted booking clerk at a minor station found his SM's duties more onerous than he had thought. If there were wagons to be cleared he might have to roll up his sleeves and do the job himself. He might also have to issue tickets, work the signal box, and

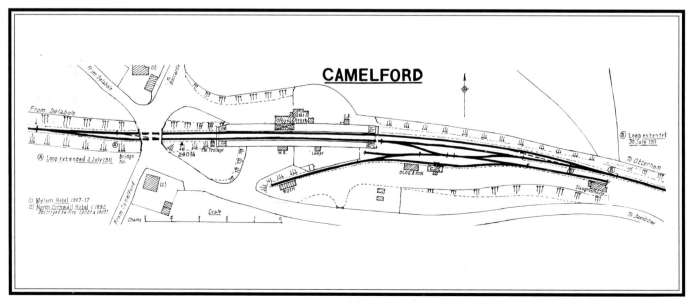

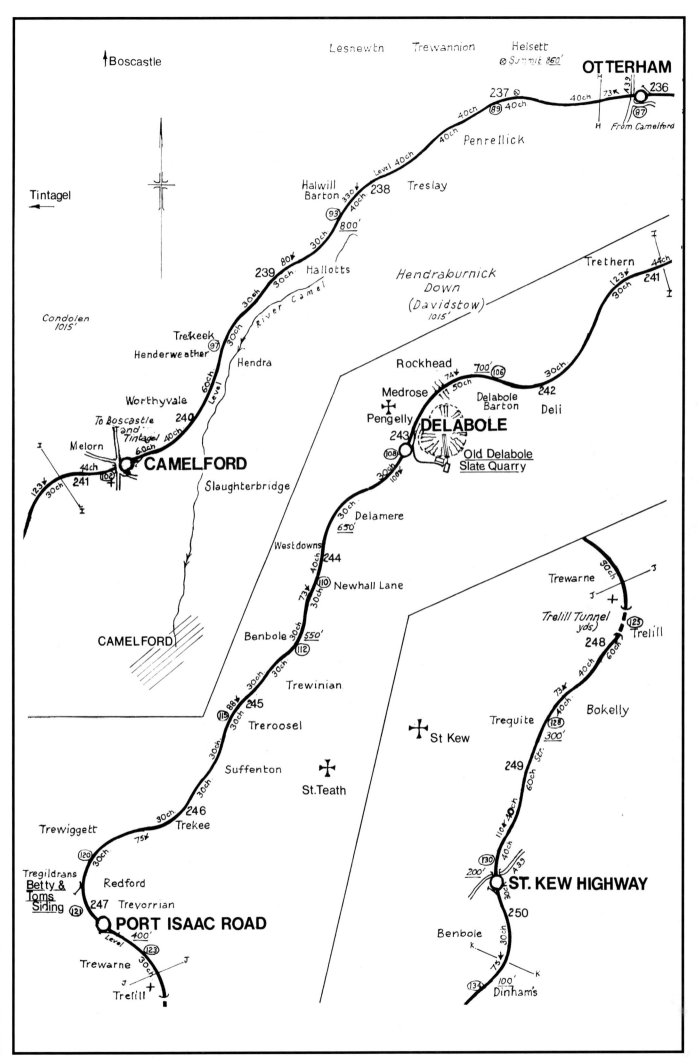

↑Boscastle

Tintagel ←

Lesnewth   Trewannion   Helsett
⊗ Summit 860'

OTTERHAM

237 ⊗   40ch   73↗   43ch   236
         40ch (89) 40ch   H   ⑧⑦
                                    From Camelford
                                 H

Penrellick

Treslay

Halwill
Barton   330↗ 40ch 238
(93)   40ch
30ch   800'

239   80↘
   30ch   Hallotts

Hendraburnick
Down
(Davidstow)
1015'

Trethern 44ch
123↗   241
30ch

Condolen
1015'

Trekeek   River Camel
(97)   30ch
Henderweather
Hendra

Rockhead   700' ⑩⑥
         74↗   50ch
Medrose ⊞   Delabole
         ⊞   Barton   Deli
Pengelly DELABOLE
243 ⑩⑧   30ch 242
(108)
30ch
100'
  Old Delabole
  Slate Quarry

Worthyvale 240
60ch Level
To Boscastle 40ch
and 60ch
Tintagel

Melorn ⊞ CAMELFORD
44ch (102)
123↗ 30ch 241

Slaughterbridge

CAMELFORD

Delamere
30ch   650'

Westdowns 244
40ch
73↗ (110) Newhall Lane
30ch

Benbole 30ch 550'
(112)

Trewinian

88↘ 245
(115) 30ch
Treroosel

Suffenton

30ch St.Teath ⊞

Trewarne
30ch J
J ⊞
Trelill Tunnel
(yds) ⑫⑤
248 Trelill

73↗
40ch 60ch
Trequite Bokelly

⑫⑧
128 300'

249
60ch Str.
110↘ 40ch

St Kew ⊞

30ch 130
130 200' A39
ST. KEW HIGHWAY

250

Benbole
k.
30ch
75↗ K
100' 134
Dinham's

Trewiggett
30ch 75↘ 246
120 Trekee
30ch

Tregildrans
Betty & Redford
Toms
Siding 247 Trevorrian
121

PORT ISAAC ROAD
Level 400'
123
Trewarne 30ch J
J ⊞
Trelill

The Camelford station nameboards were early products of the Exmouth Junction concrete works. In the yard behind is Messrs. Rush's agricultural store, but the cattle pens (centre) were virtually disused by 1964. (C.J. Knowles-Thomas)

in the earlier years walk, or cycle, to some distant farm to advise of a consignment of goods arrived. The staff at Otterham always included two signalmen, a porter (and/or junior) two booking clerks, and the permanent way men were paid here. The latter would also help unload wagons if called upon. As the volume of goods here rose, a checker was appointed. The SM in 1924 was Mr. Kail. He was followed by F.J. Lashbrooke who, by then, was controlling Tresmeer and Egloskerry stations was well. During the 1930s it was Messrs. A.E. Heard, R.P. Reeves, later on Mr Radcliffe and finally, at the closure in 1966 Mr. Bert Harding. As noted, SMs were used to mobility if they sought promotion and the latter, now made redundant, gravitated to the Plymouth area, finishing his career in the National Carriers organisation.

His station had suffered the indignities of withdrawal freight facilities from 7 February 1964 and the closure of the signal box from 7 February 1965, together with the abolition of the yard sidings and the Down loop. By 1966 there were only three trains each way, and very few passengers using them. A sad end and quite typical of this 'Beeching' decade.

Otterham to Camelford

Through Otterham station the alignment was east to west, but veered south west beyond Helsett towards Camelford. Just beyond Otterham's main road bridge the line was briefly in St Juliot Parish (of Thomas Hardy and 'Pair of Blue Eyes' fame). The author courted Emma Gifford here long before the North Cornwall came, travelling by GWR all the way from Dorchester to Launceston. In Lesnewth, where the Church is steeply below Trewenton bridge at the 237 milepost, lay the 860 ft summit point. The gradient sloped up at 1 in 73 to here, but the alignment still

snaked along with 40 chain reversing curves below the Davidstow escarpment and Hendraburnick Down. In contrast to the bare fields and hedgerows, only just to the west are the deep wooded valleys of the Valency leading into Boscastle, but four miles away on the better road from Halwill Barton. This is the edge of the Middle Culm Measures, where they give way to the Devonian rocks to the south, and why quarrying for slate and minerals equated with agriculture to the south. The ingenuity of the NCR engineers was taxed in directing the line towards the Delabole Quarry, not the easier route down the Camel Valley through Camelford town. Contour-following continued through Forrabury and Minster Parish, including a short level at Penrellick, where a small quarry was opened for stone; then a descent of 1 in 80 all the way to Camelford (station).

The underbridge at Halwill Barton (No.93), with its nasty road turn, has gone but just to the east is the infant Camel and its boggy upper reaches. A tributary had to be crossed at the 239 milepost on a fair sized embankment. Bridges followed at Trekeek and Hendra (notice the first hint of a Cornish name), then down by Worthyvale to approach Melorne where Camelford station was built. Hard by is Slaughterbridge, by its name an ancient battlefield. Legend says Arthur was mortally wounded here and Mordred was killed. At Worthyvale, Lady Falmouth erected a memorial stone to mark Arthur's grave. No doubt tourists were lured to the spot, readily accessible by train after 1893.

Camelford (240m 56ch)

Mystery surrounds the hotels formerly adjoining this station. A 'North Cornwall Railway Hotel' was built on the down side at the time of the opening, on the south east corner, by the

crossroads. It was destroyed by fire about 1900, rebuilt but again burned down about 1907. A new hotel, the 'Melorne', was erected on the opposite corner but slightly up the road towards Boscastle. Opened about 1908 it too succumbed in January 1917. The story goes that nothing was known of the last fire until the following morning, when the owning family were found huddled in a nearby barn for shelter. The shell was rebuilt into the present Melorne Farm. The presence of hotel(s) signifies the relative importance of Camelford Station. Tourists in the 1890s were not in such a hurry, and commercial travellers found them useful. There was little else at Melorne however (a Bible Christian Chapel) but the crossroads, which was re-aligned on top of the railway bridge. This dictated the siting of Camelford Station, with Boscastle and Bossiney to the north, Delabole and Tintagel to the west, Davidstow to the east and Camelford town to the south. The view to the east is dominated by the spectacular heights of Rough Tor and Brown Willy. It was one and a half miles down to Camelford, walkable although a horse bus met trains in earlier years. The LSWR subsidised another horse bus from Boscastle and Tintagel until withdrawal in 1920. Thereafter motor buses were run by Mrs. Fry (Tintagel) and Mr. Webber (Boscastle) until their contract with the SR ceased in 1930. Following this the Southern National bus company (part-owned by the SR) served this route, and into Camelford town. From 1935 the SN's 122 route (Bude/Wadebridge) fairly comprehensively covered this area and connected with many trains at Camelford Station. Combined rail and road tickets were issued to Tintagel and Boscastle into BR days.

Not only the Melorne Hotel, but the opening of the large King Arthur's Castle Hotel (1899) at Tintagel and the continuing attraction of the earlier Wellington Hotel at Boscastle brought much business to Camelford. Even royalty - Prince Albrecht of Prussia and his suite travelled by special train in 1895. Thomas Hardy came to St. Juliot again in 1913 after the death of his wife, Emma and again in 1916.

Camelford itself had not been well regarded for years. The new turnpike road from Launceston to Bodmin of 1769 bypassed it, and the Borough was disfranchised by the 1832 Reform Bill. Nevertheless the town was regarded as goal for several railway promotions; after all the population was around 2,000, it retained the County Court and the surrounding area was quite well populated to the south, in St Breward and Michaelstow parishes, the Rural District numbering about

The last summer for the North Cornwall line, and on Saturday 2nd July 1966 the 16.50 Okehampton to Wadebridge has some passengers at Camelford. In the distance are three rows of cottages built by the LSWR for its employees. On the right are Rush's agricultural stores in the goods yard. The upper quadrant SR signal arm is mounted on a pair of re-used rails, typifying the economic re-use of materials by the old companies. (R.A. Lumber)

7,000. The Duke of Bedford who owned much estate hereabouts provided the distinctive Town Hall (1806) and a Grammar School derived from the native benefactor Sir James Smith (1679). Camelford town, though bypassed this time, actually gained some prosperity through the tourist trade and the business engendered by the new station - ready availability of general merchandise from London, and wider selection of building materials was evident in new villas and terraces which appeared in the next decade.

Indicative of Camelford's status as a railhead was the provision of an awning over the Up platform, its original plain roof replaced by a more distinguished version before 1914. The Station building itself was constructed in faced Delabole stone, but the signal box and platform walls were in unfaced stone. Slate cladding was attached to the walls of the SM's house to keep out driving rain; like Otterham it can be very wet and windy up here at 700ft above sea level. A sea fog will also blank out visibility, (also very wetting!) which made spotting signals difficult for enginemen. Camelford, from 1927, took control of Delabole, Port Isaac Road and St Kew Highway. John Wildish, a former SECR man was appointed SM in 1928. What he made of his tenure, so different from his last station (Strood in Kent) can be gauged

from the fact that he fitted in quite well. As he was a Methodist even better, and a good choir master at that! His staff at that time comprised: booking clerk, goods checker, a leading porter (passed shunter) and two signalmen.

The platform loops were on a slightly easier 1 in 330 gradient, rising in the Delabole direction, and on a steady 40 chain curve reversing to 60 under the road bridge. After extensions at

both ends were made in July 1911, these loops were adequate for passing 35 wagon goods trains or, at maximum, 12-coach passengers. The section towards Delabole was re-equipped with a No 6 Tyers Tablet ('returnable') in 1923, but the No.3 was not replaced by a WR Electric Key Token until 1961. The signal box was the square, well glazed, version of the 1880s period. The Stevens frame held 17 levers to work a slightly more com-

Camelford's Down side goods yard was somewhat larger than many, but in July 1964 only a few fertilizer vans were in view. Crosfields, of Liverpool, established a warehouse in the former slaughterhouse (centre) distributing locally in the Bedford lorry. (C.J.Knowles-Thomas)

Serving as the railhead for passengers from Tintagel and Boscastle, Camelford was provided with a protective awning on the Up platform. The cast iron columns survive within the present Museum of Cycling. (C.J. Knowles-Thomas)

The exterior of Camelford station buildings in 1964. Slating over the walls of the house was an attempt to counter the effect of wind and rain in this exposed position high above the Atlantic coast. A good supply of household coal for warming fires in the house, booking hall and offices was another essential! (C.J. Knowles-Thomas)

plicated layout than usual. The down side goods yard was fed by facing and trailing points from the Down loop (push and pull). Inner siding No 2 was faced by a medium-sized country good shed, with ports both sides, stonework grey Delabole (unfaced) but with brick corners. In 1934 a new brick slaughterhouse opened at the extremity of the up siding, later used as a fertiliser store by Messrs. Crossfields of Liverpool, and acquired from the Western Co-operative Society. Right to the end of freight working, a considerable tonnage was handled and distributed by lorry. Harry Bolt, formerly in the rabbit business here, at Otterham and Tresmeer, and a member of a well-known railway family latterly conducted Crossfield's distribution. Long before, Messrs. Rush built a store for feedstuffs and agricultural merchandise at the other extremity of the long

back siding. Olde of Boscastle also had a wooden store, next to the goods shed, and handled coal as well. It came through Wadebridge Quay or Plymouth in earlier years but later went direct from the collieries.

Blewitts of Marshgate ran the slaughterhouse (leased from the SR) and meat was thence forwarded to Nine Elms. There had been a fair quantity of cattle driven up from Camelford's monthly market and two pens were provided on the dock. Two goods trains in each direction during the day brought necessary wagons, coal, cattle, seeds (including potatoes from Scotland, though early potatoes from Boscastle were sent east in late May) and road boxes. In the 1930s the 'road boxes' from Exeter and Plymouth came in on the 6.00am goods from Okehampton, en route to Wadebridge. In the 40 minutes available, they were

unloaded into the parcels store, or shunted over to the goods shed. The London (Nine Elms) box served only Launceston to St Kew Highway, having left at 9.30pm the previous night. In those days a telegram from a local grocer would have an ordered item (e.g. a special blend of tea), delivered within 24 hours, such was the role of these nominated wagons, though they carried most sundry merchandise, from beer to carpets. The 11.35am goods from Wadebridge returned the road boxes, through Camelford in the early afternoon en route for Plymouth, also the overnight fast goods train from Exeter. Although the perishable and parcels traffic was diverted to the up afternoon passenger train from Padstow in the late 1920s, the road box system persisted until 1964. By this time BR was using railheads at Launceston and Wadebridge. From the opening years calves would be sent from East Devon stations to Camelford - very urgent of course!

Mails arrived before 7.00am by goods trains from the 1890s. Camelford was the head Post Office for a wide area, and a contracted-out Mail Cart System extended from St Gennys in the north to Port Isaac in the south, also to St Breward, Boscastle, Tintagel, St Mabyn and St Tudy. This goods train also ran on Sundays, (terminating at Camelford) until 1917. Thereafter the Mails came by road from Launceston. In the Up direction the overnight despatch left by passenger train starting from Camelford at 6.30pm (again Sundays included until 1917).

Goods services ceased on 7 September 1964, but the yard was still connected until 30 November 1965, at the same time as the up block section was extended all the way to Egloskerry. Even after the passenger closure on 3 October 1966 wagons were stored in the up loop. The station buildings survive as a residence and an extension now houses a cycle museum, while down the road to Worthyvale one can observe the LSWR staff cottages. The overbridge under the crossroads has been removed - and the Chapel is a private house.

Camelford to Delabole
The road from Camelford station to Delabole simply goes straight there, not so the route of the old North Cornwall line! As near Tresmeer, complete half-circles were plotted by the Engineers. Firstly by a 30 chains radius around Tretherne Farm, then reversing to skirt the hillside above Deli, the route was brought by a 50-chain curve around to the top of the great quarry at Delabole. At least these contortions achieved a reasonable 1 in 123 falling gradient, a slight level under

Camelford, as other stations, received a coat of brown and cream paint after the original Western Region take over in 1950. It remained unmistakably 'South Western', including the medium sized country goods shed with its port structure over the siding. The large shed on the Down platform was for servicing the signal and station oil lamps. (R.L. Goodman collection)

bridge No. 106 taking the Rockhead to Camelford road. The two and a half miles between the stations was, even then, the shortest on the North Cornwall. The final curve ended in Delabole station after giving passengers a spectacular, almost frightening, glimpse into the tremendous depth of the quarry. Away to the south spread the slate spoil and on the further edge of the pit ranged the quarry haulage machinery and storage buildings.

Delabole (243m 5ch)

The fortunes of Delabole depended mainly on the great slate quarry and the employment it gave to hundreds of men of the village, as well as the surrounding parishes of St Teath and Camelford. Stretching for about a mile between Rockhead through Medrose to Higher Pengelly, it may not have brought many tourists as did Tintagel or Boscastle, but the quarry itself was, and is, an attraction in its own right. After the railway opened output of slates, and slate stone for building, rose considerably. This prosperity was reflected in new houses and an Anglican Church (St John's) though Chapelgoing was strong, there being three at one time. Outside the quarrying community Delabole stayed rural, attracting a cattle market in due course.

The station and its goods yard was placed to the north of the bridge under the street from Higher Pengelly down through Pengelly to the quarry buildings and pit head at Grove. The goods yard, though fairly extensive, was hemmed in by the western face of the quarry. The LSWR expressed concern when this face began to be worked in 1904, though it was assured by the Slate Company that it was safe. The carriage of slates by rail directly to all parts of Britain was, of course, the

prime reason for routing the NCR via Delabole. After a rather slow start (the LSWR complained!) tonnage forwarded by rail rose steadily until the 1920s. At first only a short stub siding was provided but from 1895 he LSWR (not the NCR) built a wide loading bank to take three narrow gauge Slate Co sidings. For the Earl of Wharncliffe's slate traffic from his Trebarwith quarries, another siding was laid down in 1896. By 1899 the original short siding had been extended 400 yards to the Grove area, with a gate at the goods yard end. The loading bank gradually fell into disuse and the narrow gauge sidings were removed. Slates were packed in straw in 10 ton loaded open wagons, whole trainloads being despatched in the years up to 1914. The firm was reconstituted as the Old Delabole Slate Co Ltd in 1898. After the Great War use of slate for roofing declined as clay tiles became popular. The main des-

tinations in the 1930s were to West Cornwall and the Continent (particularly Belgium). An interesting timetable note in 1927 required that slate from Delabole and Camelford to the LNER should be weighed at Woking, en route to Feltham Yard. By 1937 finished slate tonnage was down to 10000, but uses for residual slate dust had been found, as will be seen.

The engine shed lasted until 1 July 1912. An iron-framed affair, it had been sold to the Delabole Co-operative Society for £20 in 1905. It was lifted sideways and became the Society's corn store. The 50ft turntable was removed. Apart from this siding and those for slate, a siding for about 35 wagons served a cattle pen bank and the goods shed (No 2 LSWR). A store for Martyns of Wadebridge lay beyond, with an end-loading dock siding and long shunt neck completing the accommodation. The 1893 signalling included a ringed-arm signal at the yard exit for slate trains to run directly out towards Camelford.

In similar fashion to Camelford, Delabole's standard station house was, in due course, slate clad on the upper storey. The darker dressed slate stone here contrasted well with the Bath stone quoining. This house and the offices were on the Down platform, the waiting shed and signal box on the Up. The frame held 22 levers, including four spare, and housed in the 1880s-style wood and stone construction with multi-paned windows. Originally equipped with Tyers No 3 Tablets in both directions, in 1923 they were converted to No 6 (returnable) probably because of the lengthy shunt movements occurring at Delabole. From 1939 a new Up advanced starting signal (No 19) was installed towards Camelford, causing the Down home to be resited as well. In turn the Down distant was moved, ending

The tourist attraction at Tintagel is 'King Arthur's Castle', a spectacular cliff-top fortification unlikely to have housed the legendary Round Table and Camelot! The Southern Railway named its N15 4-6-0s after King Arthur, his numerous knights, his Queen and included 'Tintagel' itself (No. E745). (Commercial Postcard)

up a mile and 86 yards from the box and (uncompensated) needing a tremendous pull by the signalman to get it 'off'.

After the 1911 loop extensions a twelve coach train could be held (seven against the platform) or 32 wagons, engine and van. On one occasion during the 1963 diversions from the WR, the signalman had four trains in his care - two in the platforms and two shunted back into the yard. The water column on the Down platform was the only one between Launceston and Wadebridge. Supply was restricted for many years until a better source was eventually found. On one occasion a ballast train engine working towards Otterham ran short of water, struggling up to the road overbridge there, for the crew to 'drop' the fire. Meanwhile a road tanker was quickly filled and brought down from Davidstow. The water fell by gravity into the engine tender from the road above. After 1935, at the other (Camelford) end of the Down platform a wooden shed sheltered the two local permanent way motor trolleys.

Jack Manning drove the light vehicle with Frank Bartlett (ganger) Bill Geach (sub-ganger), Bill Gregory and Claude Lee whilst on the Port Isaac side were Sid Keat, Bill Witheridge and Tom Stanbury. Later Ford-engined trolleys able to tow a trailer were substituted, but Tablets had to be drawn for movements outside station limits.

Stationmaster Caple had the p.w. men to pay as well as another half dozen traffic staff in the early 1920s. After 1927 Delabole came under the Camelford stationmaster with two booking clerks, two signalmen, and two porters in the 1930s, but the goods guard did the necessary shunting. LSWR houses for the staff were built in Pengelly, one of the reasons (with a certain stability of employment, and wages above farm level) that attracted men to railway work in the past.

Manufacturing of household goods in large towns had largely replaced locally made products by World War One. Rural water mills grinding the farmer's corn were less and less used. Before the rise of motor road transport the railway carried practically everything, and Delabole's share would be handled in the yard and good shed. Overnight would come groceries from Exeter, Bristol and London in the ubiquitous road boxes, confectionery from Manchester and bags of flour from Avonmouth (milled from North American wheat) for local bakers. Iron and steel bars, bricks and timber would be taken straight from wagons to horse carts, later to steam wagons and, finally, to motor lorries for delivery south and west to Port Isaac, St Teath, even down to Polzeath. Coal, including the Slate Co's supplies, now came by rail instead of through Port Isaac. Some was transhipped from vessels at Wadebridge Quay and came northwards to Delabole. In 1940 a huge stack of coal was laid down in the yard as an emergency supply unloaded, it is said, by one man alone - Marnie Geach. The Co-operative Society traded in coal, corn and foodstuffs, West Cornwall Farmers in animal feeds and agriculture requirements, as did F.J. Martyn (of Wadebridge). Later Silcocks used an SR store for distributing their products. Thousands of rabbits (again!) were sent away from Delabole, a very lucrative trade. W. Pearce of Trewalder was the main trader.

Outwards a certain amount of wool went to Yorkshire in sacking bales, and in the 1940s to 1960s, sugar beet to Kidderminster. A cattle market came into its own from 1940. The Ministry of Food purchased animals brought in by Pearces, who then sent five or six wagons weekly, Easingwold, Yorks being one destination. Delabole, like Otterham, attracted military traffic during World War Two to the extent that redundant army tanks were imported to serve as targets for aircraft on the Treligga range, a mile or so to the west. With heavy traffic like this an 02 0-4-4T would be sent up from Wadebridge to shunt. About 40 wagons could be held in the yard and a train of 13 run-round inside. No wonder the Wadebridge foreman found Delabole's accommodation useful, though ten miles off! There was a breakaway on a goods train in 1949, the engine (34008) was well down towards Port Isaac Road with the leading wagons before it was discovered.

Mention of slate dust, once a by-product and then deliberately ground to powder in a large mill, has been made already. At first (from 1930) it went away in bags - 'Delafila' it was called - for use as a finish for rubber (690 tons in 1934 compared with 680 tons of slates). Bound for Brimsdown (Essex), via Feltham Yard, other loads went via the GWR to Hayes (Middlesex) to make the old '78' gramophone records. Then a 'Covhop' was tried out, confined to its own loading shed! This trial as a bulk carrier was followed by five (dedicated) 'Prestflo' wagons filled and emptied by air pressure, in the 1960s. Unfortunately the introduction of plastic 45 and 33 records from the mid-1950s badly affected business. When Delabole's freight facilities were closed the 'Prestflos' were loaded at Wadebridge from large bags taken by road, and this continued into the 1970s. Some powder was exported to Calcutta (a special load of 400 tons is recorded) via the docks at Newport (Mon.) and once, 66 tons went to Rio de Janeiro. Finally, the diamond toothed saws used in the quarry were sent to Panmuir in Scotland for resetting. The present firm, Delabole Slate (1971) Ltd., a part of the RTZ Mining & Exploration Ltd. since 1984, relies on road transport to export its powder and granules, reduced in a modern crushing plant installed in 1980. The pit is gradually being filled in by graders working on spiral tracks. The number of men now employed is much less than the 350 in 1937. About 120 tons of slate block is currently quarried (sawn, not blasted) for floor slabbing, fireplace etc. - but not for roofing!

Some alterations were made to the yard in 1930, and again in 1963, when the trailing connection to the down (No. 12 points) were clipped out. Otherwise, after withdrawal of the freight services the yard remained in-situ, until 1965.

Delabole Up platform and standard waiting shed on the left. LSW 90lb/yard rail in 30 foot lengths still exists here in the 1960s. (Lens of Sutton)

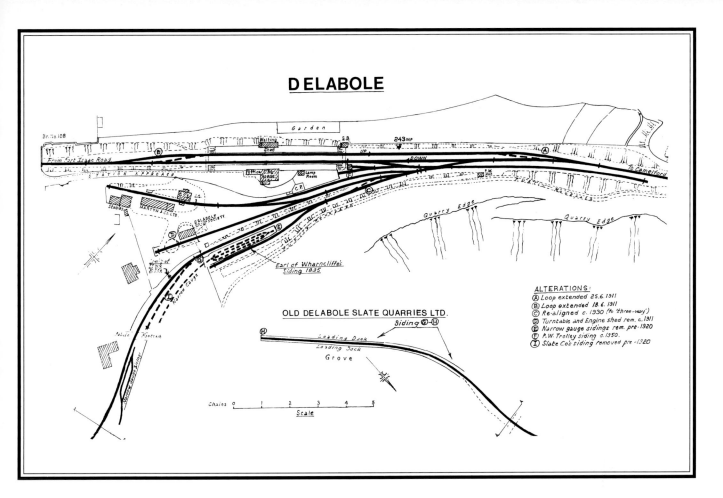

DELABOLE

OLD DELABOLE SLATE QUARRIES LTD.
Siding Ⓖ-Ⓗ

ALTERATIONS:
Ⓐ Loop extended 25.6.1911
Ⓑ Loop extended 18.6.1911
Ⓒ Re-aligned c.1930 (to 'three-way')
Ⓓ Turntable and Engine shed rem. c.1911
Ⓔ Narrow gauge sidings rem. pre-1920
Ⓕ P.W. Trolley siding c.1950.
Ⓘ Slate Co's siding removed pre-1920

Delabole to Port Isaac Road

Below Delabole the line snaked its way on a series of 30 chain reversing curves at a ruling and mainly 1 in 73 gradient past Delamere and Benbole. At Treroosal Bridge (245m 7ch) the road leads to St Teath just over a mile away and this was where the inhabitants of 1892 would have preferred a station. On the down side is the site of the once active Trewenham mine.

Beyond, at Trekee, the NCR's surveyors laid out a complete semi-circle - a left hand 30 chain curve to keep on the hillside above the deep valley at Trewarne. Down below, a quarry for blue stone had been worked over the years, but with the installation of a roadstone crusher at the railway level, Messrs. Tom Bros (1922) requested that the LSWR provide siding facilities. Served by facing points (Up) and

situated about half way round the mile-long curve (246m 66ch) it was controlled by a two lever ground frame released by the Tablet. A key held in Port Isaac Road box unlocked the gate and a scotch block inside. As it was not safe to work it by passing goods train, the siding was served by a special trip by an engine (off the pickup goods) from Port Isaac Road. Empty wagons were propelled, brake van next to the

The Old Delabole Slate Quarry Company siding was extended in 1899, thereafter directly serving the splitting shed. A few years later a special is being loaded in the Grove, to be hauled away by an Adams '380' 4-4-0, one rebuilt with a Drummond boiler and round-spectacled cab front. (Cornwall Record Office)

The Old Delabole Slate Company's narrow gauge system was converted to steam in the 1890s. Bagnall 0-4-0ST 'Sir J.T. Firbank' arrived in 1902. The standard gauge siding leading from Delabole goods yard (right) was extended in 1899. (Cornwall Record Office)

engine, to just above the points. The engine then detached, and reversing, collected loaded wagons from inside the gate, coming back out and attaching to the BV and empties. The whole train was then drawn back clear of the points and then propelled into the sid-ing. After leaving the empties inside the gate, the engine, loaded wagons and brake van returned to Port Isaac Road. The Tablet machine to Delabole was altered to No 6 (returnable) from 1923. After World War Two separate trip working was made between Wadebridge and (Betty &) Tom's sid-ing, usually for wagons of ballast. It remained operational until 1964.

It was only another quarter mile thence to Port Isaac Road. Underbridge No 121 (247m 3ch) at the north end of the station has been, at the time of

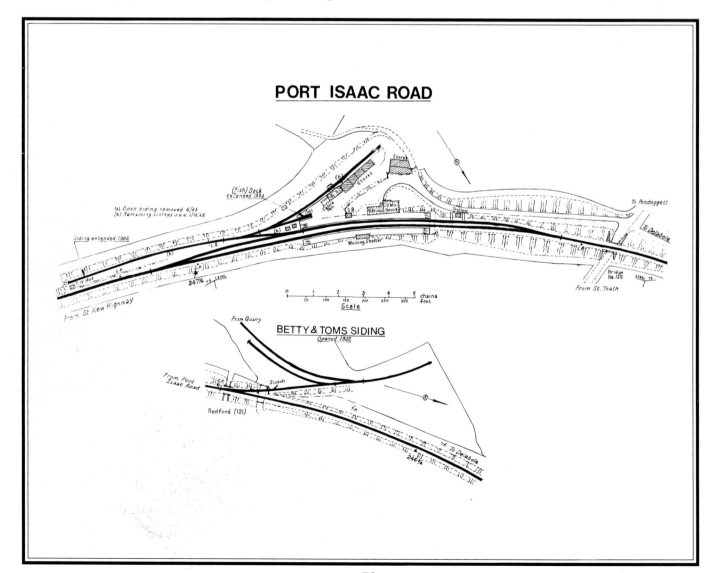

Four miles to the east of the fishing village by narrow lanes, Port Isaac Road was sited in St.Kew Parish - its remoteness discouraged passengers as this view taken in July 1963 shows. (S. Gradidge)

writing, proposed for listing as a 'scheduled' structure. Just below is a most awkward turn into the station access lane.

Port Isaac Road (247m 13ch)

Quite isolated, on a cross country road from St Teath to Pendogget which included several steep and narrow lanes, it seems a most unlikely place for a station, but with Port Isaac itself only four miles to the west of that seaside village was in mind. St Teath was relatively nearer at two miles. The Port Isaac fish trade - considerable in the 1890s - was attractive, together with tourist prospects. From opening the LSWR provided a good service for herring (which along with pilchards had declined) traded through Pawlyns who bought in the mackerel and shellfish

catches. Wagon loads were forwarded for overnight delivery to Billingsgate Market in London, an example occurring in October 1897 when 150 tons of fish was despatched to Exeter, Birmingham and London, brought by farmers' carts to the station. The spur from the goods yard was lengthened in 1902 at some cost, to avoid 'tow-roping', followed by extension of the dock in 1903. A shelf site was dug out to keep it level with the station, whereas the line to St Kew dropped sharply away at 1 in 73 in a cutting under Trewarne bridge. At one time a fair quantity of flowers and fruit also went away from this station. Growth in tourism and the building of hotels followed and Port Isaac was to draw a discerning clientele, not averse to the comparative isolation of this corner of

the Atlantic Coast. John Prout started a road service from the village to Wadebridge and Bodmin Road from 1861. Subsequently his son John was the GWR cartage agent, while son Mark took on that for the LSWR/SR. Horse-drawn vehicles were replaced in the 1920s by motor buses (which also collected mail from pillar boxes). The SR withdrew its subsidy in June 1930 and a Southern National bus then served Port Isaac. The Prout Brothers merged their businesses (which included carting building materials and fish) and the firm still operates buses and coach tours to this day.

The standard SM's house and station offices were on the Up platform, the top-glazed signal box on the same side holding a frame of 17 levers (three spare). All material used, except the platform coping (slate slabs), was dressed local stone. The building, with wider eaves protruding from the roof, presents Port Isaac Road (and St Kew) with a more attractive appearance, though it had not, 25 years since closure, received the attention of conversion to a private dwelling. On the Down platform a standard waiting shed was provided.

The yard was awkward to shunt, and brake van(s) of Up goods trains were ordered at the Wadebridge end if wagons were left outside the home signal. Visibility was restricted by the 30-chain curve through the station and, noteworthy for the North Cornwall, there was a measure of track circuiting, covering the Up loop facing Down trailing (No. 10) points, replacing a fouling bar. With an electrical release on the starting signal, shunting in the Down direction could be

Port Isaac Road and St.Kew Highway looked very much alike, but the former had its signal box on the Up platform. To the south the line from Port Isaac Road falls away at 1 in 73, but the shunt neck (extended in 1902) kept on the level. Considerable fish was sent away from this station from the start, continuing in certain measure until closure in 1966. (R.C.Riley)

Just north of Port Isaac Road is the location in May 1957 as the lined-black 'T9' No. 30717 saunters by with local Set No. 27 in contrasting red and cream, probably the 10.00 a.m. Okehampton to Padstow. (Rail Archive Stephenson)

larger consignments. It matched the station buildings' stonework. Beyond, Messrs W.T. Tucker & Sons established a farm store for the usual corn, feeds and fertilizers, also coal and seed potatoes. The yard closed in September 1964 and was clipped out of use in December 1965.

The last Stationmaster was Mr Corrick in 1927. Thereafter it came under Camelford's control. The two signalmen, also acting as porters manned the box, which here retained the Tablet apparatus (not transferred to the booking hall as elsewhere). Over the years Albert Vincent (1942-49) and others, like Arthur Beer and Ken Cory kept trains operating the loops surviving to the end of services. A booking clerk attended, though the remoteness of the area discouraged applicants for this post!

Port Isaac Road to St Kew Highway
Below Trewarne Bridge the line went to the right on a continuous 30 chain curve, dropping at 1 in 73. Just after the road from Pengenna (where arsenic mining once was active) into Trelill village crossed the line, came the entrance to the short Trelill Tunnel, with its handsome stone/brick portal. The southern portal is plainer. The countryside from here to St Kew is less

somewhat inhibited by the use of the non-returnable Tyers No 3 Table to St Kew. It was made easier in the Up direction after the substitution of a No 6 Tablet to Delabole in 1923 for working Tom's siding.

This wayside station developed quietly up to the 1930s. As well as the fish, the (inevitable!) rabbit business burgeoned after 1918 with much crating and barrowing to meet the arrival of the afternoon 'Perisher' from Padstow to Exeter. Inwards, calves from East Devon (also fish - the other way - plaice and cod from Grimsby) by passenger train, and sundry merchandise through the Road Box System, belied any notions that Port Isaac Road slept. A standard LSWR No 2 Goods Shed, a 2-ton crane within, handled

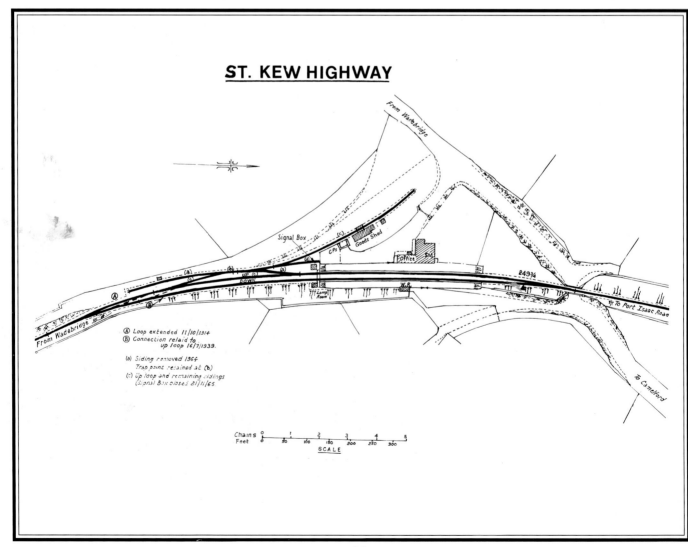

ST. KEW HIGHWAY

Ⓐ Loop extended 11/10/1914
Ⓑ Connection relaid to up loop 16/7/1939.

(a) Siding removed 1964
Trap point retained at (b)
(c) Up loop and remaining sidings
(Signal Box closed 21/11/65.

Chains
Feet
SCALE

St. Kew Highway yards in the last summer of freight working in 1964. By then the only likely traffic was coal and fertilizer, the end dock siding (centre) was already gone and sundry merchandise delivery concentrated on Wadebridge. (C.J. Knowles-Thomas)

St. Kew Highway station took its name from the settlement on the Camelford to Wadebridge road, St. Kew village lying about a mile to the north. It also served St. Mabyn to the east, and St. Minver by Prout's buses. The overhanging eaves of the station house were repeated at Port Isaac Road and Padstow. (R.C. Riley)

opened, is open to conjecture. Certainly not very many in later years, and from the 1920s the motorbus served these communities better though only, perhaps, on one or two days a week. There was already a public house on the main road from Camelford to Wadebridge, with a small settlement (which grew somewhat after the railway opened) known as St Kew Highway. This road went under the railway just to the north of the station, with a very low headroom. The bridge still stands but the A39 now cuts a wide swathe through the adjacent embankment. Most holiday trains (and the ACE) called at St Kew Highway as it was the railhead for Polzeath on Padstow Bay and the straggling settlement of St Minver down to Rock. All these places, eight to ten miles to the west, attracted visitors who in the early days were quite prepared to ride in horse brakes to the quietest beaches and cliffs in the west country - and to the golf course at St Enodoc. Sir John Betjeman came to love this corner of Cornwall and travelled by train to St Kew or Wadebridge; not surprisingly, the North Cornwall Railway is commemorated in his prose and poems.

St Kew Highway was almost the double of Port Isaac Road in appearance and layout. The stations buildings were the same, though the approach road was much less sinuous and narrow. The signal box was off the platform though at the country end, almost four-square and fully glazed in the 1880s pattern. It held 17 levers and three spare to work the loop points, the 'push and pull' connections with the goods yard and the mini-

'open' and the curvature was much less severe, in the 40 to 60 chain range. The line still fell at 1 in 73, however, from the 400 foot contour at Port Isaac Road to 250 at St Kew. On the left could be seen the farmlands of Bokelly, while on the right, well out of sight and nestling in a valley, is St Kew Churchtown, a charming little place. The road from St Kew to Bokelly via Trequite crossed at 248m 51ch. Nearly into St Kew Highway another minor road came under the railway at the north end of the hamlet, the gradient easing to 1 in 330.

St Kew Highway (249m 64ch)

St Kew village lay, not directly by road, to the north about two miles distant. St Mabyn village is southward by a tortuous road down to the Allen and up a long hill thereafter. Over to the east is St Tudy - walking distance about two and a half miles and beyond is St Breward on the edge of Bodmin Moor, at about six miles. How many local people used St Kew Highway, once

St. Kew Highway signal box stood alone off the Wadebridge end of the Up platform. it opened in June 1895, one of the last built in the LSWR 1880s style, and was equipped from the outset with Tyers Single line Tablet apparatus. The North Cornwall line down to Delabole was originally provided with the old wooden Staff and Ticket system, though with the telegraph Absolute Block safeguard. (R.C. Riley)

The Up starting signal raised for the mid-day train from Padstow to Okehampton will be lowered by the porter signalman at St. Kew Highway walking down to his box off the platform end. He would have restored the Tablet from Wadebridge East in the instrument in the booking office. (Lens of Sutton)

mum number of semaphore signals needed to work these passing places, i.e. six. Until 16 July 1939 there was a direct connection to the Down loop (resembling Whitstone on the Bude Branch), as well as one trailing into the Up. As moves from the Down entailed working outside the starting signal (i.e. withdrawing the Tablet to Wadebridge) in later years a change was made to a Tyers No 6 (returnable to the St Kew machine). The Wadebridge-end loop points were advanced 50 yards in October 1914. St Kew's signalling was modernised in 1939, the fouling bars exchanged for facing points lock and detectors, the signal posts from wood to two vertical rails latticed together and re-equipped with SR upper quadrant arms. At a late date the WR substituted Electric Key Tokens for No 6 Tablets to Wadebridge East. The first signalman was Joseph Vincent in 1895. The last, Peter Hamley, later followed his father-in-law into the box, working it as a relief man on closure in 1966.

The spur from the goods yard was lengthened at some time, proving too short for shunting movements. Otherwise only two sidings were provided, one for 15 wagons to the cattle pen and goods shed, and a short stub to the end loading dock (removed in 1939). The goods shed was an LSWR standard No 2, inside it a two-ton crane. W.T. Tucker & Son traded here until the 1930s, and again from the 1950s when they rented the goods shed as a Fertilizer store. Several wagons per week brought Silcock's products in season and, in this area, a certain amount of corn was sent away. Sugar beet went to Kidderminster in 16-ton open wagons. In these days of mechanical handlers it is difficult to visualize the amount of shovel and fork labour necessary to shift beet, coal, bricks - and, at one time, manure! St Kew served farmers' needs from St

Mabyn, St Tudy and Chapel Amble to the east, also to the St Minver parishes to the west. There were rabbits of course, to Birmingham and the Midlands, and Messrs. Inch forwarded live and carcassed pigs. Noteworthy was an early complete farm removal in pre-Second World War days, from Ashwater to St Kew Highway. The SR provided cartage to Pencarrow where Mr G Daniel acquired a tenancy. But St Kew, very much a wayside station, was doomed by the rise of competing road transport. There had been no SM since Mr Dark in 1927, supervision passing to Camelford. The yard was taken out of use (after closure in September 1964), together with the Up loop, on 21 November 1965 and the Signal Box closed.

St Kew Highway to Wadebridge

Down by Benbole the last stretch from St Kew to Wadebridge continued to fall 1 in 75. Here the 'T9' and a down train skated along, leaning from one curve to the next en route to the sea. It was quite a pull the other way, needless to say, though a 'West Country' even with four or five on, made little of these gradients. The multiple exhaust beats would echo in the woods below Hingham, the scene in direct contrast to the open hillside near Otterham. The entry into the Allen Valley could be effected only by more skilful engineering. A high embankment to cross a tributary at Bovehill, above Dinham, then under the road at Rocksea which was given a very tight diversionary curve from its original line, over another tributary before the railway arrived on a shelf built above the River Allen itself at the 251 MP. The NCR would have crossed the Allen here and come down its east side, but the 1894 deviation kept it higher up and above the west side of Lemail Wood and its old mill. There was another old mill at Hingham indicating the use made of the Allen for water power. A lot of grain was formerly grown in this area but by the time of the railway's arrival arable land had been converted to grass. The contractors had to blast their way through rock (granite) past Hingham, where once there was a hillside quarry. Past the 252 milepost the level dropped nearer to that of the river, and the one time navigable limit at Sladesbridge. The line was carried over the Wadebridge to Bodmin Road by Bridge No 141, an all-masonry structure, not brick faced as was usual. This low headroom bridge has been removed in recent years and the road widened. Remaining on an embankment and in a straight alignment, the line was carried to the north bank of the Allen and then over it by a single arch bridge. Between the Allen and the Camel is the toe of the hillside rising above

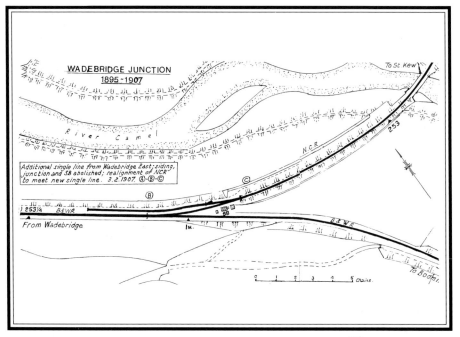

WADEBRIDGE JUNCTION
1895-1907

River Camel

Additional single line from Wadebridge East; siding, junction and SB abolished; realignment of NCR to meet new single line. 3.2.1907 Ⓐ-Ⓑ-Ⓒ

From Wadebridge

To St Kew

NCR

253

B&WR

B&WR

To Bodn.

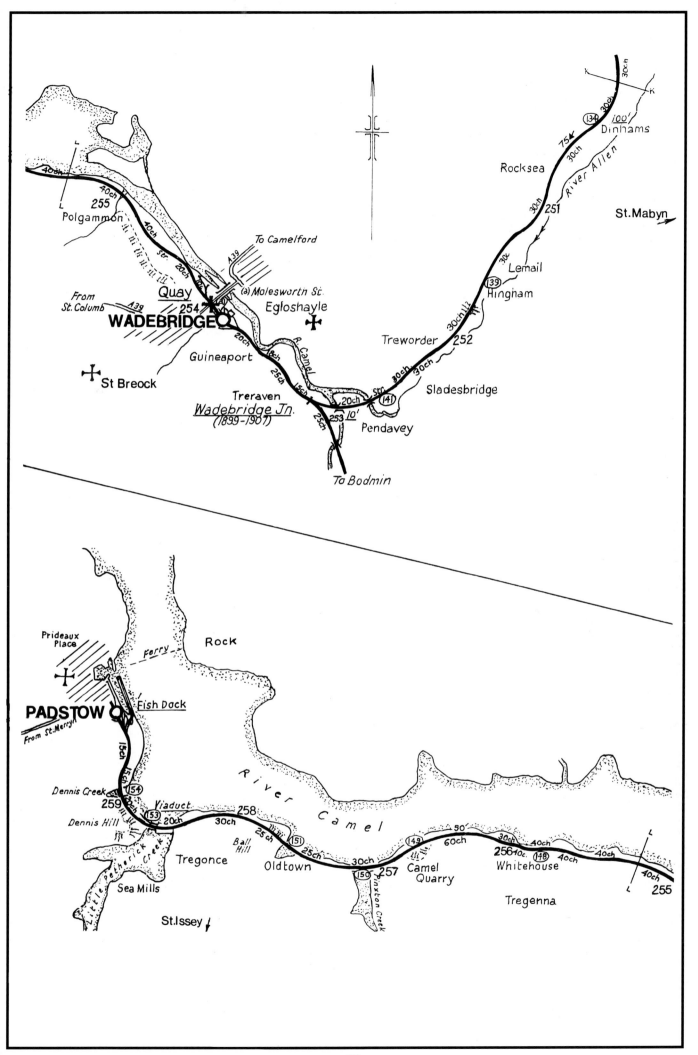

Wadebridge East was constructed in stone conforming with the central pillar style of LSWR signal boxes of the mid-1890s. After 1907 the frame held 43 levers (including eight spare), the signalmen would issue Tyers single line Tablets to St. Kew Highway and Boscarne Junction. Double line absolute block signalling obtained to Wadebridge West box. (J. Nicholas)

Pendavey Farm. A short, but deep, cutting was necessary to penetrate this before the North Cornwall line emerged over the Camel (Bridge No 144) at 252m 78ch. Rather unusual in that the main span was a pair of W.I. hog back girders (over the river) and a 9 foot W.I. plate girder over the river path. From here a sharp 20 chain curve rounded an embankment to the site of the former Wadebridge Junction, and the end of the North Cornwall Railway in 1895. All the NCR overbridges were constructed to double line standard (i.e. 28ft), only a few in some of the stations actually using this facility. As recounted, the original entry into Wadebridge was over the reconstructed single line Bodmin & Wadebridge Railway. The farm track to Treraven crossed at 253m 47ch by an overbridge (two cast iron girders), with

only 26ft between its masonry abutments, just enough for the two single lines formed from 1907. The Camel Valley widens considerably below Pendavey but the B & W kept to the south side, hugging the edge of the hillside below Treraven on a near level profile. On the outskirts of Wadebridge the Camel meandered toward the railway, thus the 1907 widening works included retaining walls both against the river below and Guineaport Terrace above. The line curved left at 20 chains and reversed into an 18 chain radius at this point, showing its B & WR origins, and thus close to Wadebridge station.

Wadebridge (253m 72ch)

Wadebridge, until then part of St Columb Rural District Council, was

granted Urban District status from April 1898. Situated each side of the ancient Camel river bridge, on the north side is the Parish of Egloshayle and on the other that of St Breock. Only part of Egloshayle was included in the new District and the railway was entirely on the south bank over the bridge. The population in 1901 was 3,470 and thus a most realistic goal for the North Cornwall Railway, backed by the LSWR. Its railway inheritance has been noted - the primitive 1834 line to Bodmin, Ruthern Bridge and Wenford, also the 1888 connection from the GWR at Boscarne. Already a town of importance, and of political influence, on the opening of the NCR in 1895 the way east was now by a direct standard gauge route for cattle shipment, granite, slates, manure and grain. Sea sand brought from Padstow was transferred to rail at the Quay and taken to inland destinations. Later a fair-sized forwarding of dairy products (not milk) fresh meat and rabbits was encouraged by the LSWR and SR. General merchandise, formerly brought by coaster from Bristol to the Quay, soon went to rail. The LSWR instituted their daily 'road box' system from London, Exeter and Plymouth; foodstuffs (including fresh fruit) were unloaded in the goods shed and distributed by cart around town and country. Soon to expand were inward loads of fertilizers, cattle feed and seeds. Two foundries in the town, Oatey & Martyn in Polmora Road, and Iron Bros. (1922 - formerly Harris) relied on the railway for materials and coal, and despatching of finished goods. Timber arrived at the Quay from the Baltic. Granite and china clay came from Wenford - and (earlier) iron and copper ore - a

On the sunny morning of 25th August 1960 the 6.30 a.m. from Okehampton (with coaches and newspaper van from the 1.30 a.m. Waterloo) has reached Wadebridge at 9.15 a.m. behind 'N' Class No.31847. After nationalization in 1948 several Bodmin Road trains were extended to Padstow. Former GWR 2-6-2T No. 4565 (St. Blazey) with a 'B' Set is on a return working calling at Wadebridge at 9.20 a.m. (R.A. Lumber)

By 1955 the WR engineers had replaced the sagging timber platform wall (this end) of the island platform at Wadebridge with concrete blocks. The 12.58 p.m. Padstow to Exeter on 4th July 1955 consists of a local 'P' Set, the returning Newsvan (from the 1.30 a.m. Waterloo) and an XP mail van behind T9 No. 30709. (R.C. Riley)

continuation of the B&WR's traffic developed by the LSWR from the 1880s.

With its shops in Molesworth Street and weekly market (as well as the Monday Cattle Market) Wadebridge was well endowed to attract country people from North Cornwall stations, and from the Bodmin direction. Horse coaches plied from St Columb and Truro, replaced by motor buses in the 1920s. The LSWR encouraged tourist traffic by excursion fares, considering Wadebridge a railhead for Newquay! Even after the 1895 connection to the east it is doubtful if the LSWR attracted many long distance passengers to and from Bodmin, and thus

away from the long-established GWR Cornish main line. In 1888 Truro became the County Town, and the centre of a Cornish Diocese and a new Cathedral, but Bodmin retained the Assizes, Gaol, Asylum and the Duke of Cornwall's Light Infantry Depot.

The 1888 station building and its single platform was transformed into a through layout with three platform faces in 1899, on completion of the North Cornwall Railway, but remained in LSWR ownership. The original platform was extended to a total of 460 feet by extensions at both ends, with a water column placed at the Padstow extremity. A cantilevered awning faced

about three quarters of the offices, but the ornate wooden footbridge to the new 1899 island platform had none for passengers. It was replaced by a stark concrete version in the 1920s. The 350ft island platform was wide enough for a large waiting room in brick with fireplace and chimney, the whole building surmounted by another cantilevered awning. The 3ft high platforms, a newer standard, originally supported by timber and iron struts, were gradually rebuilt in concrete precast parts and lastly in BR's concrete blocks. At the east end stood two water columns, essential to supply engines about to climb to Otterham (the next one was at Launceston), and to Bodmin Road. Built after the fashion of Launceston's station building, single storeyed, with a steeply-pitched roof and dressed stone walls, there was no accommodation for the SM and his family. They lived in a house opposite, in residential developments dating from the 1888 opening from Bodmin. The Town Hall also dates from this period, though it opened as the 'Molesworth Hall', its cost largely borne by that family. The Platt (or Fair Plot) between the Hall and the Treguddick Brook and the railway accommodated a cattle market. In a short while from the North Cornwall's arrival, it had proved inadequate, for before the railways arrived cattle dealing was largely unorganised. There was now the prospect of much increased rail forwarding, mainly by dealers from Exeter and beyond, and a new site was

The Beattie tanks lasted at Wadebridge for over seventy years, given their suitability for working to Wenford and on the sharp curves of the Quay sidings. In 1930 No. 3329 and a wagon of engine coal is observed by a gentleman in period baggy trousers. In the distance are the stub blocks off the turntable and the breakdown van. (R.S. Carpenter)

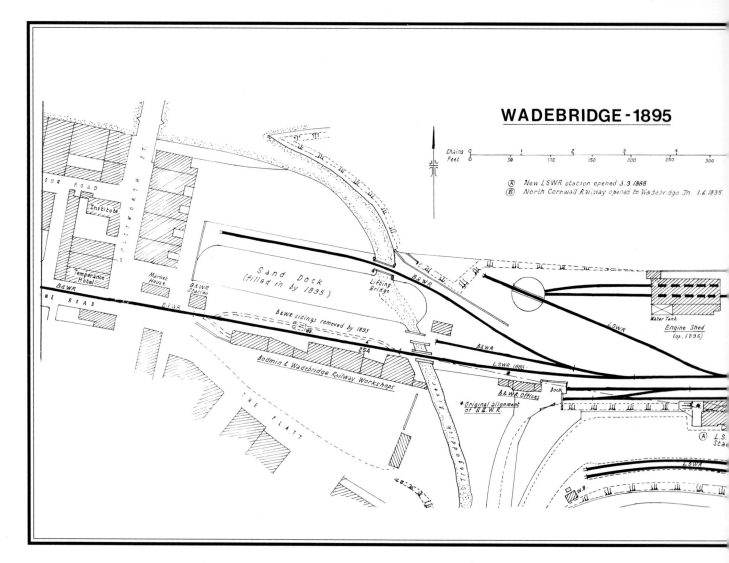

Chains 0 | 1 | 2 | 3 | 4
Feet 0   50   100   150   200   250   300

Ⓐ New LSWR station opened 3.9.1888
Ⓑ North Cornwall Railway opened to Wadebridge Jn. 1.6.1895.

(Map labels: Four Road, Institute, Walmsworth St., Temperance Hotel, Market House, B&WR Station, B&WR, NE Road, Sand Dock (filled in by 1895), B&WR sidings removed by 1895, Lifting Bridge, B&WR, LSWR, Water Tank, Engine Shed (op. 1895), Bodmin & Wadebridge Railway Workshops, The Platt, R. Tregoddick, LSWR 1888, B.& W.R., B. & W.R. Offices, Dock, *Original alignment of B.&W.R., Ⓐ L.S. Sta., LSWR)

found off the Polmora Road, again encouraged by the Molesworths who provided 8,000 loads of fill.

For the proposed Wadebridge station enlargement of 1895-8, land to the north was filled, the first structure to appear being a new engine shed, with turntable (50ft) and elevated water tank. It needed to be available for LSWR bigger engines arriving from June 1895. The Beattie 'Well' Tanks had been housed in the old B&WR shed to the west. Although various other small-wheelbase engines were tried out on the Wenford Branch services and the sharp curves on the Quay, these 2-4-0WTs survived until 1962. Until 1908 the new timber-built shed was single-ended with access solely via the turntable. Introduction of H13 steam railcars saw an extension on the east side, making it a 'through' shed with sidings joining the Up line. Over the years Wadebridge shed retained a small allocation of 'Jubilee' 0-4-2s and various 4-4-0s for the Okehampton line, and '415' 4-4-2Ts, '02' Class 0-4-4Ts then, latterly ex-GWR pannier tanks and Ivatt 2-6-2Ts, for Bodmin workings. The long-serving Beattie tanks were replaced by ex-GWR '1366' 0-6-0PTs in 1962. Always on the shed were visiting Okehampton or Exmouth Junction 0-6-0s and 'N' Class 2-6-0s (from 1925) on goods work. The 4-4-0 Classes, and the new 'West Country' Pacifics (from 1947) mainly used on passenger turns, shared the goods working as required. In the final years of steam the 'Ns' were undertaking both roles.

Isolated from its Exmouth Junction parent by 115 miles, Wadebridge motive power staff needed to be self-sufficient. Lifting crane, work benches, boiler washout facilities, sand store etc. with a staff of around forty including the enginemen, cleaners, fitters and night men - all under a Foreman - provided for this. True to type the drivers and firemen held their own self-taught locomotive instruction classes, and 'first aid'. They, and other local railwaymen, knew that their working environment could be dangerous, thus

Wadebridge in the early 1930s showing a Drummond 'L11' 4-4-0 on a Padstow to Okehampton train and an '02' 0-4-4T on a Bodmin train in the Up loop. On the right is an ex-LBSC brake van for Wenford Branch workings, and wagons of engine coal, some of which was shipped through Highbridge S & DJR. (J. Rea collection)

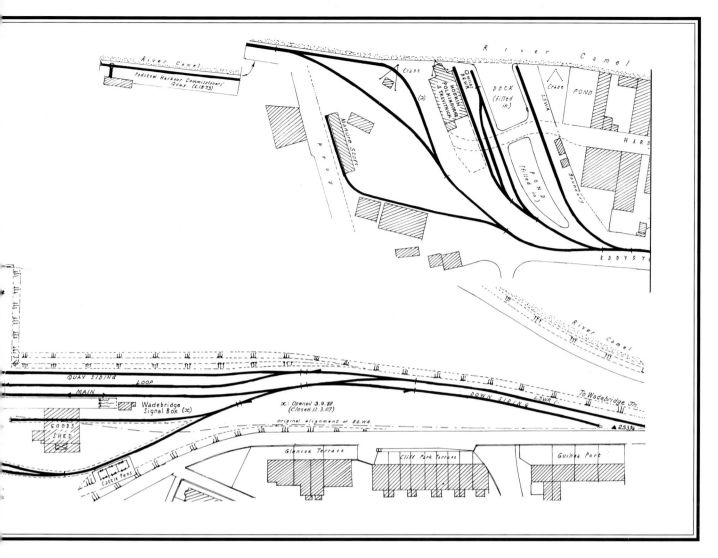

Ambulance and first aid practice were strongly pursued. Under Mr. Brown, Foreman, in the last decade 13 sets of enginemen worked in six 'links' taking in Wenford (1 set), North Cornwall (6), Bodmin (2), Rest Day Relief (1), Yard Pilot (2) and one spare. The Western Region's takeover in the BR years (Wadebridge then coming under St Blazey) followed by the emergence of diesels, widened the field of transfer and promotion, though since the Southern Railway was formed in 1923 men had come west from London and Kent. In the summer season and for the fish specials, firemen from Exeter would work from Wadebridge, lodging in the town before the last war. Post - War a dormitory coach was provided for Exeter crews working in on Friday evenings and out on Saturday morning's 'ACE'. Following its closure in January 1967, five men transferred from Wadebridge shed to Newton Abbot and four to St Blazey. Roy Wilce of Plymouth Laira, who learnt his calling on the footplate of a Wadebridge

A train from Okehampton had arrived at Wadebridge on 21st July 1948 consisting of ex-LSWR local Set No. 54, an SR Parcels and Mail van, and a T9 4-4-0. To the left of the signal may be seen the SM's office and the PW Inspector's Office, behind the guards' and porters' room. (A.E. West)

The east end of Wadebridge goods yard in July 1964 showing the cattle pens which, by then, were virtually disused. Household coal at 'summer' prices account for the 16-ton wagon loads, though some may be for the engines. The amount of merchandise passing through the goods shed (left) had declined, and was finally concentrated by the Sundries Division of BR at Plymouth, with road delivery. The Station Master's house off the Guineaport Road is behind the lower trees. (C.J. Knowles-Thomas)

Railways first came to Wadebridge in 1834 and they ended there in 1978. The Bodmin & Wadebridge 'Station' lay where stands the furthest wagon, and Lever's/Rush's store is on the site of the old sand dock. in July 1964 box vans of cattle feed and fertilizers came via the North Cornwall, but from 7th September were diverted via Bodmin Road until final closure of Wadebridge as a 'full load' depot in 1978. On the right are the ex-LNWR dormitory coach, a bogie 'Queen Mary' brake van and an ex-GWR breakdown van. (C.J. Knowles-Thomas)

moved towards St Kew by 30 yards to become 'home' signals. Wadebridge East box (from 1907) held 43 levers (ten spare) to work the switches and facing point locks, and the impressive array of signals, particularly those on the east end of the island platform (replaced by an SR bracket and arms in 1938) - mirrored by the above mentioned 'homes' 200 yards east of the box. Shunting movements in and out of the down side goods yard and the engine shed/up sidings were controlled by the signalman. His Tablet machines were No 6s for the St Kew Highway and Boscarne single lines, while Preece 3-wire instruments operated the double 'open' block to Wadebridge West.

Over a quarter of a mile towards Padstow, Wadebridge West signal box stood adjacent to Molesworth Street level crossing - its gates folding against themselves to rail, and operated by a wheel. The box held 29 levers (seven spare) and, apart from the crossing and single line block to Padstow (No 6 returnable Tablet), controlled the western end of Wadebridge station and the Quay sidings entrance points. One peculiar ancillary was an Annett's key kept in the signal box, to unlock a one-lever frame. This worked a protective catchpoint against false moves to a lift bridge over the Treguddick River. The bridge was left free to float clear on extra high tides and depended on a counterbalance system. Before any movement was made over it to the sand siding the foreman had to ensure securing bolts were in position. The siding fronted a miniature tidal dock dating from B & WR days, wherein barges of sand from the estuary were off loaded into wagons for eventual distribution to the Bodmin sand drops and inland farms.

'T9', nowadays drives an Inter City HST on the former GWR main line, but 'Art' Ferrett and Norman Wills ended their service here, as did the fitter Walter Harper and shedman Arthur Rush.

The layout at Wadebridge from 1899 remained largely constant until closure in 1966. The points and crossings at the East signal box required to be altered to serve the separation of the Bodmin and North Cornwall lines as from 3 February 1907, the number of levers in the frame increased from the original 29. Direct facing crossovers, forming a 'scissors' pattern, encompassed all movements in and out of the Main platforms (1 & 2) and the two-end-worked Up loop (No 3). From 13 February 1938 these crossovers were separated and the Bodmin line one was sited to the east of the occupation crossing. At the same time the Down outer home signals were removed and the inners

The unpretentious station at Wadebridge dated from 1888, though the dressed stone and slate roof were handsome enough in comparison with the concrete blocks of the adjoining goods shed extension. The booking office accommodation held both LSWR and GWR positions until 1915. The rear of the bookstall (left) shows a Southern National bus time-table overprinted BUS STOP. Wadebridge station was the railhead for a number of services to the north side and to St. Columb, Newquay and Truro. (C.J. Knowles-Thomas)

The Treguddick creek was tidal, consequently an arrangement of counterbalances allowed the bridge carrying the sand dock siding to rise and fall, if high water was expected. Fishplates were removed, and a catchpoint opened for protection. It was in place until October 1955, and the siding to the north side of the B & WR sand dock was shortened to suit. (L.T. George Collection)

Although the new west layout was commissioned on opening to Padstow in March 1899, a further engine spur was laid in and a facility for starting Down trains from the Up loop, became operable from June 1906. It appears to have coincided with the introduction of railmotor trains to Bodmin, with the occasional trip to Padstow. The No1 Up siding terminated for a time in a truck weighbridge (replacing the B & WR's on its quay line). The 1899 alterations were quite sweeping to accommodate the new island platform-enough land had been acquired by the LSWR before 1895 in anticipation of the NCR's arrival, although some reclamation was necessary by the river. Adjacent to the sand dock were a couple of sidings initially used by Currys as a base for constructing

the Padstow extension. From May 1899 the No 1 siding was extended from the weighbridge paralleling the Up loop to the East box (with a No 2 siding outside and another beyond, both serving a re-sited coaling bank). Another change here occurred in February 1908 when the engine shed was extended eastwards to house the railmotors and the sidings within connected with the No 1 Up siding (under East box control). In 1916 the Up siding was extended and the crossover to the loop moved east, to join the Up main close to the East box.

In the far corner between the sand dock and Molesworth Street, a siding was extended westward at the same time, down to the footbridge with another across the old B&W sand dock. The former in the 1950s held an ex-

LNWR sleeping car (No DM 198932) as the enginemen's dormitory. The latter siding was realigned in the same decade to serve a new store for Levers (cattle feeds). The sand dock had gradually silted up and was filled and levelled, and a concrete hard standing provided. The tidal bridge, catchpoint and siding beyond were removed in 1955.

On the Down side the extensive goods yard, provided in 1888, included a goods shed siding and two mileage sidings (for about 40 wagons) with hard standings, skirting the new station forecourt. A large cattle pens dock was formed and from 1899 received a second short siding on its flank. The cattle trade out of Wadebridge Market (then on the second Monday, monthly) grew very quickly once the North Cornwall opened, with large shipments to Exeter, Chichester, and by 1914, to eastern England. Wadebridge Market on its newest site became weekly, when the yard filled with cattle, the drovers and station staff struggling to herd them through the pens into the wagons. The former practice of driving cattle through the streets was ended, by hiring lorries, from the 1940s. All day the station pilot kept busy, marshalling and placing wagons in the docks.

Cattle specials were timetabled out of Wadebridge as normal events, and empty trains or wagons supplied to suit. The SM and agent had to be well briefed on likely requirements, and a Cattle Inspector would be on hand as regulations for transit of animals were very strict. Allied to the cattle farming was the fresh meat trade, started quite early on from Wadebridge to Nine Elms (and Smithfield Market) at first in ventilated box wagons but in due course in demountable containers. There was a weekly export of pigs, up to three or four wagons from farm collections by Lloyd Maunder and Blewitt (Trelill). Wool went in bales to Bradford, and sheepskins to Buckfastleigh and Yeovil. Needless to say there was a large forwarding of rabbits: George Robinson & Sons and Tonkins maintained depots and the 3.15pm Padstow 'Perishables' (with its Medway and Midlands connections) was the favourite train for these. The latter carried small consignments of primroses and violets in season, and a considerable egg trade was conducted by the Cornish Egg Depot, Robinsons (Treguddick), and Tonkins - by the container full. Wadebridge farmers could also find a profitable business in new potatoes to Covent Garden and Brentford Markets In reverse, inward loads of seed potatoes arrived from Scotland, latterly delivered over a wide area by Hammett of St. Issey. Sugar beet went to Kidderminster and Ely.

Over the top of the SR concrete fence along Eddystone Road, Wadebridge may be seen the West Cornwall Agricultural Co-operative Association's store, the 5-ton gantry crane and the Farm Industries (successors to Hoskin, Polkinhorne and Trevithick) store. To the left is the footbridge carrying a public path to the river. (C.J. Knowles-Thomas)

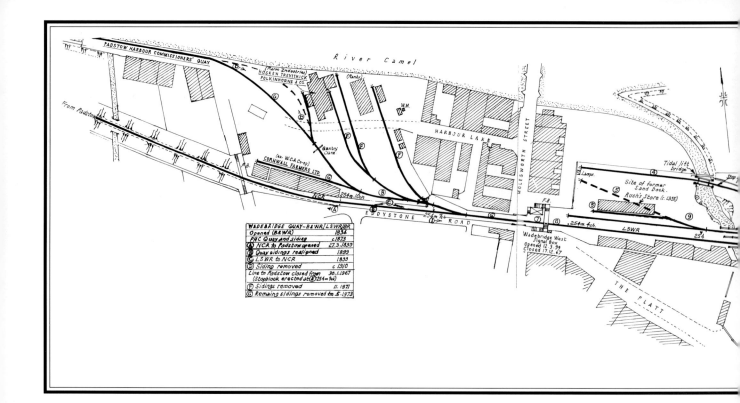

WADEBRIDGE QUAY—B&WR/LSWR/BR
Opened (B&WR)	1834
PHC Quay and siding	c.1873
Ⓐ NCR to Padstow opened	27.3.1899
Ⓑ Quay sidings realigned	1899
Ⓒ LSWR to NCR	1833
Ⓓ Siding removed	c.1910
Line to Padstow closed from 30.1.1967 (Stopblock erected at Ⓔ 254m.9ch.)	
Ⓕ Sidings removed	11.1971
Ⓖ Remaining sidings removed fm 5.1973	

Rustic slate from Trebarwith loaded in open containers, granite headstones and curbs from Wenford by road and transhipped by the goods shed 1 ton 17 cwt crane, were typical freight in latter years, seen alongside ice cream going to Newquay! Out in the yard china clay in sheeted wagons and bagged in box wagons for Staffordshire, together with granite slabs on open or flat wagons from De Lank and Hentergantick, also containerised RN stores, were marshalled from the Wenford branch for Up North Cornwall goods trains. Wagon loads of bulk rolls of paper from Sittingbourne were routed to the 'Cornish Guardian' at Bodmin. Wadebridge was the railhead for St Eval (RAF) and St Merryn (RNAS) airfields, large quantities of stores passing during the second World War and after, also for St Mawgan after Newquay's goods yard closed. The Royal Cornwall Show, held at Wadebridge in 1895, 1924, 1927 and 1957, found a permanent home at Wadebridge from 1960. Invariably farm implements and exhibitors' wares came by rail. When the Household Cavalry took part in the 1960s a whole train of green BR horse boxes transported its mounts from Knightsbridge via Kensington Olympia. Occasionally, unseen and secure, surplus coins and notes went by container to the Royal Mint from local banks, especially in the summer season. If one saw a petrol wagon or a banana van on the inward goods, they were bound for Bodmin (Esso), and for Rowes (fruit ripening in steam-heat just in time for sale).

The goods shed was enlarged in 1939, (filling the gap up to the station buildings) a result of the rising quan-

The 1834 Bodmin & Wadebridge Railway's Carriage shed and workshops lasted until 1962. The freehold here and as far as the end-on junction with the North Cornwall's Padstow extension (beyond the level crossing) remained with the LSWR until 1923, when all passed to the Southern Railway. Remaining traces of the railway here were swept away in the 1980s in favour of a supermarket and car park.

WADEBRIDGE

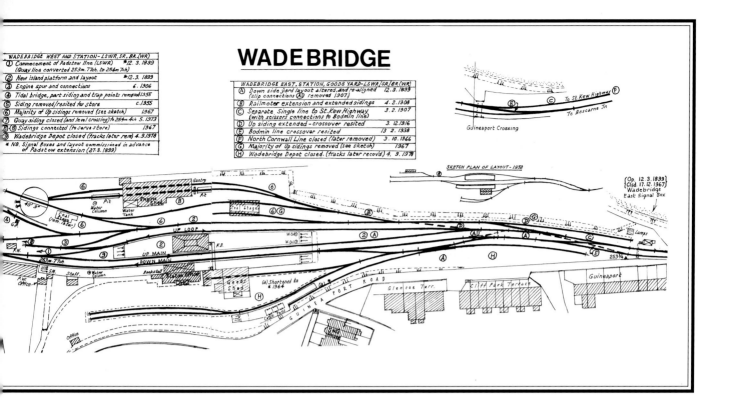

tity of sundry consignments from grocery wholesalers, and household appliances. The Nine Elms road box (from the overnight 'Tavvy' to Plymouth) came in at 12.30pm but the Exeter and Friary vans, behind the Waterloo Newsvan was earlier, at 9.15am. The return workings were on the 11.35am and 5.00pm goods. The tonnage through the shed increased from 3,767 in 1927 to 10,906 in 1944, while out in the yard (and at the Quay) about 10,000 wagons were forwarded and received - and 17,000 transferred from one goods service to another. One could not say that the Wadebridge layout was exactly cramped. There was enough room to handle the average 80 to 85 wagons a day these numbers suggest, for local traders or services from and to Padstow, Wenford, Bodmin, Bodmin Road, Exmouth Junction and the east. As we have seen the Wadebridge foreman would ask Delabole to keep wagons back. The increase in block fertilizer workings (mostly from Avonmouth) in the 1960s caused problems, with every foot of sidings in use at station and quay.

The movement of china clay from Wenford was interesting. In the 1920s the Beattie 2-4-0 survivors brought down wagons which then went direct to Padstow. After World War II Fowey and Par became the destination requiring reverses at Boscarne, Bodmin General and Bodmin Road. Through Halwill from the North Devon Clay Co was routed a daily tonnage of ball clay for Fowey. Wagons came in on the afternoon goods and the empties went back on the 5pm up service. The sundries business declined in the 1960s, the cattle traffic went to the roads, and the end of freight traffic on the North Cornwall from 7 September 1964 left Wadebridge with the remaining 'wagon load' business routed through Bodmin General and Boscarne Jn.

Having squeezed through lower Wadebridge on the converted B&WR's route and across Molesworth Street with its attendant shunting problems, the points for the Quay lay immediately beyond, leading to the physical junction between the LSWR and NCR. The crossing problems were never resolved of course, and an unwritten law forbidding obstruction exceeding two minutes was often broken, bringing renewed complaints. Some Quay shunts had to be conducted over the crossing. A Beattie tank would commence at 6.20am, and with the Padstow trains passing, plus trips into Wadebridge, hold ups were inevitable. Nothing has changed - today's motorists are frustrated here by traffic lights!

Very few trains passed Wadebridge without stopping - even fish specials from Padstow. One that did trundle through was the Armoured Train on patrol in 1940/41. Manned by Polish troops, its role was to defend the Camel estuary, also going up to Port Isaac Road on occasion. Those wartime years put a great strain on Wadebridge facilities. Peacetime holiday trains terminated at Padstow of

Molesworth Street and Hotel, Wadebridge, in the last century. Some of the earlier meetings of the NCR Directors were held in the hotel, named after the Molesworth family whose seat was at nearby Pencarrow. Sir Lewis Molesworth was a director for many years. (Commercial Postcard)

Beattie tank No. 0298 awaits departure from Padstow with an Okehampton train on 16th June 1926, but is unlikely to have gone forward with it from Wadebridge. (H.C. Casserley)

course, but here at Wadebridge evacuees and prisoners of war arrived in specials. The evacuations from London occurred in 1939, 1940 (when 580 mothers and children arrived) and in 1944 at the time of the V1 Doodlebug blitz. The prisoners of war, Italian and German, were housed in a camp where the present Sports Complex is sited. All this time the normal passenger service was well patronised. Tickets issued doubled from 42,571 in 1938 to 92,471 in 1944. Coal came entirely by rail, the tonnage rising from 7,000 to 13,000 by 1944, but china clay exports fell considerably while Continental Europe was occupied. Diversions from the GWR in 1941 (and 1963 - see later), meant that the long Penzance trains needed dividing to get them up to Delabole and from Launceston to Meldon Junction. The 'N' 2-6-0s took eight corridors. The equivalent load for diverted goods trains was 29 and two brake vans. Both operations required marshalling room in Wadebridge, and servicing of the GWR engines (43XX 2-6-0s and 51XX 2-6-2Ts) from and to Bodmin Road.

The Bodmin Road passenger trains numbered about three a day, using the running powers acquired by the GWR to Wadebridge in 1886. After nationalisation in 1948 some trains extended, from Bodmin Road to Padstow, at 7.50am, 10.05am, 6.15pm and 9.15pm, and from Padstow at 9.03am and 10.55am. Shorter WR workings continued to and from Wadebridge (some connecting for Padstow) for Bodmin General and Road, with about a two-hourly SR service Wadebridge/Bodmin North. Under the WR from 1964, a diesel railcar service operated from Bodmin Road to Padstow, and Boscarne Junction (new platforms) to Bodmin North by an AC railbus. A goods service was instituted from 1888, some of these GWR trains being 'mixed' from Bodmin General to Wadebridge. A certain amount of wagon transfer took place at Boscarne Junction sidings, mainly the clay traffic, but mostly at Wadebridge. Already noted was a cattle wagon from Otterham to Truro, and amongst other transfers, the travelling funfair owners made use of rail to take road trailers from one site to the next. Anderton & Rowlands, the St Austell proprietors, sent trailers from St Columb to Bude, via Wadebridge.

During 1971 considerable numbers of wagons still inhabited the Wadebridge yard, mostly fertilizer (290 from Severnside ICI and 162 from Cattewater out of a total of 633), basic slag from Scunthorpe and Corby and imported artificial fertilizer via Barry and Kings Lynn. Seed potatoes, in small tonnages from Aberdeen and Montrose, completed the list of inward loads. Only slate dust by road from Delabole was sent away, in former salt 'Presflo' wagons, the majority to Tonbridge and the remainder to Derby and Sunderland. BR declared that working these wagons was becoming unprofitable, through wagons being shunted and marshalled several time en route. Only recently the last vestige of 'full load' - Speedlink - has ceased, and all bulk traffic now comes into Cornwall in large lorries on expensively widened roads.

The main station layout remained unchanged while the Bodmin Road to Padstow diesel cars maintained a seven-a-day return service. On this service being withdrawn from 30 January 1967 and a stop block erected west of Molesworth Street, the existing signalling and boxes remained operational until 17 December. From that date the East and West boxes were closed. Wadebridge then existed at the end of a 'long siding' from Boscarne Junction, controlled by a wooden staff. At the closure of the signal boxes the majority of the up side was clipped out of use and subsequently removed. A small diversion was initiated at the river bridge where the old engine spur was joined to Levers siding to give adequate length for the bulk-feed wagon standage. The Quay sidings closed in April 1973 and Molesworth Street gates finally shut across the rails (254. 4ch). All remaining points were now converted to hand levers, though the

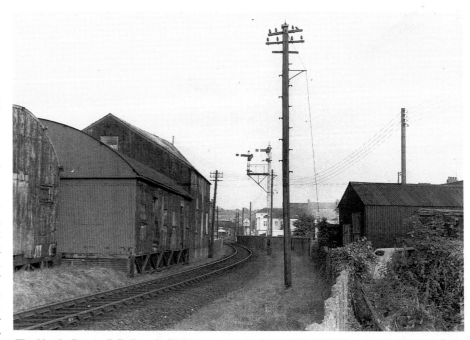

The North Cornwall Railway's Padstow extension joined the LSWR end-on just beyond the Wadebridge West Up home signals for loop and main. On the left are the traders' stores, served on their flanks by the Quay sidings. (C.J. Knowles-Thomas)

points at the Boscarne end were kept locked by a key attached to the staff.

The three ex-GWR pannier tanks (1366 Class) which replaced the Beattie tanks on the Wenford service in 1961 were themselves ousted by an '03' 204hp diesel shunter in 1965 (though not very successfully). '08' Standard diesel shunters had been tried but could not work the Quay curves. By 1976 the '08s' were proved capable of working all remaining services i.e. Bodmin Road/Boscarne Junction/Wenford/Wadebridge. Wadebridge was closed from 4 September 1978 although a brakevan rail tour went down there in the December. A headshunt was established at Boscarne towards Nanstallon to reverse the Wenford trains, but even these ceased to run in September 1983. The trackbed all the way from Wenford to Padstow, except in Wadebridge, has been converted to a foot and cycle way. Bodmin Road (now 'Parkway') to General has been revived by preservationists in recent years, but Wadebridge and Padstow are unlikely ever to see trains again.

Over the years the Wadebridge stationmaster, a Class 3 appointment, led a busy life. At one time he had 140 to pay weekly, not all under his personal control. Some 40 were drivers, fireman and shed staff, 35 in the Permanent Way department, and his own 65 clerks, porters, goods yard men and motor drivers. Up to 1915 there were GWR staff as well, a legacy of the 1888 to 1895 period. After 1927 Bodmin SR and the branch halts were added to his superintendency. The weekday services occupied his, or his foreman's attention, from 5am until 10pm. On Sundays however, Wadebridge virtually shut down, only the occasional

p.w. train working locally, or the single summer return excursions which ran from the late 1920s. Station Master in 1924 was Mr. Brown, followed over the years by Messrs Brazier, Clark and Clapp until Mr. J. Taylor in 1966.

Wadebridge Quay

The Bodmin and Wadebridge Railway started at the Quay. A fan of sidings was laid down curving sharply round from behind the Temperance Hotel, one fronting the river, one to a manure store, and one each side of a wet dock. Although isolated from its main system until 1895, the LSWR improved trade out of here, finding better rolling stock to do so. Wenford's china clay and granite traffic was transhipped to sailing coasters, the latter bringing in corn (for flour milling) coal and timber. De Lank granite was in great demand for public works in Britain in Victorian times. At the Wenford end it was brought down a cable-worked steep incline to be loaded into LSWR open two-plank wagons and a large sheerlegs tripod handled it at the Quay. Messrs Hocken, Trevithick and Polkinhorne built a commodious provender store and flour mill, followed by the Western Counties Agriculture Co-operative Society for grain and coal supplies (later taken over by Fulford Trumps). The Padstow Harbour Commissioners constructed their own quay extension with siding to the west in the 1870s. Access required an occupation crossing over the Padstow Extension from 1899, with a footbridge (1902) to preserve footpath rights to the foreshore. The river was dredged to allow berthing of deeper draught steamers; the S.S. 'Dunraven' traded in general merchandise into the 1900s, later the M.V. 'Florence'

brought flour from Ranks (Avonmouth). Rank's own premises were acquired by M. Thomas of Plymouth. Thomas became the largest of the west country slag distributors. Obtained from iron furnaces, it was much favoured by farmers as a grass fertilizer. F & J Martyn's interests in the yard were acquired by Cornwall Farmers Ltd (corn and seed), and later Farm Industries Ltd retailing farm machinery. Balers, combines, drills, ploughs, all came exclusively by rail, always noticeable in their bright colours.

The LSWR relaid and remodelled the Quay in 1916 (the inside siding and its turnouts had already been resited in 1899 to make room for the Padstow extension)and a 5 ton overhead gantry crane was substituted for the sheerlegs and the small wet dock filled in. Vessels could still use the Quay until about 1954 for occasional cargoes of coal, slag and grain (some grain was also exported) but the river silted badly thereafter. After the passenger closure in 1967 a stopblock was erected on the Padstow line short of the Commissioner's Crossing (254m 09c) and several sidings were removed in 1971. Access across Molesworth Street meant opening and shutting the gates by hand. The yard closed in April 1973, and very little remains of this once thriving and profitable corner of Wadebridge's railway activities.

Wadebridge to Padstow

The vistas for passengers along the Camel estuary were comparable with those of the Exe at Dawlish, or from Lelant and Hayle. The river gradually widened towards the Town Bar, opposite Padstow, where it was almost a mile across to Porthilly (Rock), though it narrowed again considerably beyond

Possibly the last vessel to come up to Wadebridge Quay, the ketch 'Agnes' swings on her mooring in 1955. (Author's Collection)

Approaching Padstow - the Denis Hill monument is seen above - on 14th August 1950 is '02' Class No. 30193 with a Maunsell 'P' Set from Bodmin (North). (L.T. George collection)

the Padstow to about half a mile. The mud flats seen at low water at Wadebridge give way to large expanses of sand banks beyond Whitehouse. The blue water, yellow dunes and green fields still can be enjoyed today from the same vantage points, on the walker's and cyclist's path.

After the long and straight embankment for the first mile out of Wadebridge, the NCR snaked along the foreshore on 40 chain reversing curves, over another short embankment where the stream came out of Polgammon Woods, and past the track

from Tregunna to the shore, carried on the sole overbridge (a brick-faced masonry arch at 255m 74ch). There was another short embankment before the line rounded to the left before reaching the site of the Camel Quarries through a large area of dumped waste material. Disused for some years previous to 1899, it nevertheless provided useful stone for pitching the embankments. The line then curved 30 chains to the right, damming the creek at Pinxton and cutting off the old quay within. To get round to the next creek at Old Town

(257m 57ch) a shelf had to be cut into the hillside, and then a sharper 25 chain cutting (to the left) to pass through the corner of Ball Hill. A further curve took the line around under Tregonce, in St Issey Parish, to the wide inlet at Little Petherick.

The 200 yard embankment was first bisected by a small arch before taking its 20 chain curve to the right and over the well known, 400ft long viaduct. Then it eased to a 30 chain radius in a very deep cutting through the side of Dennis Hill. The monument above commemorates Queen Victoria's Ju-

From the beach on the north side of Padstow may be seen the new fish shed and the old semi-enclosed tidal dock (left) while a row of round-ended fish wagons line the original quay (centre). The date is c.1907 and within a few years substantial sums would be spent by the LSWR in redeveloping this frontage to accommodate 60 to 70 trawlers. The proposed gates for a wet dock, however, never materialised. (R.I.C.)

A carriage siding was laid in at Padstow about 1905 and a North Cornwall period coaching set consisting of a 42 ft. bogie third, 42 ft. tri-composite and 30 ft. (6 wheel) brake van of 1880s vintage occupies it, together with a rake of open fish wagons. The contemporary salmon pink (upper) and brown (lower) panels of LSWR coaching stock may be deduced. Accommodation for cattle transfer was no more than for a country station; the wagon in the dock was equipped with a vacuum pipe or brake to run in passenger trains. (R.I.C.)

bilee of 1887. Just beyond was the last obstacle, Dennis Cove, the new embankment formed a lake but pre-railway a shipyard existed here, where was launched one of the largest vessels from Padstow (800 tons). Final curves of 15 chains bore the line right and left through another shallow cutting into the terminus.

Padstow (259m 43ch)
The sheltered inlet from the Camel had been a natural anchorage for ships from time immemorial, though the infamous Doom Bar further out into the estuary was what its name implied. Worthy of note is the Padstow Lifeboat, established in 1827, with its history of courage and tragedy. The recognisable port dates from the 1530s and it traded much with Ireland and Bristol in cloth, fish and tin, and coal from South Wales. In the 1850s it was even an emigrant departure port, mainly to Quebec. Not always called Padstow (Lodenek in the 16th century) it was briefly a borough in Elizabethan days, but since then had rested under the semi-feudal care of the Lords of the Manor, the Prideaux-Brunes whose seat is Prideaux Place above the town. We have seen how Charles Gordon Prideaux-Brune was to the forefront in bringing the railway to Padstow and Colonel C.R. Prideaux-Brune was one of the last directors of the NCR, in 1922.

In the 19th century shipbuilding dominated, but wooden sailing vessels were ousted by steam, and the last was launched from the Higher Yard in 1889. It was during this period that the Padstow Harbour Commissioners were established (1844). The population of the town in the 1890s was about 1,700, rising slightly until World War 1 but falling again in the 1920s. High hopes were placed on the new railway's contribution to Padstow as a holiday resort. The opening of the South Western, later Metropole Hotel in May 1901 as a draw for high class 'visitors' (as they are known in Cornwall) was successful, but fine summer days brought influxes of day trippers from as far as Exeter. There is no promenade at Padstow, but holiday makers were attracted to Trevone (within Padstow Parish, and only two miles distant) or to Harlyn Bay, Treyarnon Bay and Porthcothnan Bay by horse vehicles, and then motor bus. Prominent in the transport field was William Pope, who was bringing long-stay visitors from Wadebridge off the North Cornwall coach at first, and rail from 1895. He also ran buses from the new 1899 Padstow station, serving the coast towards Newquay. As Pope & Sons they were the LSWR's and SR's general cartage agents in the area, although by 1948 these were Bill Cornish and Nick Reynolds. Reynolds and James commenced Brown's Bus Services in the 1920s with motor buses, plying as far as Bedruthan. Hardy Colwill and the National Bus Co were also contending. All these routes were in the Southern National Omnibus Co's system from 1935, one or two buses being stabled at Padstow Station.

Like Wadebridge, Padstow acquired Urban District Council status by 1900 incorporating Trevone, the expanding 'village', bringing the total population to approaching 3,500 by 1939. Just over the river was Rock and Porthilly, part of St Minver, and reachable by a ferry service. With a tourist trade growing quite rapidly and the development of the fishing port, the Station Master's position at Padstow was no sinecure. First to be appointed was Mr. Buscombe, during the Great War came Mr. Watkins then, in the 1930s, Messrs Portass and White, followed by Mr Penwarden in the 1940s. Many Padstonians remember, some with awe, Miss May Cavill, a booking clerk in the 1930s and 1940s. The number of staff necessary to run Padstow was large and although loading of fish trains was by the traders' men, the railway goods checker had to be on hand. In comparison the amount of merchandise through the goods shed was much less than at Wadebridge, though coal, fertilizer, building materials and timber arrived in wagons for the local merchants, with outward cattle and Padstow's share of the rabbit trade. It has been noted that there were continuous shipments of china clay, brought by rail, up to 1936. With two signalmen, several passenger guards, porters, a carriage cleaner, the

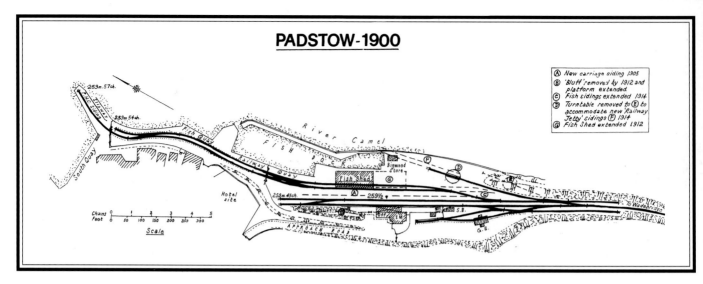

PADSTOW·1900

(A) New carriage siding 1905
(B) 'Bluff' removed by 1912 and platform extended
(C) Fish sidings extended 1914
(D) Turntable removed to (E) to accommodate new Railway Jetty sidings (F) 1914
(G) Fish Shed extended 1912

booking clerks and a goods clerk, by Nationalization in 1948 (which subsequently added road lorry drivers) it all looked pretty busy. The fish landings were, however, declining by this time, freight was passing to the roads in the 1960s and the rise of private motoring was taking toll of the extra summer holiday trains. After the withdrawal of freight trains on 7 September 1964, nearly all the sidings were taken up in early 1965. The signal box was closed from 9 January 1966 leaving only the run-round loop (for operating the Bodmin school train) to be controlled by a two-lever ground frame unlocked by an Annetts Key on the wooden train staff, in use from Wadebridge West. In spite of much protest, the diesel railcar service from Bodmin Road was withdrawn from 30 January 1967, only a few months after the Okehampton/Halwill closure.

The station layout stretched 400 yards from just inside the last cutting to the platform stop blocks at 259m 45ch, but the sidings ran towards the South Quay for another 200 yards to the end of the NCR's property. One was extended on to the PHC's pier itself. The goods yard was simplicity itself, just one siding skirting the goods shed (with a light crane within), another to the cattle and end-loading dock, with a short shunting neck to the east. The signal box controlled all movement this side. Part of this layout was even reduced in 1933, leaving one only siding by the goods shed to the dock.

The Up side and quayside sidings were much larger, totalling one and a half miles at its zenith in the 1920s. Alongside the platform was a run-round loop, but with long trains in the summer the engine would draw them right down to the stopblocks to enable at least eight coaches to be platformed. After unloading the train would be pushed back, the engine released through a levered sprung points crossover. The platform had been lengthened 120 feet at the stop blocks

end in 1912. A further carriage siding, joining the loop, was provided soon after opening. The original LSWR ground signals were replaced by SR discs and yellow arms, and the signal arms changed to upper quadrant, in the late 1930s. There were only three of the latter - the Down home, Up starting and Up advanced starting. The Down distant was fixed at caution and a long way out at Little Petherick, almost three quarters of a mile.

The development of the new quays and their sidings were described earlier. It would appear that Padstow initially would lack a turntable, for the LSWR was reluctant; there was after all already one at Wadebridge, and the subject was still under consideration in August 1899. The BoT insisted and a 50ft table was installed in 1900, on the first of three sites. No other facilities were provided for engines at this time. The siding on the South Quay pier was under control of the

PHC which complained in 1899 that rails were too near the edge. The LSWR was responsible, said the NCR, although only trucks went on the pier. A gate was installed here in tandem with one for the new road to the station. The narrow strip in front of the Custom House and the old Court House was formerly the quayside, the NCR fencing it off as far as St Edmunds Lane. An infill and a new quay face (West) was constructed here in 1899, paralleled by a siding making two (with a crossover between them), as far as the South Quay entrance. The shipyard itself had disappeared under Padstow's new station and fish sidings, but the narrow jetty enclosing the (fitting out?) basin was retained so giving some shelter to the vessels unloading to this new quay.

These two long sidings serving the fish shed, the West Quay and the one ending on the South Quay, survived until truncated at the far end in 1961.

The new South Western Hotel stands prominently above Padstow station at the top of the new approach road from the top of the town in this early 1900s vista. In the centre the 'bluff' of remaining rock would be removed in due course to provide infill for the new West Quay. Padstow station was constructed in local dressed stone and featured the pronounced eaves noticeable in the lower three NCR stations. The SM's children play in the garden while a group of sailors roll down the road. (Author's collection).

A very early view of Padstow showing the original jetty or breakwater, part of the old Higher shipyard. The 4-4-0 has a North Cornwall line train of two low arc-roofed bogies and guards brake, a high-roofed bogie coach and another guards brake. Passenger rated stock also occupies the fish sidings - a 42 ft. bogie guards brake and a 30 ft. example with a cupola lookout. The lack of accommodation at Padstow became acute at this time (a coach is stabled by the goods shed) and another siding was laid in next to the run-round loop about 1905. (R.I.C.)

There was a certain amount of ship-to-rail traffic pre-1914, and spasmodically until 1964, probably coal, but the crossover (to the east of the siding gate here) was removed by 1925. It, and a scissors crossover beyond the fish shed, enabled run-rounding of fish wagons. The northernmost siding closely bounded the 1899 West Quay, but new works from 1910 left a wider (on average) 60ft landing. Further development followed, including more fish traders' offices, one of them a quaint narrow two-storey wooden edifice and a wagon weighbridge. The fish auction shed was purpose-built by the NCR 160' x 50' incorporating a 20' cantilever awning over the loading bank and siding. It still stands, with its timber stanchions and roof trusses clad in corrugated iron. The original layout was comparatively simple, the fish sidings joining the new run-round loop which continued to a dead end near

the cutting. The turntable siding crossed it with double slips (No 12 points) leading to the single line. Movements towards the facing points in the single line were originally protected by treadle locks but the SR converted these to locking bars and inserted limited track circuiting.

The heavy works concerning the new or 'Railway' pier starting in 1911 required resiting the turntable 50 yards to the east to accommodate pointwork for the two sidings laid to the pier. The existing fish shed sidings were lengthened at the same time. The new layout was operative from August 1914. The fish shed was lengthened by 100ft to the same design and a crossover was incorporated in the new pier sidings at the seaward end. Although the second station siding for cleaning and re-watering carriages was provided before 1905, there appeared to be an embarrassing shortage of car-

riage sidings in earlier years, conflicting with the heavy fish traffic.

Much fish was carried in sheeted open wagons before 1914, but ventilated vans (with vacuum pipes or through brake) tended to be used in the 1920s. The fish was packed in ice in boxes or barrels, and the whole trade was a cold, wet and smelly business. Naturally with such a perishable commodity speedy handling was essential, and the LSWR and SR were adept in supplying wagons, not only to get it away on the specials, but to ensure an adequate supply of boxes in return. When the East Coast fleet converted to steam in the 1920s a large quantity of coal arrived by rail (some by coastal vessels) to be stored on the West Quay. In a typical season over 700 wagons of coal would be required. Despite the contraction of the fishing fleets in 1914-18, the Lowestoft (and Ramsgate) vessels used Padstow the year round and the fish trains continued. The seasonal herring trade started again in 1919, and in 1922 over 500 crew and ancillary workers were quartered in the port, supporting 52 trawlers at work. Pressure was intense to carry inland several thousand tons of fish in the eleven week season (January to March). Estimating how much, and when, exercised the skills of the Station Master and his staff. In the SR days the 3.15pm 'Perishables' could take some wagons but usually a special was laid on, a pathway being available at 4.40pm, into Okehampton at 7.26pm and Exeter 8.20, thence Nine Elms for Billingsgate Market. As with all extra traffic, railway staff enjoyed overtime payments - the Padstow fish traffic was thus very popular.

The North Cornwall Ice & Cold Storage Co Ltd's factory (1910) was owned by the Padstow Electric Supply Co,

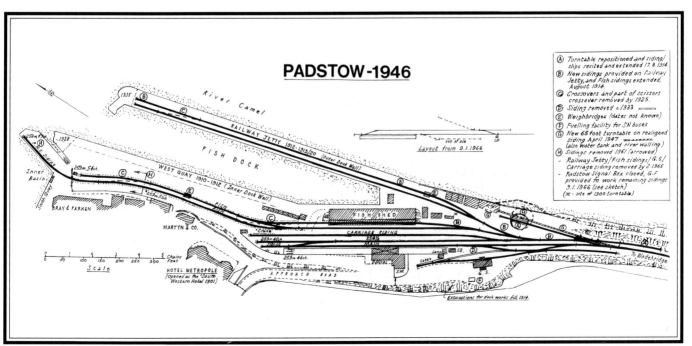

PADSTOW -1946

Ⓐ Turntable repositioned and siding/ slips resited and extended 17.8.1914.
Ⓑ New sidings provided on Railway Jetty, and Fish sidings extended, August 1914.
Ⓒ Crossovers and part of scissors crossover removed c.1925.
Ⓓ Siding removed c.1933
Ⓔ Weighbridges (dates not known)
Ⓕ Fuelling facility for SN buses
Ⓖ New 65 foot turntable on realigned siding April 1947 (also Water tank and river walling)
Ⓗ Sidings removed 1961 (arrowed)
- Railway Jetty/Fish sidings/G.S./ Carriage siding removed by 2.1965
- Padstow Signal Box closed, G.F provided to work remaining sidings 9.1.1966 (see sketch)
(x - site of 1900 turntable)

which also supplied current for lighting the quays and goods yard. It was extended in the 1920s. A further sub-business was kippers. A smoke shed (oak chips) employed Scottish girls and they lodged in the town during the season. The railway also carried a considerable quantity of boxes and barrels, something up to 300 wagonloads in the season, to the quayside. The essential fish porterage, packing and loading was the concern of the traders who rented premises on the quay. In the late 1920s about 20 were listed, chief among them Hobson & Co (Lowestoft), The Lowestoft Fish Selling Co Ltd, Pawlyn Bros. and Richard Thomas Ltd. The Great Grimsby Coal, Salt & Tanning Co Ltd dealt with ship's chandlery, while the Lowestoft Coaling Co Ltd's role was obvious. Around the corner on the South Quay timber and general merchants Bray & Parken received rail-borne traffic, unloaded on one of the long sidings, though they also imported coal by coastal vessel up to the 1940s.

Export of china clay from Padstow originated from the exploitation of large deposits on the west side of Bodmin Moor. As early as the 1880s a small amount was shipped from Wadebridge Quay brought down by B

& W wagons from Wenfordbridge. It was not until 1906 that the North Cornwall China Clay Co opened Stannon Pit, six miles from Penpont on the Wenford branch. Clay slurry was piped to driers situated there, and by 1912 50,000 tons of clay were being produced, though most of this was exported through Fowey by rail via Boscarne Junction and Bodmin Road. The 1914 improvement at Padstow enabled the LSWR to expand clay shipments. Twenty five flat wagons were built in 1914/15, each to carry eight hinged-side containers. A special 5 ton travelling crane was proposed to handle the containers on the Railway Pier, but it is unlikely to have materialised. However they were handled at Padstow, this interesting transport mode lasted only until 1923 when the wagons were converted to side-opens. China clay exports slumped heavily from 1914 and were slow to pick up again, reaching only 3,000 tons by 1933. Padstow's facilities could not compare with those of the GWR at Fowey. The last known shipment from the Pier appears to have been in 1936, though there may have been some in World War Two. Any resumption of shipments from Padstow were thwarted by political

The pedestal crane at Padstow in July 1948. Behind the two sidings to the South Quay are the fish traders' offices (A.E. West)

considerations in 1946, which saw to it that all clay went through Fowey and Par, and not a 'nonregistered' port like Padstow.

By 1950 the fish trade at Padstow was moribund and rail freight was declining. The line of 16-ton wagons on the jetty may be coal for Wadebridge engine shed, or household coal at summer prices, which was sustaining traffic at this end of the system. 'N' Class No. 31837 is attached to the coaches for the 12.55 p.m. to Okehampton and Waterloo. The single coach (right) was an LSWR 'Ironclad' relegated to departmental use. (T. Gough)

Chapter Four
ALL STATIONS FROM OKEHAMPTON

From July 1886 passenger trains from and to Okehampton were diverted to Launceston's new station and Holsworthy received only a 'branch' shuttle from Halwill (now 'Junction'). Main line trains from Devonport were running via the GWR 7.55) and from Okehampton (off the 5.50am Waterloo) arriving at 2.03pm.

The 8.24am Okehampton originally ran only on the last Wednesday in each month for Launceston Cattle Market, but reverted to a goods train until 1890. The 9.00am from Waterloo the Friday Market. Third Class ordinary fares from Waterloo were 36/7d and First Class 70/3d.

Of consequence for the future of the North Cornwall line was the horse coach leaving Padstow (Ship Hotel) at 8.25am and running via Camelford

On a sunny afternoon in July 1959 guard, shunter and signalman relax after dealing with meat containers, XP van and bogie van off the 3.13 p.m. Bude. 'T9' No. 30338 has just attached these vehicles to the 4.52 p.m. Plymouth to Waterloo, via Eastleigh, in Okehampton's Up platform and stands near the 1935 signalbox. (R.C.Riley)

through Yelverton to a junction at Lydford and only two of these, the 10.20am and 2.55pm, were reasonably fast to Waterloo. Downwards, the 11.00am and 2.30pm reached Okehampton in five hours, and brought Launceston to about seven hours from the capital. Five trains ran in each direction between Okehampton and Launceston, but Holsworthy did have one departing at 12 noon (Waterloo arr caught up a 6.25am slow train at Crediton and exchanged portions. The 9.00 went on to Devonport and the 6.25 to Torrington. This fulfilled the 'Parliamentary' requirement of an all stations service for Third Class passengers at 1d per mile. Cheap fares were sold for Launceston Pannier Market on Saturdays (5/0d from Exeter, 2/3d from Holsworthy and 1/0d from Ashwater). It was 5/0d to Exeter for (11.20am) connecting with the 1.50pm train from Launceston. Downwards a coach was waiting at Launceston station for passengers from the 9.00am Waterloo at 4.00pm, leaving for Padstow at 4.15pm. From 1875 the 'Vivid' coach had run from Launceston GWR to St Columb, but from 1881 the North Cornwall Coach Co's 'Pioneer' took over. As the North Cornwall Railway steadily extended westward the

Principal passenger services : 1886						
		am	am	pm	pm	pm
Launceston	Dep	7.50	10.30	1.50	2.50	6.45
Okehampton	Arr	8.54	11.32	2.45	3.56	7.51
Exeter	Arr	9.59	12.32	4.21	5.10	9.23
Waterloo	Arr	2.34	5.20	10.09	10.09	-
		am	am	am	am	am	pm
Waterloo	Dep	-	-	-	9.00	11.00	2.30
Exeter	Dep	7.15	8.50	-	1.48	3.20	6.50
Okehampton	Dep	8.24	10.02	11.50	2.54	4.25	8.30
Launceston	Arr	9.26	11.09	1.01	4.00	5.25	9.35

		Passenger Services : November 1895							SUNDAYS
		am	am	am	am	am	pm	pm	
Waterloo	Dep	-	-	5.50	9.00	11.00	1.00	3.00	
Exeter (Q.St)	Dep	-	9.05	10.48	1.45	3.10	5.15	6.38	
Okehampton	Dep	-	10.19	12.13	3.03	4.07	6.06	8.34	
Launceston	Dep	8.23	11.22	1.12	4.03	4.56	7.17	9.35(a)	
Wadebridge	Arr	9.41	12.37	2.32	5.22	5.59	8.36	-	
		am	am	am	pm	pm	pm		pm
Wadebridge	Dep	7.05	9.18	10.20	1.20	2.40	6.05		-
Launceston	Dep	8.25	10.43	11.45	2.25	4.02	7.20		6.45(b)
Okehampton	Dep	9.41	12.02	1.05	3.29	5.14	8.30		8.30
Exeter (Q.St)	Dep	10.25	12.45	2.10	4.15	6.00	9.28		9.28
Waterloo	Arr	2.33	5.00	7.52	8.14	10.15	-		-

a: Extended to Tresmeer (arr 9.54 pm) on Fridays.   b: Starts from Camelford 5.59pm

NCC Co's connections retreated until they ran only from Wadebridge to Haloon (St Columb Road GWR) and to Newquay, Atlantic Hotel. The LSWR opened a receiving office in Broad Street, Launceston in 1885. The GWR was running a horse bus from Bodmin Road to Padstow in the early 1880s.

Hidden in the timetables were useful changes at Halwill and Okehampton which, in time, stimulated local communication across Devon, particularly to the Markets. Special rates were available to 'regrators' or 'higglers' who collected dairy products e.g. butter from outlying farms for sale in the latter. In 1888 a local train actually ran through from Holsworthy at 1.15pm arriving at Launceston at 2.30pm.

A pattern of ordinary services established in the late 1880s lasted until closure in 1966, except for connections from the early morning Waterloo trains, which no longer applied post-1914, and a better spread of the afternoon trains from the capital at 1.00pm and 3.00pm with consequent changes in the west.

Tourist traffic grew steadily in the summer months and there were two through trains to Okehampton from Holsworthy, at 10.20am and 12 noon in 1890 through changes at Halwill downward. A Sunday service of one up train leaving Launceston at 6.45pm

(7.00pm Holsworthy) commenced. It also carried mail (as did its weekday equivalent). Down line early mail despatches were always carried in goods trains.

By the end of 1893 Delabole was the terminus. It was equipped with a turntable to permit the '395' 0-6-0s and the new 'Jubilee' 0-4-2s to run correctly back to Launceston and Okehampton. There were still five trains each way weekdays and, from 1893, one on Sunday evenings starting from Camelford at 5.40pm also carrying mail. Most Okehampton connections were reasonably smart, but passengers off the 3.00pm Waterloo were subjected to a 35 minute wait. At first

Leaving Ashbury on the afternoon of 4th August 1964 was Standard BR 2-6-4T No.80037 with the 3.10pm Padstow to Exeter Central, one of the few local trains to go beyond Okehampton. The vans carried urgent and perishable goods, the white insulated containing meat, but the origin of the 6-wheel milk tank is not clear, no creameries existing on the Bude and Padstow lines. (P.W.Gray)

their train went to Delabole (arrive 10.43pm) but was cut back to Tresmeer in 1894, and then only on Fridays, for the regrators, the coaches going back empty to Launceston. Holsworthy continued to have branch trains from Halwill Junction. Due to the unconsolidated track, trains were restricted to 25mph Launceston/Tresmeer, and 20mph Tresmeer/Delabole.

In the summer period of 1894 the 8.25am from Okehampton, which had reverted to a goods train until 1890, was run as a passenger (mixed if required) running to Delabole and, turning round between 10.26 and 11.45am, arriving back at 3.14pm. With variations this purely local service appeared to be dictated by the needs of Launceston Market. There had been a gratifying increase in passenger traffic since 1890, with Launceston's receipts especially good. Another evening train was put on from Okehampton at 6.00pm, to connect with the retimed 1.00pm from Waterloo. After arriving at Delabole 7.55pm, it too returned, this time running through to Exeter Queen Street to arrive at 11.20pm.

Even with these extra services, there appeared on the timetable the germ of the future holiday expresses in this 1894 summer. The 4.07pm from Okehampton off the 11.00am ('Alexandra') from Waterloo, missed out Ashbury, Ashwater, Tower Hill and Egloskerry, arriving at Delabole at 5.46pm compared with 6.25pm the previous winter. Hardly an 'express' at an average speed of 30mph, it of course had to slow down at the 'missed' stations to exchange single line staffs. A similar up train left Delabole at 1.45pm connecting to Waterloo (8.16pm).

Although Wadebridge had been enjoying a passenger service since 1888 from Bodmin and Bodmin Road on the GWR, (seven trains each way, including two mixed, were plying in 1894), its citizens had to wait until 1895 for a direct way to Exeter and London. As from 1 June the newly completed North Cornwall line had the basic five trains each way extended from the previous Delabole terminus. Another down train was put on, leaving Launceston at 8.23am. It also carried the mails off the early goods train from Okehampton. Many years later it actually fitted the end timings of the 1.30am Waterloo Newspaper train.

The Waterloo 11.00am's connection, the 4.07pm from Okehampton, now continued during the winter of 1895/6 to miss out some of the wayside stations, but passengers from east of Okehampton could be set down at Ashbury, Ashwater and Otterham. The 1.20pm from Wadebridge called only at Port Isaac Road, Delabole, Camelford, Launceston and Halwill Junction. It would take up London passengers at St Kew, and for Exeter and beyond at Otterham. Holsworthy continued to be served by branch trains from Halwill Junction, but the 6.06pm from Okehampton (off the 1.00pm Waterloo) had portions for both Wadebridge and Holsworthy. The mail was taken upwards on the 2.40pm from Wadebridge and the evening train from Launceston. The latter also ran on Sundays, but still from Camelford. The down mail on Sundays was on a goods train leaving Okehampton at 4.38am (Camelford 6.46am/Holsworthy 5.28am).

Noteworthy, in view of the eventual importance of the stuff, was a note in the Working Book stating that the 6.05pm from Wadebridge "will have a vacuum meat van attached for conveyance on the London goods". Wadebridge, in 1895, was quite inadequate to handle the new service, the GWR trains from Bodmin, and from that year the restored service from Bodmin LSWR. It would be two years before the single platform was supplemented by a new island platform.

To Padstow 1899
Unlike Bude, opened the year before, Padstow's facilities were simple. Engines were provided by Wadebridge and serviced there, with consequent light engine running and use made of 'mixed' trains comprising passenger vehicles, loose coupled wagons and a brake van. With trains extended off the North Cornwall line, and one or two locals from and to Bodmin, up to a dozen movements a day traversed the 5 3/4 mile extension. The mixed trains were restricted to 25 mph and spent 15 minutes on their journey compared with 10 for normal passenger trains. Since the 1889 Regulating Act there were fewer 'mixed' about, and those apparently mixed trains seen with additional vehicles on the North Cornwall proper (and elsewhere) might be through vacuum braked, with some of them, at least, 'piped'.

There were now seven down North Cornwall trains terminating at Padstow in the summer of 1899, the usual five 'stoppers' but one limited to calls only at Halwill Junction, Ashwater, Launceston, Camelford, St Kew Highway and Wadebridge. Again, the previous 4.07pm off Okehampton, connecting from the 11.00am Waterloo, with arrival at Padstow at 6.20pm, would stop specially at Ashbury for passengers off the 11.00am express, and at Tresmeer on Saturdays. In this season the last train no longer ran beyond Launceston (arrive 9.28pm). The balancing up limited-stop train - it could hardly be called an express - was the 1.04pm from Padstow. Port Isaac Road had a stop, but St Kew's for London passengers only. Camelford, Launceston, Ashwater and Halwill followed but only on Saturdays for Otterham and Tresmeer. With the change at Okehampton, total time elapsed was 7 hours 15 minutes. Compare this with the 10.25 am SO 'ACE' Padstow to Waterloo through train in 1938, which took 6 hours 17 minutes including a run nonstop from Launceston to Exeter St Davids.

For many years national newspapers, which then had limited circulations in the west country, were loaded onto the 6.10am Weymouth and Exeter train, delivered sometime during

The rebuilt LB&SCR 'E1/R' class worked the Torrington line from 1928 until 1953. No. 2096 has brought a cattle van and ex-steam rail motor 'gates' coach into the bay at Halwill in the 1930s. (Lens of Sutton)

101

Passing the east of Meldon Quarry on 9th May 1961 is the 9.56am Okehampton to Padstow behind 'T9' No.30313. The rear two Maunsell 2-coach 'P' Set and XP van will be detached at Halwill for Bude. On the left is the abutment for a bridge once taking narrow gauge spoil trucks from the quarry to a tip. (S.C.Nash)

the afternoon. The widely read 'Western Morning News', printed in Plymouth, travelled by goods train at first. Later the LSWR ran a special to Exeter in the night hours, transfering bundles at Okehampton (later at Yeoford or Bow) to the first down goods to Launceston.

The first through coach was arranged by Sir Sam Fay (LSWR General Manager) to run in the 1.00pm Waterloo in the winter of 1901/2. Probably one of the 1898 tri composites with lavatory accommodation, it returned on the 8.54am from Padstow (Waterloo 5.20pm). Then it was taken off, but with pressure from the North Cornwall Board was restored in September 1904, this time in the 11.00am from Waterloo, as an 'experiment' until Christmas. But the success of the tourist traffic induced the LSWR to

provide not just through coaches, but from 1900 a complete through train, Waterloo to Bude and Padstow, and from 1907 with a restaurant car. These were the forerunners of the 'Atlantic Coast Express' and are dealt with under that heading.

Meanwhile the stopping trains plodded across Devon and Cornwall taking two hours for the 62 1/4 miles from Okehampton to Padstow. Nearly all the trains were, by 1905, dividing and attaching a Bude portion at Halwill Junction, although this operation could take up to twelve minutes in the up direction, uncoupling for Bude and attaching the local tank did not take as long. Okehampton was always under criticism - the platforms were 'too low' and up connections took too long. Provision of an up bay was refused by the LSWR. Right up until 1964, pas-

sengers had to hang about while their empty North Cornwall was shunted out the way of the Up Plymouth arrival. Although there was a Down bay, there never was but the barest shelter on that side.

The fashionable railmotor made its appearance at Wadebridge in 1906. Two were allocated to the Bodmin branch, though in 1909 three services were extended to Padstow during the day. Apart from delivery and overhaul journeys there was no question of them running on the steep gradients of the North Cornwall.

An 11.10am from Waterloo (1914) trailed the 'North Cornwall & Bude Express', its connection arriving at Padstow an hour later. In summer, however, the 1.00pm Waterloo included a through coach each for Padstow and Bude, as did the 8.20am

Passenger Services : Summer 1899 - Weekdays									
		am	am	am	am	am	am	pm	pm
Waterloo	Dep	-	-	-	5.50	9.15	11.00	1.00	3.00
Okehampton	Dep	-	8.15	10.19	12.13	2.43	4.07	6.10	8.37
Launceston	Dep	7.48	9.21	11.17	1.08	3.38	4.56	7.19	9.28
Pardstow	Arr	9.31	10.55	12.44	2.45	5.07	6.20	8.43	-

NB. The Sunday up mail train continued to start from Camelford

		am	am	am	pm	pm	pm
Padstow	Dep	6.50	8.54	10.20	1.04	2.1	5.40
Launceston	Dep	8.25	10.42	11.53	2.25	4.02	7.20
Okehampton	Arr	9.21	11.38	12.47	3.13	4.57	8.14
Waterloo	Arr	2.33	4.40	7.52	8.16	10.15	-

In August 1963 the 8.30am Padstow comprising No.34083 '609 Squadron', van and 'P' Set enters Halwill. A local set from Bude waits to be attached at the rear. The engine of the 9.00am from Torrington has propelled its coach away from the platform (right) to the distant run-round loop. (P.Paye)

		am	am	pm	pm	pm
Okehampton	dep	-	10.04	1.08	3.47	7.45
Launceston	arr	7.45(d)	11.02	2.05	4.51	8.38
Padstow	arr	9.01	12.22	-	6.06	9.55
Padstow	dep	8.35	12.38	2.20	3.00	5.22
Launceston	dep	10.06	2.06	3.52	4.30	6.55
Okehampton	arr	11.08	3.04	5.11	5.26	7.56

from Padstow (Bude 9.26am). Reasonable connections were available at Halwill Junction, morning and evening, between Bude/Padstow trains right up to 1914. Several locals ran to and from Bude specially for this in July and August, and an 8.00pm from Padstow train connected at Okehampton for the Plymouth line. Thus in the summer of 1914 seven trains crossed North Cornwall each way, though the last down train terminated at Launceston. The Sunday service continued to be out of balance, there being only the evening mail train from Camelford in 1909 (but from Launceston in 1914) to Okehampton, thence to Exeter Queen Street.

Local Services in World War One

Trains continued to run in 1915 as they had in 1914, apart from cancellations due to troop movements. In 1916 and 1917 withdrawal of engines for Gov-

ernment service and provision for extra cattle trains, put paid to the summer extras and some locals on the

Bude branch. Still, a basic five trains each way plied between Okehampton and Padstow, the last serving only to Launceston. The railmotors at Wadebridge were withdrawn leaving only three extra passenger trains, and two mixed, each way to Padstow in April 1917. The limited Sunday service ceased from January 1917. Further reductions in May 1918 included the 1.12pm from Okehampton (from the 5.50am Waterloo) and some much later arrivals ensued at Waterloo for Up trains from the west. The 2.15pm Padstow passengers in June 1919, for example, although into Okehampton at 4.47pm, had to wait until the Plymouth train came in at 5.21, eventually getting to Waterloo at 11.24pm - a

On a warm afternoon in 1956 a Launceston family return home from Tower Hill. The driver of the 'U' Class 2-6-0 is about to exchange single line Tablets with the signalman. (B.Tunbridge)

103

The second Down morning train from Okehampton (9.56am) calling at Delabole in 1961. A parcel/mail van leads a pair of Bulleid and Maunsell corridor coaches. The driver and fireman of 'T9' No.30719 have just exchanged with another crew and the engine shows signs of hard work on its lower smoke box door. In later years the station house received a cladding of slates. (R.C.Riley)

nine hour journey! Of local interest, the 7.38am from Launceston stopped at a one coach platform at Meldon Quarry to 'take up wives of company servants going to Okehampton'. The 3.00pm from Waterloo made connection at Yeoford Junction, rather than Okehampton, in 1918 and 1919, and its Bude connection from Halwill ceased to run. It was the summer of 1921 before restorations could be made, but the rather lavish service the LSWR had provided for its rural passengers and purely local tourism to 1914, never really returned again.

Between the Wars 1919-1939
Thinner fare greeted locals in North Cornwall for the summer of 1919 - only a minimal service. From Padstow at 8.10am, 12.30pm, 2.15 and 5.30pm, from Okehampton at 10.10am, 4.08pm and 6.38pm. The 8.08am from Launceston was mixed from Wadebridge to Padstow and took nearly two hours for the 36 mile journey. Launceston retained its early morning (Up) and late evening Down) trains to Okehampton. They were in the hands of superannuated locos, Beattie 4-4-0s and Adams '460' Class bearing the main burden.

By the summer of 1924 the through holiday trains were back, the new Southern Railway steadily restoring them as engine power and rolling stock permitted. Locally, the midday (Exeter) Okehampton to Launceston/Bude train was running again. This train became important by the end of the decade as it also included vans for return loading. From 1927 the trains ran separately, the 2.45pm from

Padstow was also a 'Perishable', as it was termed, and now ran through to Exeter Queen St, where some vans were transferred to the 7.30pm fast goods train to Nine Elms, others going via Templecombe to the Midlands. As the herring business picked up again at Padstow, the 2.45pm could become heavily loaded at times. The summer of 1924 saw a through Brake Composite (1st/3rd Class) in the 3.00pm from Waterloo going through to Padstow, the Okehampton local train being extended beyond Launceston for this purpose. It is likely to have returned on the 8.20am from Padstow, the next morning. These extra summer period through coaches which graced local services were typical of LSWR and SR concern for passengers, and inconceivable in today's set train formations.

Since the demise of the Railmotors in 1917, locals from Wadebridge to Padstow were in the hands of the surviving Adams 4-4-2Ts, some running to and from Bodmin, as before. There were four of these, supplementing the North Cornwall trains - one mixed, thus likely to take cattle to and from Wadebridge Market. Most cattle wagons were vacuum braked, and in those days not only mixed trains would convey them. Passengers would have to wait at a rural stop, like Tresmeer, while the engine trundled off to the cattle dock to fetch and attach a truck deemed to be urgent.

While the 3.00pm from Waterloo gave a connection right through to Padstow in 1927, the 1.00pm connection from Okehampton served only Bude. No through coaches were in-

cluded in either, as before, but the 8.35am from Padstow (9.42am Bude) and the 11.00am from Waterloo (both named the 'Atlantic Coast Express' the previous year) were now including them summer and winter. When the through train ran in the summertime the name was transferred to it. In 1928 the North Cornwall saw its first Sunday train since 1917, but it was an excursion from Padstow to Exeter-'well filled' with passengers, said the local newspaper. Even if a Sunday train service had been instituted in the 1920s it would have been unsustainable. No shops were open, nor places of entertainment and, in the eyes of the predominantly Methodist population, travelling on the Sabbath was not to be encouraged in any event. However, times were changing as the above report shows. World War Two gave Launceston a regular timetable service, even extended to Delabole for one summer (1953), but it would have been still unremunerative to run trains in the thinly populated areas between Launceston and Wadebridge.

While the five basic services underlaid the North Cornwall's passenger service all through the 1930s, they were modified in the summer months in timings, loads, and even destinations, by the presence of the through trains from and to Waterloo. This was especially so on Saturdays when this long and slender route could be near capacity and, though crossing loops were reasonably well placed, any out of course running spelt trouble. Southern signalmen knew their trade, however, and the phones would be hot as they regulated late runners past

104

the local goods and 'Perishables' patiently waiting at the starting signals. The Padstow station master not only had his Waterloo and locals, but fish trains as well to contend with from September. The Wadebridge shed foreman had to provide the 4-4-0s, some in pairs, and take care of Exmouth Junction engines and his own at the end of the day, while the Halwill staff put the through trains together, or divided them for Bude and Padstow. The 10.00am from Okehampton was one of the trains with limited loading to keep it on time through North Cornwall, as the holiday trains passed it at Halwill, Launceston, Delabole and St Kew. The 2.20 up from Padstow was crossing the down trains at St. Kew, Port Isaac Road, Otterham, Launceston and Halwill. On Saturdays the last down train was extended to Delabole, Waterloo passengers changing at Halwill from a through coach to Bude. The stopping trains which normally took the 'Atlantic Coast Express' through coaches to Padstow, only served up to Okehampton on Saturdays. With a mixture of holiday trains and local trains, some with through coaches attached, local passengers had to be aware of missed stops, like Egloskerry or Tower Hill. Luckily for them the station staff were adept at calling out such things, loudly and in dialect perhaps, but at least the natives could understand, even if the poor Londoners might not!

Local Passenger Services in World War Two

As August 1939 wore on the unsettling threat of war crept over the country. The winter timetable due to commence on 25 September would have lasted until 30 May 1940. During August a through excursion from Padstow (dep. 9.45am) to Bude (12 noon), returning to Padstow quite late at 10.56pm, ran each Sunday. The Bude line was now getting three services each way on Sundays in summer (until 10 September that year). The situation became unreal as people cancelled holidays. Reservists were being recalled to their Depots and Government plans to evacuate Britain's big cities were being activated. Not waiting for a reply to the ultimatum to Hitler over the invasion of Poland, the evacuation of school children started from London on 31 August and was completed by the day War started on 3 September. Many main line services and summer extras were cancelled, the stock diverted to evacuation specials. Waterloo, regarded as inviting congestion as air attacks were expected, was avoided. The children (and teachers) were brought by bus and Underground to Vauxhall and Wimbledon. Destinations in North Cornwall were Bude, Launceston, Camelford and Wadebridge and Southern National and local operators' coaches distributed the evacuees to the country areas. The expected bombing did not

materialise then, as it turned out, but it did in 1940 and 1941, and again in 1944.

The SR continued the summer timetable until 10 September, but with many cancellations. A drastically curtailed and decelerated service was then instituted but, under pressure, the company restored many trains on Monday 18th. Another timetable was issued from 16 October, entitled 'Emergency Passenger Services', given more publicity but revised again on the 28th! The 1.00pm Waterloo ceased but its connection (the 5.50pm to Padstow/Bude) continued to run. The 10.35am departure provided through coaches to Bude arriving at 5.09pm, Launceston 4.44pm and Padstow at 6.19pm, being a revised, but now nameless 'Atlantic Coast Express'. The Up coaches now left at 11.28am (Bude) and 10.05am (Padstow), combining at Exeter Central with the 12.25pm Torrington, leaving at 2.30pm. The 1.05pm Padstow arriving at Exeter at 5.03pm, gave passengers a long wait there, not getting them to Waterloo until 10.30pm! The 3.00pm Waterloo, retimed to 2.35pm, connected to Launceston (9.09pm) and Bude (9.26pm) and the early morning trains from these towns departing at 8.22am and 8.02am respectively were retained, with a connection to Waterloo (arr. 2.35pm). A 60mph limit on the main line, and additional stops, dictated the longer service times. On 1 January 1940 the Waterloo departures were eased to 10.50am and 2.50pm, and Up West of England arrival times to 2.35pm, 6.35pm and 10.08pm, but journeys remained between 8½ and 9 hours to and from far Padstow. By 1944 the through coaches ran weekdays from Padstow (8.30am) and Bude (9.35am) and arrived back at 5.09pm and 6.19pm. On the local scene the two afternoon up 'Perishable' trains

from Padstow to Templecombe and Bude to Okehampton still ran, being regarded as essential food suppliers to the big towns.

The 1.25am London Newspaper train, another essential (together with the overnight 'Tavvy' fast goods) remained intact throughout the War. For years the Newspaper vans had been transferred to the 6.0am goods at Okehampton, reaching Bude about 8.50am (though 7.15 in 1938) and Padstow at around 9.0am. Although through coaches were running to Plymouth in the 1930s, there had been inexplicable gaps (sometimes unadvertised). An early morning train from Launceston had taken on the Padstow Newsvan at about 8.30am (7.44 in 1938) but it seems a local two-coach set was running unadvertised in the early War period from Halwill, and probably Okehampton, from 1940. Bowing to pressure from servicemen on leave, mothers visiting evacuee children, etc. an advertised connection was made from Okehampton from 5 October 1942. The (now) 6.42am goods became 'mixed' and the 8.34am from Launceston took the 2-set on to Padstow arriving at 9.52pm. In 1944 this train was also 'mixed' between Launceston and Wadebridge. A connection to Bude arrived at 7.55am but no longer with a bogie Newsvan, the papers being transferred at Halwill.

Most of these services were hauled by 4-4-0s, mainly 'T9's of which 20 were now allocated to Exmouth Junction and the western depots. The M7 and 02 0-4-4-Ts remained on the Bude and Bodmin locals. The four-each-way North Cornwall trains at this period compared favourably with the 1938 timetable and, as elsewhere in Britain, became well used in the War years, with nine trains (two mixed) services Wadebridge/Bodmin SR, and Padstow. GWR locals from Bodmin

Wadebridge and Bodmin trains strengthened the service to Padstow and were, for years, in the hands of Adams 'O2' Class 0-4-2Ts. On 3rd September 1954 No. 30203 leaves Wadebridge for Bodmin (North) with a two coach Maunsell 'P' Set, several wagons and a goods brake van. The B&WR original alignment was on the extreme left, the reverse curves dating from 1888 and Wadebridge East signal box from 1899. (R.C.Riley)

Padstow on 15th July 1960 with T9 4-4-0s No.30717 departing with the 12.55pm to Okehampton (the two rear coaches for Waterloo), and 30719 waiting to work the 3.13pm 'Perishables' to Exeter Central. (R.C.Riley)

continued to ply from Bodmin Road into Wadebridge behind their 2-6-2 tanks. This was a most useful link in wartime Cornwall, which would come into its own during the Plymouth 'Blitz', as we shall see.

The 'Phoney' War, as it was known, lasted about nine months, many evacuees returning to London, but with the invasion of the Low Countries, then France, in May 1940 the situation changed dramatically. The SR found itself at full stretch in May and June with the Dunkirk evacuation. Troop trains had already arrived in the west in 1939, and many more were to follow.

In spite of restrictions, cancellations and exhortations *Is Your Journey Really Necessary?* rail travel burgeoned. There was little alternative to it - and the local buses. Surprisingly, the 10.50am Waterloo actually included a Dining Car set through to Padstow, daily, from February 1941 to January 1942. If traffic was heavy the set was included in a 10.59am relief, also having four coaches to Plymouth and Brake Composites for Sidmouth, Exmouth and Bude. The return journey was in the 8.30am from Padstow, the erstwhile 'ACE' pathway now restored but slower. By October 1944 the 10.50am Waterloo and 8.25am Padstow were shown to have a 3-coach corridor set indicating a continuing demand west of Exeter. The 8-hour journeys resulted from the 60mph limit, additional stops and difficult manoeuvres with long trains at Waterloo. During the bombing in 1940 and 1941 Waterloo, and Clapham Junction carriage sidings, were repeatedly hit and Wimbledon was resorted to as a

terminus on many occasions. In the winter of 1944/5 the last train into Launceston (9.35pm Okehampton) was extended on Fridays to Otterham for Servicemen stationed at Davidstow airfield. Interestingly, from the mid-1930s, the Meldon Quarry staff and their wives were accommodated by the 1.20pm Okehampton to Bude/Launceston which stopped at the Quarry Halt. This train was piloted by an M7 tank (off the front of the 11.37 Exeter Central) on Saturdays.

From Halwill, the 'M7' took the rear portion to Launceston, returning light engine, taking up duty as the 'new' engine for the Bude branch. The 'old' Bude M7 went light from Halwill to Okehampton and thence to Exeter as leading engine on the 2.35pm to Plymouth.

The London 'Blitz' in 1940 and 1941 brought further evacuation specials. In June 1940 580 people arrived at Wadebridge, 276 at Camelford and at Launceston 550, and many others came away to escape, or were actually bombed-out. Again, the V1 'Doodlebug' menace in 1944 resulted in more evacuations, including specials from the Kent coast. The Southern Railway handled all this and the various troop trains, ammunition trains and, after the Invasion of Normandy in 1944, an influx of Prisoner-of-War trains. The latter terminated at Holsworthy, Launceston and Wadebridge. The North Cornwall line escaped direct bombing and no incidents are known though late, very late, running often occurred as a result of actions in London and Exeter (1941). Plymouth Friary station suffered quite severe bomb damage too.

The Slow Decline to Closure

Rail travel remained paramount in the years succeeding World War Two, petrol rationing persisting until the 1950s though bus services increased quite considerably. The latter were not a serious threat to the North Cornwall as few roads paralleled it. The Bude/Holsworthy to Launceston - Plymouth routes creamed off some traffic but as we have seen, the Southern National's Bude to Wadebridge route actually coordinated with rail at Camelford. More serious were Blake's services from Delabole to Plymouth, though the firm was bought out by the Southern National in 1952. The Southern Railway's holding in the National Co was 'nationalized' from 1 January 1948. The other portion, owned by Thomas Tilling Ltd, was bought by the British Transport Commission soon after. Little change ensued in the following 18 years until the railway closed, but the Southern National (now Western National) abandoned its depots at Bude and Delabole in 1971. The successor to the North Cornwall Coach Company horse route from Wadebridge via St Columb Major to Newquay existed into the 1950s. The SN was then running a near-hourly service from Padstow station forecourt for Treyarnon, Constantine, Harlyn and Trevone (sometimes extended to Newquay) which annexed the territory claimed by the North Cornwall directors as theirs 60 years before. On the trainless Sundays the Southern National ran three buses each way from Padstow to Wadebridge, Bodmin and Bodmin Road.

To work trains along the North Cornwall required quite a complicated roster of locomotives 'duties', engines and men supplied by Exmouth Junction, Okehampton, Launceston and Wadebridge sheds. Typical of these was Exmouth Junction duty No 593 of 1960, though the 'N' Class 2-6-0 employed was outstationed at Okehampton for mixed traffic, as the following shows. It left Okehampton shed at 6.00am and attached to the overnight Waterloo to Padstow coaches and newspaper van, 'road boxes' and a number of goods wagons and brake van. Exmouth Junction men who had travelled as passengers on the train from Exeter thus relieved the Okehampton pair at 6.05. The train left at 6.20 for Launceston where the Exmouth Junction men were relieved by Launceston's early shift at 7.55am. The latter then drove the 'N' through to Padstow, the Waterloo train being shunted into the middle sidings, and the engine turned. Wagons were assembled for a 10.10am goods to Wadebridge where more shunting took place before this engine was taken to shed at 11.30 for ash cleaning and servicing. Coming off at 12.49 the Launceston men exchanged their 'Woolworth' for the 'T9' now detaching from the 12.58pm Padstow to Okehampton. However, at Launceston the early shift men were relieved by the local second shift at 2.15 (who had booked on at 2). The train was terminated at Okehampton Up platform, but the through coach to Waterloo in the 1950s was dealt with by the station pilot, for attachment to the up Plymouth train. The 'N' went on shed from 3.18 to 4.00pm for turning etc, emerging at 4.05 to attach to the 4.24 local passenger to Bude in the bay. At Bude between 5.28 and 6.00 any necessary shunting was done and the engine turned again (6.05 to 6.50pm) before going into the bay to attach to the 7.05pm passenger (and mail) to Halwill. At the latter the Launceston men now handed the 'N' over to an Okehampton crew at 8.30pm. Then it was time for it to make the final haul by piloting the 5.00pm goods from Wadebridge on to Okehampton where the engine went on shed at 9.06 for the night.

It can be seen that although only one engine was involved over a 15-hour period, it needed servicing and turning several times, with eight men involved. In the background were the traffic staff, the guards, signalmen, stationmen, permanent way and signal and telegraph men, let alone night shedmen in the locomotive depots. At this date at the turn of the 1960s, probably of the above trains hauled by the 'N', only the overnight Waterloo to Padstow train earned its keep by virtue of the high-value newspapers and merchandise it carried and the fares passengers might pay for a journey of up to 260 miles.

British Railways was already making an operational loss by this time and such a long straggling rural line

like North Cornwall, still equipped with signal boxes at each of its ten stations, would not now be profitable. Nevertheless a reasonable passenger service was still offered in the early sixties, the 1960/61 winter timetable showing that Launceston and Camelford enjoyed a public transport offering not available today.

While the 1.10am Waterloo passed down into Cornwall behind the 'N' 2-6-0 as we have already seen, at Launceston the first Up train started away at 8.20am behind another 'N' going through to Okehampton. At Halwill a local 'P' set of two coaches was added from Bude, both portions affording a good connection to the first Up Plymouth to Waterloo fast train. Meanwhile at Padstow the 8.30am 'Atlantic Coast Express' three-coach set left behind a 'West Country' 4-6-2, an all stations train to Okehampton in the winter months. At Halwill a Brake Composite coach was placed on the rear by the Bude engine (a 2-6-2T) as its contribution to the eventual 7-part train which arrived at Waterloo mid-afternoon. Following all the activity at Halwill, the 9.56am from Okehampton trundled in behind a 'T9' 4-4-0 with a bogie van and two 'P' sets, the rear one for Bude. It called at all stations in the tradition of North Cornwall 'stoppers', taking 2 hours and a quarter - an average of 27mph. Even in the short reign of the diesel cars, the average was not above 33mph and they had little to obstruct their passage in 1966. On the rising gradients from Wadebridge to St Kew the latter only managed 30mph, though this rose to 42-45mph down the opening valley from Tower Hill to Launceston. The slow progress of these stopping trains, the circuitous route and lack of population near stations, had become an anachronism by 1965 in view of the rise in private motoring. In the climate of the 1980s, with a more sympathetic public view of rail travel, a speedier 'Sprinter' might make a more attractive proposition, but a large subsidy would have to be forthcoming.

There were no trains from Padstow to Okehampton after the 8.30am 'ACE' departure until the 12.58pm. A 'T9' off the 9.56am Okehampton took the latter to Wadebridge (changing for an 'N' on Duty 593), consisting of a through brake composite for Waterloo, and a 'P' set. The mid-day mails from Launceston (and from Bude at 1.55pm) were loaded into the guards/luggage ends en route for Exeter. The Bude coaches were attached, as usual, at Halwill and the train was into Okehampton at 3.13pm. The Brake Composite was attached to the rear of the afternoon Plymouth train (Waterloo 8.00pm).

Every weekday afternoon the two Up passenger and 'Perishables' left Bude and Padstow soon after 3.00pm. In their heyday both were 'T9'-hauled and references have been made already to them already. Operating in-

dependently, the Bude train terminated at Okehampton where its van was attached to the following 3.13pm Padstow, bound for Exeter Central. Containers of meat from both lines (Holsworthy/Launceston/Halwill) were transferred to the 4.15pm Bideford Goods to Nine Elms, leaving Exeter Central at 7.30pm. The express road van from Padstow was forwarded by this train or the following 5.25pm semi-fitted goods from Torrington to Nine Elms, (10.40pm from Exmouth Junction). The number of meat containers had grown considerably by this time and, after the demise of the 'T9s' in 1961, this duty (Okehampton No.599) was taken over by the 'N' class engines, well able to take the six or more wagons on the tail, and this train also conveyed the empty Newsvan to Exeter, en route to Clapham Junction. Both engines on these 'Perishables' carried the Okehampton/Padstow headcodes. It seems that any 'T9' or 'N' working out of Okehampton kept them up all day regardless of branch, which was a little confusing for photographers at Halwill, but not to the local signalmen. Passengers took (and take) little notice of headcodes anyway!

The 6.00pm from Padstow similarly was a heavy loader for its Wadebridge 'T9', taking the evening North Cornwall mails in a bogie van, and another from Bude at Halwill. Three or more vacuum-braked box wagons - the returning road boxes for Exeter and Bristol (and Plymouth) - completed the train (a single 'P' set) from the Junction to Okehampton, where the vans and wagons were transferred to the 7.20pm Plymouth - Exeter Central passenger. This last Up Padstow train passed the last Down train, the 5.51pm from Okehampton, with another 'T9', at Tresmeer, a cameo which hardly changed in 60 years. Imagine a drizzly wet winter's evening. Dim oil lamps light the platforms, local people back from Launceston market preparing to walk a mile or so to Tresmeer village or towards Warbstow, some lucky to be fetched in a pony and trap, or (later) a motor car. Parcels to be dropped off, Cornish voices in the dark, the single line Tablets handed to the drivers. Then with a toot of the whistle one 'T9' sets off with a resounding bark up and around to Otterham, while the other drifts off down the hill to Egloskerry. Signal restored with a clank of levers, final bell codes as the lines clear and Tresmeer shuts down for the night.

Not the last train down to Launceston though. A connection was made off the 3.00pm Waterloo to Plymouth leaving Okehampton at 7.45pm. An 'N' Class this time with a 2 set for Launceston and one for Bude. It left Halwill at 8.20 and terminated at Launceston at 8.42pm. At Halwill itself the passenger services may have started at 7.00am but the early signalman was on duty at 5 for the goods and mails. After eight o'clock in the evening the 5.00pm Wadebridge up goods was still shunting about the yard in the last hour, before leaving for Yeoford about 8.30pm.

The Sunday service for 1960s summer was much the same as from 1940 onward, except that in these postwar years a through Brake Composite ran to Bude from the 11.00am Waterloo (and back at 9.45am) with connections for Launceston passengers (5.17pm arrive, 9.50am depart). In 1953 attempts were made to serve the Camelford/Tintagel areas by extending the service to Delabole. Launceston should have had a BR Standard 3 2-6-2T for this work, but in the event a WR Churchward 2-6-2T (No. 4583) was borrowed. Standard No.82013 was known to have been on this duty on 9th August and 6th September. On 26th July, off shed at 9.30am, 4583 did a morning stint from Launceston to Bude, back to Halwill then on a 11.30am departure right down to Delabole where it ran round its 2 set between 1.33 and 1.52pm (buses connected to and from Camelford to Tintagel and Boscastle). There was little profit on these extensions to Delabole and they were not continued in 1954. A bus service (SN Route 418) Delabole/Camelford/Tintagel/Boscastle/Otterham Station/Launceston ran on the five Sundays in August 1954 taking two hours each way to connect at Launceston (arr 2.30pm, dep 5.25pm). Looking forward into the final years, Bude and Launceston continued to get a train service in the summer periods until September 1965. For Bude only, a single return bus by Southern National Co.(No 129) ran to and from Okehampton in the winter of 1963/4, 1964/5 and 1965/6. From summer 1965 five DMUs made four return trips between Exeter Central and Bude, Launceston served from Halwill by dividing or attaching at Halwill.

The Change to Diesel Railcars 1965-66

The Western Region took control of the route west of Salisbury (Wilton South exclusive) from 1 January 1963, but Southern Region rolling stock continued to penetrate on both express and local workings, even to Padstow. Exmouth Junction locomotive depot and its allocation became WR (83D) but for the first year little difference could be noticed. A newly-created Plymouth Division of the WR began to find its feet during 1963 and plans were made to integrate the former SR into the Paddington - Penzance services. In the background, nonetheless, Dr. Beeching was calling for statistics of British Railways operations in just such places as Devon and Cornwall

and this same year his 'Report' was published. There was to be little hope that the North Cornwall line would survive. Traffic was seriously declining.

April 1964 consequently saw the posting of closure notices for Okehampton to Bude and Wadebridge passenger trains. (Freight closure was announced in June to take effect from 7 September). The summer 1964 timetable, to take effect from 15 June, was to be the last 'Southern' one, with NC local trains connecting to and from Waterloo. The Monday to Friday basic five Up trains from Padstow at 8.48am to Exeter Central, 9.35am to Waterloo, 1.00pm to Okehampton (no longer including a through coach to Waterloo), 3.10pm 'Perishables' to Exeter and 6.20pm to Okehampton, were completed by the early 7.55am from Launceston. Downward, the 1.10am Waterloo 'News' no longer conveyed TCs for Padstow (though the Newspaper van in the 6.25am Okehampton continued). The 10.00am Okehampton, 3.32pm (following the 'ACE' coaches at 3.08pm) and the 5.55pm still ran, the last two terminating at Wadebridge at 5.25pm and 7.48pm. The last train (8.20pm Halwill, connecting through Okehampton from the 3.00pm Waterloo) terminated, as of yore, at Launceston. Bude local portions continued to be taken from Okehampton/Padstow trains (and vice versa) but the Monday to Friday 'ACE' Bude coach had ceased to run after September 1963.

The decline in use of North Cornwall local trains was borne by the figures put forward by BR in its closure proposals. Few walked nowadays to Tower Hill or Port Isaac Road, the latter so isolated that it was probably unknown to a younger generation. Rising car ownership disregarded the railway as an anachronism, its fares 'expensive', but useful perhaps in an emergency! Yet many local people, particularly school children and shop workers in Launceston, Holsworthy, Bude and Okehampton, relied on it even in 1964. The handful of Maunsell 2-car 'P' sets, now approaching 40 years service, were supplemented by later 1940s Bulleid coaches, a smattering of BR (Mark 1s) and some ex-GWR stock which kept the service going until the onset of diesel railcars or perhaps anticipated closure. The 10.00am, 1.30pm (Bude) from Okehampton and the 1.00pm and 3.10pm from Padstow still conveyed parcel vans. Meat now saw a declining reliance on the railway as a carrier to all parts of the UK. Road transport was beginning to nudge into this business, as it did on the freight side, spurred by its own 1964 closure notice.

Together with the cessation of freight services the local scene changed considerably from 7 September 1964. Although there was still some semblance of the previous four/five trains North Cornwall service, it was

DOWN		WEEKDAYS						SUNDAYS
		(a)	(b)	(c)	(d)	(e)	(f)	(g)
		am	am	am	am	pm	pm	am
Waterloo	dep	1.15	-	-	9	-	-	
Paddington	dep	-	-	5.30	10.30	12.30	2.30	10.30
Exeter (Cen)	dep	5.10	8.55	10.42	1.19	(3.05)	5.45	2.31
Exeter (St.D)	dep	5.18	9.00	10.48	1.24	3.35	5.50	2.45
Okehampton	arr	5.57	9.46	11.36	2.01	4.21	6.35	3.25
Okehampton	dep	6.15	10.00	12.10	2.04	4.30	6.55	4.25
Halwill	dep	7.04	10.33	12.50	2.32	4.58	7.30	4.56
Bude	arr	(7.25)	(11.15)	13.25	(3.21)	5.35	(8.14)	5.43
Launceston	arr	7.36	11.00	-	2.55	(6.40)*	8.00	-
Wadebridge	arr	9.00	12.07	-	4.00	-	9.00	-
Padstow	arr	9.15	12.17	-	4.10	-	-	-

Extract from timetable 4 October 1964 to 3 January 1965

(a)   1.15am Waterloo - Plymouth Passenger and News. (Calls only at St Davids from Exeter Central to Okehampton)

(b)   8.00am Axminster to Plymouth (DMU)

(c)   5.30am via Bristol. 08.10 Salisbury to Plymouth DMU

(d)   Through train Exeter Central to Padstow. Calls only at North Tawton to Okehampton

(e)   3.35pm Exeter (St Davids) to Plymouth. Also connects with 10.25am Brighton - Plymouth (Okehampton arr 3.43pm). Bude arrival times are from connecting branch trains from Halwill.

(f)   2.55pm Salisbury to Plymouth (DMU)

(g)   2.45pm Exeter St Davids to Plymouth. Southern National bus Okehampton to Bude.

*   Connection from Halwill (dep 6.18pm)

Extract from timetable 4 October 1964 to 3 January 1965								
UP		WEEKDAYS						SUNDAYS
		(a)	(b)	(c)	(d)	(e)	(f)	(g)
		am	am	am	pm	pm	pm	am
Padstow	dep	-	8.48	11.05	-	3.45	6.20	-
Wadebridge	dep	-	8.58	11.20	-	3.56	6.33	-
Launceston	dep	7.52	10.06	12.24	-	5.00	7.40	-
Bude	dep	(7.35)	(9.40)	(12.00)	2.40	(5.35)	(6.35)	3.00
Halwill	dep	8.13	10.32	12.48	3.19	5.24	8.06	3.47
Okehampton	arr	8.46	11.07	1.20	3.53	5.58	8.42	4.18
Okehampton	dep	9.03	11.10	1.32	4.29	6.29	9.00	4.46
Exeter (St.D)	arr	9.45	11.58	2.12	5.11	7.17	9.40	5.15
Exeter (Cen)	arr	9.51	12.02	2.25	(5.23)	7.30	(10.02)	(5.31)
Paddington	arr	1.15	3.10	-	9.05	10.40	-	9.45
Waterloo	arr	2.13	-	6.13	9.13	-	-	9.13

(a)   Calls at Meldon (SO) for wives of railway staff. Connects with 07.50am Plymouth - Salisbury (DMU) and with 10.08am Exeter (St.D) - Paddington.

(b)   Through train Padstow - Exeter (Central). Connects with 12.01pm Exeter (St.D) - Paddington

(c)   Connects with 12.20pm Plymouth - Exeter (St.D) DMU and with 2.20pm Exeter (St.D) - Waterloo.

(d)   Connects with 3.15 pm Plymouth - Exeter (St.D) DMU, 5.57 pm Exeter (St.D) - Paddington and 5.20 pm Exeter (St D) - Waterloo.

(e)   Connects with 5.15 pm Plymouth - Eastleigh and (FO) 7.47 pm Exeter (St.D) - Paddington.

(f)   Connects with 7.43 pm Plymouth to Exeter (St.D) DMU

(g)   Southern National bus Bude to Okehampton. Connects into 3.45 pm Plymouth to Exeter (St.D) - limited stop DMU. Also connects with 6.07 pm Exeter (St.D) - Paddington and 5.30 pm Exeter (St.D) - Waterloo.

Exeter Central connected off the 10.30am Paddington to Penzance at St Davids, and a 8.48am from Padstow ran through to Central, connecting to the 3.10pm arrival at Paddington. No missed-stops on the North Cornwall from now on, but the Down train was swifter by calling only at North Tawton after St Davids, producing a respectable 5 hour, 39 minute journey to Padstow. On the last day of steam haulage (3 January 1965) the 1.19pm left St Davids behind Class 3 No.82039, three coaches and a van. Eric Youldon of Exeter sadly relates that 82039 was in poor condition. A stop at Bow to raise steam and again at North Tawton - extended for the same reason. How far 82039 went with its special headboard 'LAST REGULAR STEAM PASSENGER TRAIN EXETER TO PADSTOW' is not known. Sister engine 82040 was on the Halwill/Bude connections. The 2.40pm Bude to Okehampton was passed at Dunsland Cross by Class 4 No.75025 (tender first). On his return from Bude, Eric changed at Halwill into the 3.45pm from Padstow behind yet another Class 3, No 82042. For the record his train to Exeter (5.15pm Plymouth to Eastleigh) was in the charge of 'Hymek' diesel No.D7099, suggesting what was afoot for the following Monday. It was also at this date that the WR insisted on the 24-hour clock timings.

From 4 January 1965 the 'steamers' lay cold in the sidings at Exmouth Junction and the diesel railcars took over. Based at Newton Abbot, the service they now provided required to start and finish at the Exeter end, only the 18.55 Okehampton to Wadebridge and its return trip, the 08.48 Padstow next morning, stabling overnight (a three-car multiple unit). The 06.15 Okehampton (connecting still from the 01.10 Waterloo to Plymouth Newspaper train) came ECS from Newton. At Halwill a single railcar was detached to form the 06.50 to Bude and at

now integrated with the Paddington/ Penzance main line, rather than Waterloo. Local steam working had to continue, however, until diesel railcar coverage could be organised by the WR. The first conversion was the Exmouth branch from September 1963. On the SR main line only the 1.10am Waterloo News and Passenger and the through Brighton/Plymouth trains came through Okehampton and showed any signs of 'express' running. A two-hourly service Waterloo/St Davids with limited stops east of Salisbury was supplemented by an all stations Salisbury/ Plymouth or Ilfracombe service maintained by WR three-car diesel sets. The latter were timed to connect at St Davids with the Paddington trains, further providing Okehampton connections for Padstow/Bude by steamhauled trains in a timetable cast for the proposed diesel railcars. Although locomotive haulage of freight had been largely separate from passenger until September 1964, quite a drastic change in engine duties was instituted. For the most part, the Okehampton/ Padstow/Bude workings became self-contained, worked as before by BR Class 4 2-6-4Ts and the SR 'N' 2-6-0s. The Class 3 2-6-2Ts hitherto con-

fined to the Bude branch appeared in NC workings as did some BR Class 4 4-6-0s by December. The latter were unable to turn at Launceston or Bude owing to their length. Betraying some recognition that the Padstow line still existed, a 1.19pm through train from

The 'lightweight' Pacifics were designed by O.V.S. Bulleid with haulage of North Cornwall holiday trains in mind. In 1947 a 70ft vacuum-powered table was installed in order to turn these 4-6-2s. No.34036 'Westward Ho' is at Padstow in 1959; though there was a turntable and water column, coaling and servicing took place at Wadebridge. (Colour Rail / A.E.R.Cope)

The general view of the east end of Wadebridge on 3rd September 1954. On the right 'Woolworth' 'N' Class No.31848 is being coaled, in the Up loop is Class 02 No.30203 (long an inhabitant of Wadebridge) on a Bodmin North train, while Beattie 2-4-0WT, No.30586, shunts the goods shed. (R.C.Riley)

Launceston another single car detached to go forward at 07.55 to Padstow. The 'main' train (a two or three car set) returned to Okehampton as the 07.52 from Launceston. The timetable remained generally similar to the September 1964 issue, except for minor adjustments. Bude/Halwill trains were now 'shuttles', but during the afternoon some were running separately to Okehampton and back. The 15.45 Padstow to Okehampton was retarded to 15.15 (and the 16.35 Bude to 16.05). Bude did quite well, getting two evening Up services at 17.47 and 20.25 hours, making seven up and eight down trains per weekday, at least for Halwill. Samples of units employed in March 1965 were: 15.15 ex-Padstow: single car; 13.19 ex-Exeter Central: 3 car 'suburban' unit; 16.30 ex-Okehampton (to Bude): three car 'suburban'; 09.40 Bude to Halwill: single car. Day tickets were offered from Padstow (70 shillings), Launceston (54/6), and from all North Cornwall stations to London. The return for latter travellers was the 01.10 Waterloo overnight train.

Not all the services were diesel car workings. Until April 1965 the afternoon Okehampton (12.10) and the return 14.40 from Bude 'Perishables' employed diesel locomotives (a Hymek or NBL D63XX) and coaches/vans.

Steam reappeared for one day on Sunday 5 September 1965, a special organised by the Great Western Society to celebrate the Centenary of GWR Launceston Branch arriving from Exeter at Launceston (via Lydford and Lifton) behind Ivatt Class 2 2-6-2T No. 41283. After terminating in the GWR station 41283 propelled the train back to the spur junction and came across into Launceston (ex-SR). After running-round its train in the down loop, the tank left for Halwill and proceeded to Bude, before returning to Exeter.

The first casualty under 'Beeching' was the Torrington to Halwill line passenger trains. This light railway of 1925 never aspired to show in the Southern Railway's comprehensive Waterloo to the West of England timetable, but then it was hardly attractive to passengers, with its mixed trains and slow progress. Nonetheless there was always a connection at Halwill with the Up 'ACE' and from the 1.00pm Waterloo. It managed to dieselise for its last winter of 1964/5, a single car working from Barnstaple Junction to Halwill mid-morning and late afternoon. The mixed trains trailing wagons of pit props and china clay into Halwill had ceased from 7 September 1964 and the line closed altogether south of Meeth after the 18.20 left Halwill on the evening of 27 Feb-

ruary 1965. A brief re-opening occurred on 27 March for an enthusiasts' railtour - 'The Exmoor Ranger'.

From 1 March the early morning DMU combination was advanced to 06.25 from Okehampton but kept the same timings beyond Halwill. In spite of uncertainty over closure proposals, the Okehampton/Bude line service remained quite generous, and Launceston shared this to a degree. For the summer timetable, starting on 14 June 1965, a Sunday service was restored from Exeter Central to Bude, four trains each way with Launceston getting a single car twice from Halwill (turning round at 10.27/11.07 and in the evening at 18.56/19.15 hours). The surprising inclusion of a Saturday holiday train from and to Paddington serving Bude (and Ilfracombe) resulted in several diesel locomotive-hauled workings. Coaches came in from Newton Abbot arriving at Bude at 09.04 and the Down Paddington stock returned as a public train at 16.54. The North Cornwall line, beginning to look woebegone (Otterham had lost its crossing loop already), was less fortunate. The service was reduced to three down trains, at 06.25 and 10.05 from Okehampton and at 15.35 from Halwill (also Halwill to Launceston at 18.18 and 19.08 hours), and three up, from Wadebridge at 08.57, 13.50 and 17.30

(Launceston extras at 07.52 and 19.50). The outlook was not inspiring. There was no connection to the Bude/Paddington train and passengers on the 13.50 had to wait at Halwill from 15.20 to 16.01 for the Bude-Exeter Central car to appear! Small wonder long distance passengers were deterred, and local users discouraged by fewer trains and continual re-timings. During the winter of 1965/6 the lone Sunday service Bude/Okehampton reverted to a Southern National bus. The weekday 15.35 from Halwill with Wadebridge was retarded to 14.35, but did connect with the 13.20 from Exeter St Davids to Bude with its fast running to Okehampton (less the call at North Tawton).

North Cornwall and Bude services were not expected to last beyond March 1966, some prospective upcountry passengers actually being told they had ceased. Even the Plymouth Divisional Office was under threat of closure. None of this uncertainty was encouraging, but until Ministerial consent for closure, the trains had to run. From 18 April 1966 an 'Emergency Timetable' was introduced, and by this time consent had been given, so a terminating date of 3 October was included (last trains Saturday 1 October). North Cornwall simply got a morning, afternoon and evening train each way, but Bude continued to enjoy eight return services (five connecting at Okehampton). Three single (or twin) cars were sufficient to cover workings, none completely confined to either route. The flexibility of diesel units could be illustrated by the 06.25 Okehampton (ECS from Newton Abbot) which dropped a single car at Halwill for Bude and another at Launceston (to return at 07.48) before proceeding to Wadebridge. The car, arriving at Launceston at 19.21, was attached to the 18.40 from Wadebridge, in turn to the 19.25 from Bude, all going through to Exeter St Davids (the only train advertised to do so) thence ECS to Newton Abbot.

By this time only Ashbury, Halwill, Launceston, Egloskerry and Camelford retained their loops, even though Halwill only had booked crossings. It was all very sad as the weeks melted away. Enthusiasts and locals decided to join the dwindling band of regular travellers paying for day returns - Okehampton to Bude: 10/-, Halwill to Launceston: 4/8d, Delabole to Wadebridge: 3/6d or even Wadebridge to Paddington for £4/12/0d. Meanwhile the substitute bus timetables were under preparation for October, but some places like Tresmeer and Port Isaac Road would never again enjoy six-days-a-week, four or five-services-a-day public transport.

Diesel locomotives had already invaded Wadebridge from 1961. NBL D63XX (later Class 22) based on St Blazey replaced the 45XX 2-6-2Ts on the Bodmin Road trains, but the successors of the '02s' continued on the former SR services to Bodmin North. On 7 September 1964 the WR set up a revised pattern which left Bodmin North with a 'shuttle' to and from a new short platform at Boscarne Junction, and a longer one opposite, on the General line. Single unit diesel rail cars called at the latter on a service Bodmin Road, Bodmin General, Boscarne, Wadebridge and Padstow. (Grogley and Nanstallon Halts now got a call by every train). The single cars (latter Class 122) returned to St Blazey nightly but the innovative AC 4-wheel railbus for Bodmin arrived on Mondays and stabled at Wadebridge until Saturday. A set of coaches was retained for school traffic, kept at Padstow. For many years Bodmin Harleigh School pupils had used the train from Wadebridge to Bodmin SR, but from May 1948 the '02' and SR stock were diverted to Bodmin General. In 1957 a Secondary Modern School opened in Wadebridge and numbers increased, coming from both directions. 45XX 2-6-2Ts worked the afternoon service, but Padstow extensions were not always advertised to the public. '02s' worked the Bodmin Road in latter years, replaced by WR 57XX 0-6-0PTs and then, in 1962, by the Ivatt 2MT 2-6-2Ts.

Although the shadow of 'Beeching' crept across these branches as well as the North Cornwall, it is surprising to note the extensive services now provided. Even Sundays had a bus service (but not provided by BR). During the summer of 1965 the AC railbus took one return trip to Wadebridge, and was used on 'guided tours' Padstow/Bodmin North in the summer of 1965 and 1966.

From 4 January 1965 the few North Cornwall DMUs mingled with the Bodmin/Padstow services, but from 7 June were cut back to Wadebridge, except on Saturdays. There were not many connections from/to Padstow and in the last timetable (1966), they were down to the 08.41 and 18.46 arrival and 08.45 departure services. Passengers, it would seem, from Padstow and Wadebridge, were also directed towards Bodmin Road and Paddington, though even here connections were indifferent. Padstow's layout was reduced to a single run-round loop and siding, signalling by a train staff and key, in 1965. This combined service from Bodmin Road lasted four months beyond the North Cornwall's closure. The last day of service was 28 January 1967, the farewell crowds accommodated in a three-coach train hauled by NBL No D6309.

Passenger Transport after Closure in 1966
The stay of execution for the railway in 1966 enabled British Railways to arrange for some, if not entire, coverage of the North Cornwall route by public transport. The South Western Traffic Commissioners were asked to invite applications from local bus and coach operators. There was to be a subsidy from BR (but in reality paid by the National Bus Company) for a limited period. It was not difficult to attract offers for Okehampton/Bude and three were considered. W.J.O. Jennings of Queen St. Bude, established for many years in the Kilhampton area and now operating tours from Bude, put forward an 'express' service of six return journeys (weekdays), D & M Perrie of Halwill was another contender, also Okeridge Motors (Okehampton). Perrie's proposals had more stops than the trains, including Stratton. The eastern end showed stops at Halwill Junction, Ashbury Cross, Maddaford (Thorndon Cross). The Southern National Com-

					(a)				
18 April to 1 October 1966									
Weekdays (SX) 18 June to 3 September						**Sats 18 June to 3 September**			
Exeter (St D)	dep	5.22	10.13	15.45	17.27	5.22	10.26	15.5	17.34
Okehampton	dep	6.25	11.45	16.50	18.30	6.25	11.25	16.50	18.30
Halwill	dep	6.51	12.1	17.15	19.00	6.51	11.55	17.15	19.00
Launceston	dep	7.22	12.31	17.37	*****	7.17	12.17	17.37	19.21
Wadebridge	arr	8.20	13.30	18.34	-	8.15	13.15	18.34	-
Padstow	arr	8.41	-	18.54	-	8.27	13.59	18.45	-
		(a)				(a)			
Padstow	dep	-	8.45	-	-	-	8.30	14.05	18.25
Wadebridge	dep	-	8.57	14.25	18.40	-	8.57	14.25	18.40
Launceston	dep	7.48	9.56	15.27	19.45	7.53	9.56	15.27	19.45
Halwill	arr	8.11	10.19	15.50	20.08	8.16	10.19	15.50	20.08
Okehampton	arr	8.47	10.58	16.25	20.46	8.50	10.58	16.28	20.46
Exeter (StD)	arr	9.47	11.51	17.20	21.36	9.44	11.57	17.21	21.36

(a) To/From Bude

pany did not apply, and the winner was Jennings because of, it seems, the better fleet of coaches and reliable garaging, at the right end. This firm initially provided the six return journeys (and an extra in the summer) from Okehampton station, now the railhead, and Bude (Strand). The Sunday service, hitherto run by the SN Co, was transferred to Jennings and would run year-round. Until 1980 the Exeter/Okehampton leg was provided by Devon General. The coaches still operate, modified in timings and number of journeys, after 25 years. Following closure of Okehampton in June 1972 they were extended to Exeter St Davids (and into the city). The service remains essentially an 'express' in spite of additional stops.

It was a very different story from Halwill to Wadebridge. Bus substitution for the entire route was never considered, though a considerable but not very parallel, length was covered for a few years in a limited form between Okehampton and Delabole. A three-a-day return service was applied for by the Southern National Co., operating from its Delabole garage, and was granted. It went nowhere near Halwill, going directly from Okehampton by the A30, through Lifton, to Launceston Square. It avoided Egloskerry, Tresmeer and Otterham. A local school bus proprietor took pains to point out in 1967 that he went through Egloskerry and Tresmeer (village) in term-time to Launceston. In 1969

Okehampton departures were only two: at 11.35 (Delabole arr 13.36) and 16.25 (Delabole 18.26). From Delabole there were departures at 09.20 (Okehampton 11.30) and 14.05 (16.15). This service (No 406, later 366) was discontinued on 31 December 1969. Existing Southern National Services in this area were never very competitive with the railway, except the cross-countries (with Western National) from Bude and Bideford through Launceston and Tavistock to Plymouth. Perrie applied for and was granted a licence to run a weekday service from Halwill through Ashwater village and Tower Hill to Launceston, one each way morning and evening, but this lasted only a year or so.

The 'coastal' service Southern National No.122 continued to operate, as prior to October 1966, between Bude, Boscastle, Tintagel, Camelford, Delabole (and St Kew Highway) and Wadebridge. Only minor modifications, due to the closure, concerned connections at Camelford and Delabole to and from Okehampton buses, and at Wadebridge (rail). Noteworthy was the extension of the last bus (in 1967) from Okehampton to beyond Delabole on summer Saturdays. Journey time throughout to Wadebridge was two and a half hours for a fare of 7s.6d. In the southwest corner the Port Isaac/Port Isaac Road Station/Wadebridge Station daily services (SN No 133) of two journeys each way continued in 1967. (There

were also services from Polzeath to Wadebridge). The Southern National routes were amalgamated with Western National in 1968, but on the precipitate closures of Bude and Delabole garages on 31 July 1971, these parts of North Cornwall became bereft of public transport except for some limited services taken up by Frys of Tintagel, and Prouts of Port Isaac.

Wadebridge remained a railhead (and Padstow for Harlyn Bay etc.) until the withdrawal of the Bodmin Road to Padstow diesel car service from 30 January 1967. A bus service was thereupon substituted between these points, initially eight weekday journeys each way, the existing Sunday road service continuing (until 1980). This route (WN No.55) is still maintained with a not unreasonable frequency.

It may be surmised from the above that after 25 years the route of the North Cornwall is poorly served by public transport, especially toward Exeter/London. Only Bude/Halwill/Okehampton and Wadebridge/Padstow retain daily and connectional services to the BR system at St Davids and at Bodmin Road (now Parkway) respectively. Launceston has been especially unlucky since 1969 for transport direct to the centre of Exeter, even the Royal Blue coaches have deserting it for Plymouth and the A38 road.

A DMU trundles into Tower Hill on the 11.55am Halwill - Wadebridge train on 3rd August 1966. The Down side loop is now out of use and the signalling removed. (R.A.Lumber)

Chapter Five

THE LURE OF THE NORTH CORNISH COAST

Tourist traffic was already quite heavy along the coastal road (today's A39) in the summer months of the early 1890s. Mention has been made of the North Cornwall Coach Co's successive connections from Launceston, and finally Wadebridge. Operating to the north were Brendon's coaches, based at Bude and from 1895 both firms were offering an integrated two-day tourist service Ilfracombe/Newquay, actually using the new railway from Camelford and Wadebridge, from July to September.

ber. The LSWR offered some 37 combinations for travel and accommodation in 1914.

A 'fast four-horse Coach' ran every weekday until 5 October, though the horse-brakes connecting Tintagel with Camelford Station and with Boscastle were not shown. The coaches ran into and out of Clovelly. About 8,000 passengers were sampling this system every summer in the 1890s, lured by "seventy miles of Coaching through the romantic scenery of the North Coast of Devon and Cornwall, in di-

rect communication with Through Fast Trains over the London & South Western Railway". Arrangements were much the same in 1913, but the 'season' ran only from 2 June to 30 September (20th, north of Bude). In fact this horse-coach tourism lasted until the early 1920's. Through rail and coach tickets were issued only for the northern leg from Waterloo and Exeter etc. to and from Bude. In 1913 the single through fare from Bude to Newquay was 13/9d (1st Class) and the Boscastle/Tintagel to Camelford Station local fare was 1/6d single. Earlier and later timed horse buses were connecting these places with Camelford trains, as well as between Padstow (up to 1899) and Newquay with Wadebridge. Horse brakes could be hired from Port Isaac Road by giving notice.

Excursions at Weekends and Bank Holidays

While the coastal tourist business expanded, the LSWR were running weekend excursions to and from the West of England on Fridays, Saturdays and Mondays in July, August, and September, special trains arriving at whichever railhead was currently open, though it was 1899 on the opening to Padstow before coaches ran through, obviating changes at Okehampton. Excursion tickets were available on

DOWN JOURNEY		
Ilfracombe Station	Train dep	9.15 am
Bideford Station	Train arr	10.30 am
Bideford Station	Coach dep	10.30 am
Bude (Falcon Hotel)	Coach arr	3.00 pm
Bude (Falcon Hotel)	Coach dep	10.15 am
Boscastle (Wellington Hotel)	Coach arr	1.15 pm
Boscastle (Wellington Hotel)	Coach dep	4.20 pm
Camelford Station	Coach arr	5.20 pm
Camelford Station	Train dep	5.28 pm
Wadebridge Station	Train arr	5.59 pm
Wadebridge Station	Coach dep	6.10 pm
Newquay (Atlantic Hotel)	Coach arr	8.30 pm

In the distance is the quarry as 'U1' Class No.31904 comes off the country end of Meldon Viaduct on Saturday 26th August 1961 with the 3.55p.m. from Okehampton. As well as local sets for Bude and Padstow, the third and last coaches are 'through' from the 11.15a.m. Waterloo. (S.C. Nash)

the 9.00am from Waterloo in 1886 to Launceston for Wadebridge and Newquay. Returning from Padstow, the excursionist had to be up early for the 5.10am 'conveyance', to be in Waterloo at 5.15pm!

From 1899 through special weekend excursion trains definitely started running to and from Padstow. Leaving Waterloo at 7.40am, Exeter Queen Street was reached at 1.03pm in 5 1/2 hours compared with 3 1/2 hours by the best expresses! At Halwill the down service divided for Bude, and for Padstow an arrival at 4.40pm. Upwards departure from Padstow was at 7.40am, Bude 9.00am and Exeter 11.35am, giving a 4.37pm arrival at Waterloo - these on Mondays and Saturdays. Overnight Saturday excursion trains were also run at the height of the season before 1914, and it would appear that a connecting passenger coach was attached to the Sunday 4.33am goods and mail from Okehampton (and one from Halwill to Bude). Being a goods train, the passengers would have had to wait at Meldon Junction while wagons were attached! While usually terminating at Camelford (though later back at Launceston), the train continued with the coach to Delabole arriving at 6.18am, if required.

It is not certain what types of carriages were employed on these excursions. Almost certainly bogie stock, but non-lavatory. The lengthy timings indicate this with stops at Andover, Salisbury etc. and no refreshments

either. Nevertheless excursions were obviously popular. Cornish people (and Devonians!) had migrated to work in London, many still do, consequently at Easter and Christmas the LSWR pushed itself to the limit to provide extra trains, and special excursions. In 1910 on both the 23 and 24 December the normal 11.00am was formed into two divisions. The second left at 11.05am for Plymouth and Padstow only. The latter portion was reformed as an express at Exeter Queen Street leaving at 2.30pm arriving at Padstow at 5.21pm. On Christmas morning at 12.45am an excursion left Waterloo for Padstow and Bude, with a Plymouth portion on the rear. The arrivals at the resorts were at 9.01 and 7.56am respectively. The following Easter on the Tuesday and Wednesday before the holiday, an 11.05am from Waterloo served Padstow, Bude, Exmouth and Sidmouth only. It called at Salisbury, Exeter, then only at Launceston, Otterham, Camelford, Port Isaac Road and Wadebridge. On Thursday 13 April an 11.30am excursion left for Plymouth, Padstow and Bude - all stations from Exeter but omitting Ashbury, Tower Hill and Egloskerry, and the 1.00pm carried through coaches, one for Padstow, one for Bude. During the evening a special 7.00pm took coaches for Padstow, Plymouth and Torrington. Arrival at Padstow was at the unearthly hour of 4.00am! This next day, Good Friday, saw yet another excursion leaving

Waterloo at 12.30pm for Plymouth, Padstow and Bude. In 1912 a dining saloon was included in the 11.05am Second Division on 23 December working all the way to Padstow. As it was needed again for the next morning's 11.05 Waterloo, it was worked empty all the way back to Clapham Junction, leaving Padstow at 6.20pm. Arriving on Christmas Eve it spent Christmas Day at Padstow (and presumably the crew as well) and was then taken empty to Exeter on 27th, en route to Bournemouth for use on the 28th. There is less evidence of this sort of working in the 1920s and 1930s, though the timetables indicate overnight excursion trains, especially Fridays/Saturdays. Christmas and Easter holidays had lengthened somewhat. Trains always ran on Christmas Day, but only for early-hour arrivals in North Cornwall.

Motor Buses and Charabancs Compete in the 1920s

Brendons' horse - coach excursions ceased in 1922 though there was as yet no direct competition from the motor charabancs beginning to appear after World War One. The co-ordination with the LSWR at Bideford, Bude and Camelford also ended. A serious motor bus contender was the Hardy-Colwill Company of Bideford. By 1925 its red and white buses were operating along the coast as far as Newquay. To the south the Devon Motor Transport Co had established themselves in Okehampton, but their Launceston

The Southern Railway intended to use more powerful locomotives on the lines west of Exeter from the 1940s. Up to 1939 pairs of 4-4-0s hauled the heaviest of the holiday trains on the North Cornwall and Bude lines, but after 1945 these Bulleid light axle-weight 'West Countries' could handle up to eight coaches with ease on the Cornish and Devon gradients. On Tuesday 4th August 1964, No. 34107 'Blandford Forum' is coming by East Bowerland, near Maddaford, with the 11.05 a.m. Waterloo to Padstow with Set 565, a mixture of BR Mark Is and Bulleid coaches. By this time Bude no longer had through coaches from the Monday-to-Friday 'ACE'. (P.W. Gray)

The Atlantic Coast Express headboard on Bulleid Pacific No. 34110 '69 Squadron' was mounted at Exeter Central, this engine working through to Padstow, then returning next morning. On 12th May 1961 the (winter) formation is two for Padstow and a brake composite for Bude, as the train approaches Maddaford Moor Halt. (S.C. Nash)

local route failed to compete with the railway. The Southern Railway showed more concern when, in 1927, the National Omnibus & Transport Co., already in Somerset, acquired Hardy-Colwill. Moves were already afoot by all four main line railway companies to obtain an interest in the omnibus field. Parliamentary powers obtained in 1928 enabled the SR to buy into the National Co. and as from 1929 the Southern National Co was formed, with an office in Exeter, to operate buses in the Southern Railway's territory, the latter owning 51% of the capital. There was a similar arrangement between the Western National Co and the GWR, (which had run buses on its own account for many years). A successor to the coastal horse and coach route appeared in the 1930s when an Ilfracombe-Newquay ('Cornish Riviera') service commenced. Both ways it stopped over at Bude for about an hour for lunch and called at Camelford and Wadebridge stations. The Southern Railway did not influence the National Co's operations and there was little or no conflict along the North Cornwall line. Indeed, a Bude-Wadebridge service connected at Camelford station for Camelford,

Tintagel and Boscastle, as we have seen, and there was even a service by Prouts from Port Isaac to Port Isaac Road, a successor to wagonettes. Through bookings were available to Boscastle, Tintagel and (via Padstow) to Bedruthan and Trevone, also Wadebridge to St Columb Major. Interavailability between train and bus (but note - a supplementary charge was payable by those returning by train) was permitted between Padstow and Wadebridge, St Kew Highway, Delabole and Port Isaac Road to Wadebridge, and Wadebridge to Camelford. Long distance travel from London by coach became possible post - World War II when the Royal Blue (owned, ironically, by the two National companies!) started serving Polzeath, Camelford, Wadebridge and Padstow in the summer months. In the end the rise of private motoring in the 1960s really killed the holidays-by-rail traffic. People in cars became the new 'tourists' in North Cornwall. Their intrepid forebears slowly traversing the Atlantic coast in the coach-and-fours, lodging in style at the Falcon at Bude or the Wellington Hotel at Boscastle, have been replaced by a restless nation staying in overnight accommoda-

tion or parking their caravans at approved sites. For those who do not motor, only Bude, Padstow and Wadebridge are effectively served by substitute bus services from rail heads, and 'package' coach tours have taken care of the rest.

Though charabancs multiplied in the west country in the 1930s, infiltrating the coastal resorts formerly the preserves of the railways, the latter did not sit back. Reference has been made to the opening of the North Cornwall line for an excursion in 1928. It must have proved successful as it was repeated in the following summers-not greatly so, however, for the only ones booked in 1932 were from Bodmin to Paignton and Exmouth to Padstow. A so-called Half Day Excursion left Padstow at 10.10am and returned at 11.02pm. Presumably the half day was the time spent at Paignton between 2 and 7pm, on that Sunday 28 August. While the branch signal boxes were open the Exmouth train came down into Padstow at 2.16pm. Again, the evening signalmen saw this train away at 7.25pm. The Wadebridge engine crews exchanged footplates at Okehampton in the morning and Ashbury at 9.15pm that night. It is interesting to note that the Okehampton-Bude line was open on most 1930s summer Sundays in August and September, handling a variety of excursions from as far away as Bournemouth and Bristol. Bude received its first regular Sunday services in the summer of 1937, and Launceston from 1941.

The Summer Holiday Trains and 'The North Cornwall & Bude Express'

The 'Atlantic Coast Express' antecedents dated back to 1900 when the LSWR began running a 'North Cornwall Express' from July until the following September. It left Waterloo, Mondays to Saturdays, at 11.10am, called at Okehampton at 4.10pm and, after shedding a portion for Bude at Halwill, arrived Padstow at 6.40pm. It called beyond Okehampton to set down London passengers at Ashbury; then Halwill, Ashwater, Tower Hill (special arrangement 'by signal when required to take up passengers for Wadebridge and Bodmin'), Launceston, Tresmeer (Saturdays only), Otterham (London passengers set down), Camelford and the rest of the stations to Padstow. It shared the train to Exeter Queen St with a Sidmouth coach, and a portion for Plymouth leaving Queen St ten minutes later at 2.35pm. In the opposite direction portions left Padstow at 12.45pm and Bude at 1.48pm, with provisos to stop at St Kew Highway ('by signal to take up for

London passengers only'), Otterham ('for Exeter and east'). Otherwise stops were made at all stations to Okehampton though only on Saturdays at Tresmeer and Egloskerry. Hardly an express west of Exeter, but with a four hour timing it was not very fast between there and Waterloo either. In the winter of 1900/01 the 10.50am from Waterloo was advertised as the 'Plymouth and North Cornwall Express' but a change was needed at Okehampton (3.24/3.40pm) with a Padstow arrival at 6.10pm. Already from 1896, as we have seen, the connections from the 11.00am Waterloo and the 1.20pm from Wadebridge were making limited stops, some to take up and set down as described above, recognising the tourist potential in North Cornwall.

Consider the situation with the line open all the way to Padstow from 1899. The LSWR management having subsidised the completion of the North Cornwall, and to Bude (1898), wanted to maximise revenue, for tourism had grown considerably and the horse-and-coaches along the coast were carrying several thousands in the summer period. The integration between them and rail is described earlier. This was the era of the 'Grand' hotels. In due course would open the 'Grenville' at Bude, the 'King Arthur's Castle' at Tintagel and the 'Metropole' (originally the 'South Western') at Padstow. Large houses were constructed with many rooms, suitable for

letting for long periods in the summer. The well-off Edwardians on holiday with large families, sometimes 'Colonials' on leave, would travel with servants and quite a mountain of luggage though rolling stock in use at the turn of the century was not really adequate, especially for the long distance to Padstow - 260 miles from Waterloo. The GWR had already improved its running to Newquay and Ilfracombe and a start was made in 1900 in building bogie corridors for the Exeter line. By 1907 complete new sets with dining saloons, some from 'Eagle' trains, were available for the 'North Cornwall and Bude Express'. Until 1908 there were no gangways at the ends of the Padstow six-coach (two dining saloons) and the Bude four coaches. Presumably the latter's passengers made do with luncheon and tea baskets. The 'express' end of the journey was improved. Drummond 'T9' 4-4-0s were coming into use from 1899 and the 11.00am Waterloo was arriving in Exeter at 2.57pm in under four hours. From 1906 the Exeter arrival was 2.36pm and in the 1909 summer 2.15pm. By dint of non-stop running from Exeter St Davids to Halwill Junction (to detach the Bude portion) Padstow was now reached at 5.02pm. Calls were made only at Launceston, Camelford and Port Isaac Road to Wadebridge. The up train left Padstow at 11.00am, and calling additionally at Otterham, and also at Okehampton, reached Waterloo at 5.12pm. To and

'Battle of Britain' 4-6-2 No. 34078 '222 Squadron' with the 8.30 a.m. Padstow 'Atlantic Coast Express' leaves Launceston on 25th July 1964. The train appears to be a Bulleid 'R' three-coach set, a BR Mark I coach and a Bulleid Brake Third. Even as late as the 1960s, loading was still quite heavy in the summer months, mainly from Padstow, Wadebridge, Camelford and Otterham. This train would take on two or three through coaches from Bude, also a very popular resort, at Halwill. (Lens of Sutton)

from Exeter reliance was placed on Adams '460' 4-4-0s, but the weight of the new rolling stock forced larger engines to be used in North Cornwall. From the 1906 season Drummond S11s Nos. 397 and 398 were stationed at Wadebridge for this work. Apart from the summer expresses, it was usual to include through coaches on the 1.00pm Waterloo and the 8.20am Padstow, but pre-1926 there was no real equivalent of the regular weekday 'Atlantic Coast Express' with its collection of TCs (Through Carriages) for many destinations. For the next years the 'NC & BE' ran each summer (then extending into October to a certain extent), Restaurant (or 'Dining') cars invariably included in the Padstow portions.

The 'North Cornwall & Bude Express' with its Padstow and Bude portions was timed thus in 1914, with non-stop running Exeter St David/Halwill Junction and stops only at Launceston, Otterham, Camelford and Port Isaac Road. (see table)

In July 1920 a 10.00am from Waterloo was put on, with a 'Luncheon and Tea Car' to Padstow (arr 5.06pm) and a portion for Bude (arr 4.08pm). After Okehampton it called only at Halwill Junction, Launceston, Otterham, Camelford and Port Isaac Road, to Wadebridge. The Up train with similar stops left Padstow at 9.10am (Bude 10.05am) and arrived Waterloo at 4.30pm. The 11.00am Waterloo (and the 8.15am Padstow) did not appear to include through coaches at this time. From 1921 the 'West of Englands' were timed out of Waterloo at 9.00am, 11.00am, 3.00pm, and 6.00pm. The 11.00am commenced a Saturday-only combination that year to include Brake Composites (LSWR) for Padstow, Bude and Torrington. 1922 and 1923 saw the 10.00am running once more and the 11.00am, with Brake Composites again on Saturdays. There was also a 10.55am through train to Bude on August Saturdays in 1923.

1924 saw the Luncheon Car terminating at Exeter Queen Street, stops

The Atlantic Coast Express from 1926

The formation of the Southern Railway Co in 1923 was followed by a coordinated attempt to allay criticism, particularly by London commuters. J.B. Elliot had been appointed Public Relations and Advertising Assistant to Sir Herbert Walker, and by 1925 attention was being paid to the West of England services. Already the Urie Class N15 4-6-0s were named after King Arthur and the Knights of the Round Table with No. E745 as 'Tintagel'. Tintagel in reality is the village (Trevenna) and the cliff castle, though 'Camelot' (E 742) may, or may not, have existed. The 'King Arthurs' were now the principal motive power between Waterloo and Exeter Queen St. The 11.00am Waterloo and the 12.30pm from Exeter with its North Devon and North Cornwall feeding services were about to receive new SR corridor coaches and it was decided to name them, the SR Magazine for July 1925 setting out a competition for the title. Guard F. Rowland of Torrington suggested the 'Atlantic Coast Express' and his winning submission earned him three guineas. The inaugural train left Waterloo on 19 July 1926 at 11.00am behind No E779 'Sir Colgrevance' for Plymouth and Ilfracombe. At 11.10am the Padstow/Bude train departed behind No E776 'Sir Galagars'. At Exeter the Dining Car pair was detached, then between Exeter St. Davids and Halwill this 'ACE' ran non-stop behind an S11 4-4-0. The Bude portion was detached (arrive 4.42pm), while the main train ran on to Launceston, Otterham, Camelford, Delabole, Port Isaac Road, Wadebridge and arrived at Padstow at 5.41pm. The Up train left Padstow at 8.35am and

			North Cornwall & Bude Express : 1914			
	DOWN			UP		
WATERLOO	dep	11.00 am	Padstow	dep	10.55 am
Exeter (Q.St)	dep	2.21 pm	Bude	dep	11.52 am
Halwill Jcn	arr	3.28 pm	Halwill Jcn	dep	12.42 pm
Bude	arr	4.08 pm	Exeter (Q.St)	arr	1.42 pm
Padstow	arr	5.06 pm	WATERLOO	arr	5.11 pm

Outside the period from 18 July to 29 September the 11.00 had some resemblance to the future 'ACE', with its Ilfracombe and Plymouth portions. Padstow and Bude coaches called at all stations below Okehampton, Padstow being reached at 6.14pm. In the Up direction it left Padstow at 8.20am, into Waterloo at 3.17pm. During the summer the 1.00pm Waterloo also carried TCs for Bude and Padstow on a daily basis (weekdays). It is not clear when these coaches returned, possibly on the 12.47pm from Padstow (1.48pm from Bude), though ECS working was not uncommon on the LSWR.

World War I did not seriously affect the services until 1917, and it appears that summer extras ran in 1915 and 1916. Drastic economies from 1 January 1917 left the local services in North Cornwall slower and thinner and more cuts in May 1918 reduced London connections to three (including the Launceston short workings) each way. The most serious was the 1.12pm Okehampton to Padstow and the 6.40am Wadebridge (below Launceston). A good deal of LSWR main line stock was on the Continent in 1919, including some Dining Cars in leave trains from/to Bari (Italy) to Calais.

as in 1920 and Okehampton was now being passed in both directions. The 1.00pm and the 3.00pm Waterloo conveyed through coaches to Bude and to Padstow, the latter arriving on the coast at 9.42pm.

The 9.30 a.m. from Bude had arrived at Halwill at 10.10 a.m. The engine ran round the 3-coach Set No. 781, then drew it back onto the Bude line. After the 8.30 a.m. Padstow had gone into the Up loop, No. 80039 then propelled the Set on to its rear. All the coaches (including Set No. 838 and a corridor third) from Padstow were Bulleid stock, even the single brake composite in the foreground. This was the 8.52 a.m. from Torrington which had arrived at 10.18 a.m. behind Ivatt Class 2 No. 41283. In the bay is another Class 4 tank No. 80038, the second Bude engine which would work down to Launceston and back during the afternoon. (P.W. Gray)

The combined train to Waterloo climbing the 1 in 73 to Ashbury (left) while No. 80039 has retired to take water at the end of the Down bay, then to await the Bude portion of the 10.00 a.m. Okehampton. On the left of this picture is the Junction Hotel; in the centre are the shops and agricultural stores, while on the right is the brick built SR slaughterhouse (on lease and still active in 1964). On the right the white building is a Devon police house all of which shows the business which grew up around the railway over the years. (P.W. Gray)

Bude at 9.45am and eventually arrived at Waterloo at 3.39pm. These were the Monday to Friday trains. On Saturdays a Dining car was in the Bude portion (dep 11.00am) and this combined with the Padstow (10.00am) portion at Halwill, and then ran non-stop to Exeter St Davids. It left Queen St at 1.10pm, called at Salisbury, and arrived at 4.29pm.

Not all coaches on the 'Atlantic Coast Express', or the 'ACE' as it was popularly known, served the Atlantic coast. Those to the East Devon resorts, Seaton, Sidmouth and Exmouth would carry roof boards 'Waterloo-West of England' and the 'ACE' boards were strictly for the Padstow, Bude and Ilfracombe vehicles. Also, with several trains running per day, only one would

carry the title each way. The 'ACE' was an 'express' strictly between Waterloo and Exeter. The exhilarating runnings to Salisbury and on Honiton bank could hardly be matched west of Exeter, though some fast running was possible between Coleford Junction and Okehampton. The 38 miles between Exeter St Davids and Halwill would be covered in about 60 minutes by non-stop holiday trains. By 1960 the upper limit was 85 mph but slowings were necessary at Crediton (45 mph), Coleford Jn (40 mph), Okehampton (45 mph) and down to 10 mph for taking the Tablet at Meldon Jn (after 20 over the viaduct). 10 mph was the official limit for taking the Tablets at the subsequent passing loops, though this was often honoured in the breach with some deft swapping and sore arms from catching the hoops. The maximum possible speed on the North Cornwall itself was 55 mph, though it is known to have been exceeded on several occasions in late running. The line was improved considerably in the 1930s by introducing better transitions off the curves and raised canting (superelevation) up to five inches in places.

From 1928 the through (Mondays to Fridays) Waterloo to Padstow/Bude train ran each summer at 10.40am (10.35 from 1932). The usual starting

Waterloo, or Okehampton passengers, had not been required to change at Halwill, for the most part. Holiday trains or locals would consist of North Cornwall and Bude portions divided or combined at this junction. In the last summer of steam, on the morning of Saturday 22nd August 1964, the 8.30 a.m. 'Atlantic Coast Express' from Padstow arrives behind 'N' Class No. 31846, while a portion from Bude waits to be attached by Standard Class 4 2-6-4T No. 80039. (P.W. Gray)

times from Padstow were 9.40am and 10.38am from Bude. Dining Cars were included from 1933, now in the Padstow portion, and the typical formation of the 9.40am from Padstow was (in 1930): LSWR corridor brake 3rd, SR corridor 3rd, two SR corridor Brake Composites. At Halwill the Bude portion, one SR corridor Brake Composite, SR corridor 3rd, LSWR corridor Brake Composite, SR corridor 3rd, was attached to the rear. A SR Dining Car and Open 3rd were attached at Exeter Queen St.

While it can be seen that LSWR corridors were still in evidence (and continued to be employed until the mid-1940s), most coaching stock was by now of Southern Railway design. The Brake Composites which figured so often in the 'ACE' formations dated from 1926 and 1930. Other corridors, not in sets, were formed from a growing fleet of 'loose' vehicles and marshalled at Clapham Junction yard to an annual summer programme. New SR dining cars appeared in 1934, paired with 'open' third saloons. All this new stock was equipped with Pullman gangways and buckeye couplings.

By 1932 holiday travel from Waterloo was enough to warrant separate trains to and from Padstow and Bude on Saturdays. The 10.45am Waterloo left St Davids at 2.16pm, running non-stop to Launceston (3.33pm) then only Otterham, Camelford, Delabole and Port Isaac Road to Wadebridge, arriving Padstow at 4.57pm. The Bude trains were: Waterloo 11.00am, detached from a Plymouth portion at Okehampton and running non-stop to Holsworthy, and an Up train following the same pattern in reverse after leaving Bude at 10.40am. The Saturday afternoon trains from Waterloo would also include through coaches to Padstow and Bude. From 23 July to 10 September (the dates for the foregoing) there was an extra at 12 noon on Fridays (Padstow 7.03pm), a 2.00pm (SO) to Plymouth connecting to Padstow (8.36pm), and a 3.10pm (SO) relief to the 3.00pm which included through coaches to Bude, the usual Okehampton to Launceston 2-set being extended to Delabole (9.24pm).

The new 'ACE' was not confined to the summer months. In the winter of 1926/7 the 11.00am Waterloo commenced its well-known role as a provider of through coaches to many destinations in Devon and Cornwall. The ten 59-foot Brake Composites appearing in August and September 1926 were just sufficient to serve Seaton, Exmouth, Torrington, Padstow and Bude each way daily. They contained four third, two first and a guard/luggage compartment. After detachment from the Plymouth portion at Okehampton at 3.42pm, the (all stations) Padstow coach arrived at 5.59pm (and the Bude coach at 4.57pm). The Up departures were at 8.35am and 9.45am respectively. It is not clear whether these coaches ran during the winter 1927/8. With only ten BCs (Brake Composites) there may have ben problems, but another 50 were constructed in 1930 (with large windows on the corridor side) and from July were utilised in the 'ACE' portions. Usually one BC was sufficient for Padstow in the winters of 1930/1 to 1938/9, but occasionally two, as traffic required. In 1935 six two-car sets were formed for West of England and Swanage services. The usual formation leaving Okehampton was a local (LSWR) 2-set and one or two BCs (or 2-set as above), and the Bude BC.

In the final pre-war summers of 1937 - 1939 the Saturday ACE 10.40am Waterloo/9.40am , 10.40am Padstow/Bude were running from early June to mid-September. Holiday travel was reaching new heights and it is worth seeing how the SR coped with the demand in the 1938 summer timetable. Many Britons now enjoyed holidays with pay, and 'visitors' descended in large number on Ilfracombe and Newquay, but Bude had also become very popular, so much so that the SR

The Western Region provided a final through service to Bude, but from Paddington, not Waterloo, in 1965. Part of this went to Ilfracombe, but an NBL No. D6342 Diesel-Hydraulic hauls BR Standards and ex-LMS corridors forming the Exeter Central to Bude portion on 21st August 1965. A diesel unit connecting to Wadebridge is in the Bay, but the goods yards had not seen any traffic since the previous September. (R.A. Lumber)

improved the layout there in 1939 to accommodate trains up to 16 coaches. The Wadebridge East crossovers were moved eastward in 1938, and signalling simplified, probably to improve the operations there. The coves and beaches facing the Atlantic from Crackington Haven and Polzeath to Harlyn Bay and Constantine also attracted the discerning and they used Otterham, Camelford, Wadebridge and Padstow as railheads.

The 1938 summer timetable extended from 3 July to 24 September (Sundays). Overnight travel was rare in these parts, but a down train had run on Friday nights/Saturday mornings for many years, with inducement fares, as an 'excursion'. The debut of Monthly Return tickets, widely avail-

able, had replaced the latter by 1938. There was only one nocturnal train that summer. On Friday 29 July, an 11.00pm Waterloo to Plymouth train detached a portion for Bude to arrive there at 5.16 the next morning.

From Monday to Friday the 'ACE' departed Waterloo for North Devon and North Cornwall at 10.35am with a Dining car bound for Padstow (arrive 4.24pm). The 5 hour 49 minute journey was helped by non-stop running from Exeter St. Davids to Halwill, and then calls only at Launceston, Otterham, Camelford, Delabole and Port Isaac Road to Wadebridge. From Exeter Central the Corridor 3rd and Dining Car pair for Padstow, also the Corridor 3rd and Corridor Brake Composite for Bude (detached at Halwill

at 2.47pm) were headed by a pair of 'T9' 4-4-0s. The equivalent Up train left Padstow at 9.40am and Bude at 10.40am, combined at Okehampton with a Plymouth portion and arrived Exeter Central at 12.40pm then, in due course, at Waterloo 4.12pm. Although the 11.00am Waterloo to Plymouth only connected to Padstow (5.36pm) and Bude (4.54pm) from Okehampton, the 1.00pm Waterloo included a Brake Composite for Padstow. The Plymouth portion detached this at Okehampton for the 5.50pm stopping train to Padstow and Bude.

On Saturdays this service was much expanded, the 'ACE' running as a 10.35am to Ilfracombe and Torrington, 10.38am to Padstow, 10.40am to Bude and 11.00am to Plymouth (Padstow and Bude). The afternoon departures were also enhanced. (see table below).

The formation of the 10.38 to Padstow included a 4-car Dining Car set in a formation of ten coaches and was worked forward from Exeter by two 4-4-0s, one of which was detached at Camelford or Delabole. Beyond Launceston, as on the other weekdays, Egloskerry, Tresmeer and St Kew were passed by, limited to 10mph for Tablet exchanging. The 11.00am passengers changed into the local ex-LSWR two coach sets for Padstow and Bude, but the 1.00pm Waterloo detaching five Corridors at Exeter, two for Plymouth, a Corridor 3rd and Brake Composite for Padstow and a Corridor Brake Composite to Bude, appears to have gained another local Set from Exeter through to Bude on Saturdays, as well as one attached at Okehampton for Padstow. The 2.00pm Waterloo had yet another North Devon and Plymouth extra, with a Corridor

DOWN		NORTH CORNWALL SERVICES (9 July - 24 September 1938)							
		(a)	(b)	(c)	(d)	(e)	(f)		(g)
		am	am	am	am	pm	pm	pm	pm
WATERLOO	dep	10.38	10.4	10.4	11.00	1.00	2.00	3.00	3.06
Exeter (Cen)	dep	1.58	2.06	2.06	2.16	4.28	5.24	6.41	6.40
Okehampton	dep				3.30	5.28	6.28	7.35	7.47
Halwill	dep			3.18	3.59	5.57	6.55	8.22	8.20
Bude	arr		3.45	3.45	4.54	6.02	7.31	8.58	8.58
Launceston	arr	3.23		3.36	4.21	6.24	7.11	8.34	8.42
Padstow	arr	4.43		5.00	5.36	7.38	8.22		

(a)   ACE to Padstow. Non-stop Exeter St.D (2.04pm) to Launceston. Dinign car to Padstow. Not after 10 September 1938.

(b)   ACE Bude. Not after 10 Sept 1938. Dining car to Exeter. Non-stop from Exeter St Davids (2.06 pm) to Holsworthy (3.05 pm)

(c)   ACE Bude and Padstow (17 & 24 Sept 1938). R. car to Exeter. Non-stop between Exeter St D (2.06pm) and Halwill (3.14pm)

(d)   ACE Plymouth. Dining car to Exeter. Change at Okehampton for Padstow & Bude.

(e)   Ilfracombe (Dining car). Through coaches to Plymouth, Padstow and Bude.

(f)   Plymouth. Dining car to Exeter, through portion to Padstow.

(g)   Plymouth. R car to Exeter, through portion to Bude. N. Cornwall connection (not advertised) extended to Delabole (9.25 pm)

3rd coming off at Okehampton for Padstow, again attached to the local sets for there and Bude. Illustrating the pressure on the Southern extending into mid-afternoon, the 3.00pm Waterloo was run in two parts, if necessary, during August. At 3.06 a three-coach Corridor Composite set (Plymouth), two Corridor 3rds (Bude), a Brake Composite and Dining Car (Exeter) - also three coaches for Exmouth - followed the 3.0pm in (publicly) the same timings. The local Sets were attached to the Waterloo-Bude coaches, with division again at Halwill. On these Saturdays, whether in the 3.00 or 3.06 timings, the usual Launceston local Set was extended to Delabole, arriving at 9.25pm (thence ECS back to Launceston).

Just as the last hopefuls departed for the Atlantic coast, happy (and

Highway, Tresmeer, Egloskerry and the other stations missed out by the following 'ACE' services beyond Launceston and Holsworthy. The 10.25am and 10.40am (Bude) were again hauled by pairs of 4-4-0s, usually 'T9's but 'L11's and 'S11's as available. The 'N' Class (and the 'U1's drafted in from 1937) monopolized the Plymouth and Ilfracombe trains. The 12.30pm Padstow through coaches were reinforced by a local Set to Okehampton joined by a portion from Bude (also with a local set) at Okehampton.

Halwill's staff were kept pretty busy on these Saturdays, and well into the evenings! LSWR Corridor gangways were now equipped with adaptors to fit the 'Pullman' versions on SR stock, but coupling and uncoupling the SR 'buckeyes' and hooking screw cou-

plings off local Sets into them was time consuming. Okehampton was hard-pressed at times, especially for producing and disposing of engines. At Padstow and Bude the preparation and assembling of up trains (re-watering and cleaning), restocking of the Dining Cars - then contracted to Frederick Hotels - brought overtime for staff there. Down trains required berthing, and the motive power foremen needed to ensure the engines were to hand and disposed of at the right time. To cover all turns, locomotive firemen from Exmouth Junction would lodge overnight at Bude, Wadebridge and Launceston.

Although Sunday travel was not universal in the 1930s as it is today, by 1937 both the Padstow and Bude lines were regularly open in the summer months for excursion trains. Starting that year, three trains each way were advertised (July to September) between Okehampton and Bude. The 3.35pm from Okehampton connected from the 11.00am, and the 9.15pm from the 4.00pm Waterloo. Passengers from the 10.10am Bude could arrive at Waterloo at 3.50pm, and from the 2.05pm at 8.22pm (with a long wait at Okehampton for the Plymouth train to appear). The 1939 summer timetable was similar, but it was 1941 before Sunday trains, including Launceston, re-appeared and they were extended into the winter periods. Christmas and Boxing Day attracted a Sunday service and, looking ahead somewhat, on 26 and 27 December 1954, the North Cornwall line actually *gained* a connection from the 4.00pm Waterloo, terminating Padstow at 11.44pm - the latest known!

UP		(a)	(b)	(c)	(d)	(a)
NORTH CORNWALL SERVICES (9 July - 24 September 1938)						
		am	am	am	pm	pm
Padstow	dep	-	8.40	10.25	12.30	2.20
Launceston	dep	7.42	10.10	11.51	1.54	3.50
Bude	dep	7.22	9.40	-	1.30	3.04
Halwill	dep	8.09	10.34	-	2.22	4.20
Okehampton	arr	8.37	11.06	-	2.53	4.49
Exeter (Cen)	arr	9.54	11.49	1.16	3.43	5.47
Waterloo	arr	2.02	3.30	4.43	7.28	10.08

(a)   *Change at Okehampton from Padstow, Launceston and Bude.*

(b)   *ACE non-stop Holsworthy (11.01 am) to Okehampton (attach Plymouth portion)*

(c)   *ACE . Non-stop from Launceston to Exeter (St.D)*

(d)   *Padstow (inc R. car until 17 Sept), also Bude except 24 Sept (change at Okehampton) and Plymouth*

bronzed!) holiday visitors were arriving back at Waterloo. The 'ACE' Up line series on these 1938 Saturdays started with the 10.10am from Ilfracombe, 10.22am Torrington, 10.25am Padstow, 10.30am Ilfracombe, ending with the 10.40am Bude (and Plymouth) all, except the last, with Dining Cars from the coast. Many passengers did use the early morning Launceston and Bude train; in those days the Saturday change-over system in hotels and boarding houses dictated vacation of rooms, often by 10.00am. The Southern National buses were coordinated to connect from (and to) Tintagel and Harlyn Bay etc. (carrying luggage on their roofs in those days) and taxis crowded the forecourts at Padstow, Bude and Wadebridge. The all stations 8.40am from Padstow and Bude (9.40am) with non-corridor local sets to Okehampton (connecting to Waterloo) accommodated those returning from St Kew

'West Country' Pacific No. 34030 'Watersmeet' brings the Padstow portion of the Friday 11.00 a.m. Waterloo 'ACE' into Otterham on 15th July 1960. The leading vehicles are in a Bulleid restaurant/buffet set (not in use) for the next day's Padstow Up 'ACE' working. Bowler-hatted Inspector Smith of Exmouth Junction is on the footplate of 'T9' No. 30719 waiting to leave on the Up loop with the 3.13 p.m. Padstow 'Perishables'. The wagons in the yard indicate the considerable fertilizer traffic to selected North Cornwall stations at this time. (R.C. Riley)

The Last Twenty Years 1945-1965

In comparison with the First World War, when extra services continued to run in the summer of 1915, the 1940 timetable showed none. The local passenger service from Okehampton, left largely intact, had to cater for those who came to Cornwall for holidays (and there were quite a few), and a much increased demand due to petrol rationing, evacuation and servicemen's travel. Continuation was not so basic as the SR restored through coaches and trains to meet demand up to 1945, as noted earlier.

When peace came in 1945 the SR was not nearly as short of resources as in 1918, but demand almost outstripped its ageing coaching fleet. Long queues formed at Waterloo for down trains on Saturdays in 1946 (they were *a mile-long* at Paddington) to meet a pent-up demand for seaside holidays once again. Many ex-servicemen brought their families to show them the scenes of their wartime postings. The weekday 10.50am Waterloo had already regained its Brake Composites to Padstow and Bude, with the former returning at 8.25am, making an eight hour journey to the capital in 1946. During the summer of 1947 a 12.20am Saturday relief train to Padstow and Bude could be laid on to ease the pressure on the 1.25am Newspaper train, which had gained through coaches to Padstow since 1942. The 10.50am Waterloo was relieved by a 10.20am on Saturdays. Well patronised, it was reported running on 10 July as a thirteen-coach train (ten, including Buffet-Restaurant pair for Padstow, and three for Bude). The 12.20 ran nonstop from Halwill to Launceston and again to Otterham. The 10.20am omitted Okehampton and minor stations. Over the years these were usually Maddaford Moor Halt, Ashwater, Tower Hill, Egloskerry and (sometimes) St Kew Highway.

Roof boards were officially restored from September 1947, new Bulleid stock and the employment of the 'West Country' 4-6-2s giving the 'At-

The 'Atlantic Coast Express' in one of many portions, or whole trains, served the North Cornwall line and Padstow from inception in 1926 until (except World War Two) 1964. in July 1959 Bulleid Pacific No. 34036 'Westward Ho' is about to leave at 8.30 a.m. for Exeter and Waterloo with a mixture of Maunsell and Bulleid corridors. (A.E.R. Cope)

lantic Coast Express' a new look, to use the contemporary term. The 'West Countries' could now turn, following the enlargement of Okehampton and Padstow turntables in 1947.

As in pre-Second World War days the weekday 'ACE' was multi-portioned again, though with differences. In 1948/9 winter timings and formations were: Waterloo dep 10.50am, Salisbury dep 12.36pm, Sidmouth Junction 2.11pm, Exeter Central arrive 2.29pm. At Salisbury a Seaton coach, and at Sidmouth Junction, Sidmouth and Exmouth (via Budleigh) coaches were detached. At Exeter the Restaurant car pair was removed and the train divided. After the Torrington and Ilfracombe coaches left at 2.34pm, the Plymouth, Padstow and Bude coaches (2+2+1) departed at 2.42pm. There were calls at St Davids and North Tawton to Okehampton where the Plymouth TCs were detached. It was then: 3.55pm all stations to Padstow (including Halwill to detach the Bude

Brake Composite), Launceston 4.52pm, Wadebridge 6.01pm and Padstow 6.22pm. Upwards the Padstow departure at 8.25am was followed by the Launceston call at 9.54am. Bude passengers endured a rather lengthy shunting process at Halwill whereby their through coach (on the front) and local Set were run-round by the 'M7' tank, then drawn back well clear of the up platform. This allowed the Padstow 'ACE' coaches (one Third Corridor and a Brake Composite) behind their 'West Country' to sweep round the curve from Ashwater and enter at 10.22am. Nine minutes were then taken up to attaching the Bude Brake Composite, and local set (through to Okehampton). The buckeye couplings required a resounding clash to engage after an agonizing slow approach! At this time there was no up Plymouth portion, so after a call at Okehampton (10.59/11.01am) and in contrast to the down journey, it was all stations (except Newton St Cyres)

NORTH CORNWALL SERVICES (Saturdays only 21 June - 20 September 1947)									
		(a)							
		am	am	am			am	am	am
WATERLOO	dep	12.20	10.20	10.50	Padstow			8.25	11.15
					Wadebridge	8.15	8.40		11.29
Okehampton	dep	5.30		3.55	Bude	9.05	9.35		12.15
Halwill	dep	5.58	3.13	4.30	Halwill	10.04	10.31		1.00
Bude	arr	6.49	3.55	5.09	Okehampton	10.42	11.05		1.37
Launceston	arr	7.33	4.51	6.01					
Padstow	arr	7.42	5.00	6.21	WATERLOO	3.25	*4.36*		6
(a)	*Runs when required*								

122

for an arrival at Exeter Central for 12 noon. The North Devon portion arrived at 12.28 and the combined train, with a Restaurant/Buffet set, went forward at 12.35pm to reach Waterloo at 4.36pm. From 1952 a Plymouth portion (dep Friary 9.59am) became the main train from Okehampton. It was now necessary for the station pilot to draw the North Cornwall coaches back into the Military sidings. The attachment process, as at Halwill, was repeated, all this occupying 22 minutes with much making and unmaking of the vacuum brakes, and attendant testing by the crew and guard. No wonder passengers felt they were not getting very far, and slowly at that!

In the Down direction it was a much simpler task to divide the 'ACE' at Sidmouth Junction Exeter, Okehampton and Halwill - the forwarding engine just backing on to the coaches left by the main train in the down platforms.

The Mondays to Fridays 'express' was restored in the summer of 1949 as the 10.35am from Waterloo (including a Restaurant/Buffet to Padstow on Fridays). With calls omitted at the stations mentioned before, Bude arrival (two coaches) was 4.20pm, Padstow's four coaches terminating at 5.17pm. The Restaurant Car was detached at Exeter (except Fridays) and a Plymouth portion at Okehampton. The up version of this 'ACE' left Padstow at 9.52am, Bude 10.58am, Exeter 12.50pm (Restaurant/Buffet) and arrived at Waterloo at 4.36pm. On Saturdays a 7.36am Waterloo to Padstow and Bude was running (with a Restaurant Car in 1950-53).

During the winter of 1949/50 the midday local train from Padstow, conveying the returning Newsvan and parcels van(s) was timed at 12.50pm for departure, and now included two coaches (returning from the overnight Newspaper train) for Waterloo. These went forward on the 4.30pm from Exeter. At this time of the year the through coaches on the 'ACE' and the 'News' were essentially 'local' west of Okehampton, hence a preponderance of all-stations calls (including Maddaford Moor). The consequential inconvenience of retimings on local trains at this end was, however, contributing to the loss of working people to buses and cars from the mid-1950s. There seemed to be little effort to study its effect, and the transfers of control from and to the Southern and Western Regions in 1950 and 1958 hardly helped. The Southern revamped the 'ACE's' point-to-point timings for the summer of 1952 and introduced its first 60 mph schedule between Waterloo and Salisbury. The 10.50am departure was restored to the familiar 11.00am. Padstow was reached at 4.54pm (vice 5.19pm) and the 8.30am up 'ACE' portion, though still leaving in the 12.30pm combination from Exeter, now arrived Waterloo at 3.40pm instead of 4.20pm.

The ACE's Waterloo departure now adhered to 11.00am until 1964 on Mondays to Fridays in the summer months. From 1959 there was an (at first unadvertised) separation, in July and August, when the Ilfracombe/

The King Arthur's Castle Hotel at Tintagel, built by Sir Robert Hardy and managed by a Mr. Taylor in the early years, opened at the turn of the century. It reflected the desire to accommodate high class visitors to the Atlantic coast following the opening of the railway to Camelford in 1893. Much of the material and furnishings were brought by John Fry's wagons from Camelford goods yard. (Author)

DOWN		am (a)	am (b)	am (c)	am (c)	pm	pm
WATERLOO	dep	12.45	1.15	10.35	11.15	1.00	3.00
Exeter (Cen)	dep	4.3	5.10	2.02	2.46	4.48	6.37
Okehampton	dep	5.22	6.25	-	3.40	5.51	7.40
Halwill	dep	5.54	7.16	3.07	4.17	6.26	8.18
Bude	arr	6.34	7.35	3.54	4.55	7.00	8.52
Padstow	arr	7.26	9.20	5.00	6.00	(d)	(e)

SATURDAY 20 JUNE to 5 SEPTEMBER 1964

(a) Through coaches to Ilfracombe, Torrington, Padstow and Bude
(b) Not advertised to Salisbury
(c) Through coaches to Padstow and Bude
(d) Wadebridge arrive 7.48pm
(e) Terminates Launceston at 8.42pm

UP		am	am (c)	am (d)	am (e)	pm	pm
Padstow	dep	(a)	(b)	8.30	11.00	1.00	-
Bude	dep	7.58	9.00	9.30	11.45	2.01	3.35
Halwill	dep	8.49	9.54	10.22	12.45	2.51	4.20
Okehampton	dep	9.35	10.22	11.00	1.11	3.40	5.06
Exeter (Cen)	dep	10.28	11.40	11.56	2.10	4.30	5.54
WATERLOO	arr	2.11	3.10	3.23	5.24	8.10	10.08

(a) Launceston depart 8.20am
(b) Wadebridge depart 8.10am
(c) Through coaches from Wadebridge, Bude, Mortehoe & Woolacombe 18 July to 29 August
(d) Through coaches from Padstow and Bude (attached at Halwill).
(e) Through coaches from Padstow and Bude (attached at Okehampton).

Torrington service departed at 11.05am. In the Up direction the Padstow/Bude separate train would run only on Mondays and Fridays (except during the height of the season). Padstow departure was generally at 9.30am and from Bude at 10.20am. In both directions local stations, as previously mentioned, were omitted. Generally no Restaurant/Buffet services were included, except on Fridays, when the 11.00am took (an unadvertised) pair through to Padstow convenient for a return on the busier Saturdays. Noticeably, on summer Sundays, though not named 'ACE', a through Brake Composite served Bude (arrive 5.23pm) and departed at 9.45am. Launceston benefited by con-

nections at Halwill. The missed-stops by the weekday schedules were catered for by the earlier 8.30am from Padstow, and a Down local from Okehampton varying from departures at 4.36pm in 1949 to 3.32pm in 1964.

The early 1950s were boom years for the 'ACE' and holiday trains, especially on Saturdays. The Western Region ran so many extras, funnelling them from the north and London through Taunton, Exeter and Newton Abbot, that it found itself in quite a fix on occasion. The Southern, coming the 'other way' through Exeter, was required to thread through the Western between St Davids and Cowley Bridge Junction - a potential source of delay. No evidence has been found

of advertised through coaches or trains from the Midlands or north to the Okehampton line. This would have meant reversal in St Davids, and the LSWR/SR were there only by sufferance. Changes of train there, especially on busy Saturdays, were discouraged, thus the Atlantic Coast from Westward Ho! to Harlyn Bay tended to become largely a London and Home Counties holiday preserve.

Rakes of LMS and LNER coaches did arrive in troop trains during World War Two, and after, especially to Bude, where the Army continued to maintain an anti-aircraft gun practice camp for Territorials. Up to sixteen coaches worked in that direction, assisted by the 1939 signalling alterations at Bude, whereas the North Cornwall could handle but twelve, rarely more than ten and usually eight coaches or less, in its loops. Ironically the Western Region's crack express, the 'Cornish Riviera' was diverted over the North Cornwall when the line was blocked at Wivelscombe. It was Wadebridge's role to divide it (and other Penzance services) into portions capable of 'N' Class haulage over the summits at Otterham and Meldon Junction. Short platforms, short loops (e.g. Launceston), restrictive signalling particularly where electrical release on starting signal was coupled to the (non-returnable) No 3 Tablets and infrequent water columns mitigated against long trains. In 1938 the pilot 4-4-0 (usually one of two 'T9s') on ten coach Down trains was detached at Camelford or Delabole, and at Meldon Junction or Okehampton from Up

The Southern National Omnibus Company tied its No. 122 coastal stage route Bude/Wadebridge to rail services at Camelford station for Camelford town, Tintagel and Boscastle. In June 1957 a single decker is leaving Boscastle on the 'new' road - necessarily keeping to the right hand to negotiate the hairpin bend. (Author)

In August 1939 the 10.40 a.m. (SO) Waterloo to Padstow through train is arriving at Wadebridge at 4.45 p.m. 'T9' No. 703 would have had assistance from Exeter to Camelford or Delabole with the ten-coach train which included a four-car dining set. On the right are several vans strung out from the goods shed, viz: LSWR ventilated, SR ventilated and an insulated (SR or LMS) probably to load meat, and (furthest) a GWR fitted van. (E.S. Youldon collection)

trains. Post-war 'West Countries' needed no assistance up to eight coaches, but two 'N' 2-6-0s were booked for eight or more. Tablet exchangers were unknown on the LSWR and SR. Consequently some deft hand exchanges took place at the lesser stations like Egloskerry - not always at the regulation 10mph! With some relaxation of restrictions on Meldon Viaduct in 1949 two 'N's were seen at Exeter on the 10.35am Waterloo in 1953, Nos. 31846 and 31841. Similarly 31836 and 31838 on the 10.45am Padstow - hauling nine coaches and 31833 took the 11.45am Bude through to Exeter. By this time the fleet of 'T9's was dwindling, and the 'L11's and 'S11's were going. From 1957 more use was being made of the 'West Counties' on these services.

The Southern Region continued to provide a fairly generous summer timetable as of yore, contemplating even in the early 1960s faster schedules and introducing new BR coaching stock, but the 'Beeching' threat loomed and control by the Western Region came in 1963. The new mobility of long distance motorists, aided by an expanding 'bed-and-breakfast' trade, would soon eclipse train travel. Even 'Luggage in Advance', carted by the railway to and from home and away

addresses, through coaches, connection buses, ready-waiting taxis, came to be regarded as cumbersome. Not that the motor car could travel much faster to the coast. The notorious Exeter Bypass and the narrow A30 through Honiton and Okehampton were headline news. After the 1952 accelerations Padstow, with the 3 hour 5 minute Waterloo-Exeter 'sprint' and an hour to Okehampton together with the omitted local stops, was still over six hours from Waterloo. This was rarely bettered, though remarkably in the winter of 1964/5 a 5 hour 40 minute journey was possible off the 10.30am Paddington, by a change at Exeter St Davids.

In 1963, timed at 11.00am from Waterloo, the through summer Mondays to Fridays train shed the Restaurant/Buffet set at Exeter Central. Calling only at St Davids, North Tawton, Okehampton and Halwill it then omitted the usual minor stations to Wadebridge, arriving Padstow at 5.00pm. The Up service left Padstow at 9.33am with a similar pattern of stops and timings. BR figures compiled in support of closure proposals throw interesting light on the 11.00am on Saturday 13 July 1963. 87 were in the train at Halwill (or joined it), twelve alighted at Launceston, twenty six at

Camelford, thirty six at Wadebridge and twenty six at Padstow. The numbers joining it were only two at Launceston, but fifteen at Wadebridge. The 9.33am took on sixteen from Padstow, twelve joined at Wadebridge, five at Camelford, five at Launceston, twenty eight at Halwill (eighteen from the 10.20am Bude connection) and there were sixty seven continuing (or alighting) at Okehampton. Very few people (if any) used the other stops. The Mon/Fri numbers averaged thirty going through in comparison, even the 12.30am Waterloo Saturday morning bringing only sixteen for Port Isaac Road (a party?), six for Wadebridge and nineteen for Padstow. The all-stations 8.30am Padstow (and 9.30am Bude) produced one hundred and ninety eight at Okehampton on the Saturday, all going forward in the through coaches. The 7.28am Waterloo to Padstow only had thirty two people on board at Halwill, nearly all for Camelford and Wadebridge.

This, the penultimate summer service from/to Waterloo, showed only too well the deterioration of usage compared with only ten years earlier. Small wonder the WR calculated there would be little hardship if summer holiday trains were curtailed, though nearly two hundred passengers with their suitcases, would be an embarrassment at Okehampton.

The 1964 summer service retained most of the extras, the period lasting from 15 June to 6 September. The 11.05am Waterloo 'ACE' ran Mondays to Fridays, as before, also the 10.35am (SO) to Padstow (still running non-stop from St Davids to Halwill). Through coaches had ceased to serve Bude from June 1963 (also Torrington and Plymouth) on Mondays to Fridays. The Southern Region was still providing the stock for the three through trains (or portions) each way, happily in familiar green livery and, by now, there had been an influx of BR Mark 1 coaches in three car sets. The 11.00 or 11.05 Waterloo to Padstow 'ACE', also the 10.35am on Saturdays, consisted of a mixture of these and odd Bulleid coaches up to 5-set. Bude still retained through coaches on these summer Saturdays (usually two or three) but there were no more separate trains. The 'West Countries' were in charge, a BR Class 4 2-6-4T (and some 'N' Class) mostly working Halwill/Bude. On the final Saturday, 5 September, the 11.00am Padstow 'ACE' left with six BR Mark 1 coaches behind 34023 'Blackmore Vale'. A BR Class 3 tank brought up two coaches

from Bude and attached them at Okehampton. The 'Atlantic Coast Express' had lasted thirty eight years and the old 'North Cornwall Express' had started in 1900. The halcyon years had been the late 1930s when Padstow and Bude both would have 'Refreshment' car trains, with down trains arriving late into Saturday evenings, while the attractions of Bude were such that a Waterloo, Salisbury to Exeter train then ran non-stop to Holsworthy!

The through coach rather lost its identity west of Okehampton on the regular 'ACE', as it pottered through Tower Hill and St Kew, yet it was only five hours or so since it left the sight of 'Big Ben' and the tenements of Lambeth. It would leave a London fog and enter a different, soaking wet one, covering the high ground at Otterham. But the 'Southern' was always associated with sunshine, and the 'ACE' between capital and seaside promised the joys of paddling in rock pools, giant sand castles or a walk along the cliffs. This intimate link has gone forever.

This was not quite the end of holiday trains, however. Recognising perhaps, that a few hundred passengers presenting themselves and their lug-

gage at Okehampton and Exeter St Davids would present problems, the WR instituted a summer Saturdays through train to Ilfracombe and Bude. This was part of an 11.05 Paddington, and ran each Saturday from 19 June to 4 September 1965. Routed via Westbury, Yeovil and Exeter Central, it arrived at Bude at 16.11. Upwards it left Bude at 1.055 and the five-coaches and the Ilfracombe portion duly arrived at Paddington at 16.10, by the same route. Engine power in the west was either an NBL 63XX or Hymek 70XX. The Bude through train had no North Cornwall connection, but Saturday London connections with a change at Exeter St. Davids, otherwise London connections from Paddington involved one change, at Exeter St Davids.

In 1966 there were no through trains in the 'emergency' timetable, except that Bude gained a 14.15 from Exeter Central, and an 11.10 up train to Exeter on Saturdays 18 June to 3 September. Fast running St Davids/ Okehampton and omission of Maddaford Moor and Ashbury stops by these railcar connections were the last vestige of any concern for holiday passengers to North Cornwall. Ironically neither gave nor received connections to or from the Padstow line!

Wadebridge Quay in the 1880s, then owned by the LSWR after the legalities of 1886 confirmed its purchase of the B&WR in 1846. It had opened in 1834 and the siding emerging from between the houses (left centre) curved sharply to each side of the two docks and to the river frontage (right). The two sheerleg cranes were for loading granite blocks from wagon to dockside, thence to ships' holds. The terraces in Eddystone Road (centre right) echo the use of the De Lank granite for the lighthouse, moreover for some of London's bridges, and smaller products were still being sent (by rail) up to the 1960s. (R.I.C.)

Chapter Six

FERTILIZERS, CATTLE, MERCHANDISE AND COAL BY TRAIN

During the 1880s the LSWR was dispatching 'fast' goods trains from Nine Elms depot every night, including a 10.30pm to Exeter. Wagons from the latter were put on to a 5.30am to Devonport, again 'fast' - though in reality limited-stop - calling at Okehampton at 6.18am. In turn for Holsworthy and the new 1886 Launceston branch, wagons were formed into a 6.43am goods train. More shunts at Halwill, performed by the Launceston engine (having come up at 6.40) enabled wagons to arrive at Launceston at 9.30am. Before this activity Halwill was already alive with the noise of buffers as a 2.45am from Devonport was sorting. It had brought mail from Yeoford (transferred at Okehampton) coal and merchandise from Plymouth, and a transferred road box from Exeter. In 1886 and 1887 it apparently ran as a 'mixed' train on the last Wednesday of the month from Okehampton to Launceston.

The 1889 Railway Regulation Act severely curtailed the running of mixed trains. Up to then a passenger coach might well be at the rear of a line of loose coupled wagons. After 1889 the coach had to be behind the engine and equipped with automatic brakes. All mixed trains then had to be listed in the WTT. Several trains were mixed between Wadebridge and Padstow, in due course, and in 1914 the 5.20am goods from Halwill to Wadebridge could convey a passenger coach on most Mondays. There is a distinction between mixed trains as regulated and those 'apparently mixed', which include goods wagons with vacuum brakes or a through pipe. Even the latter have to comply with regulations on the number of axles allowed.

The opening to Delabole brought a necessary reorganisation to the goods service. From December 1893 a through train commenced running from Exeter Queen St. leaving at 1.00am, seven days a week. It conveyed mail, road boxes and urgent traffic and was limited to 25 wagons from Yeoford to Camelford where it terminated at 6.50am. A supplementary train left Okehampton at 7.38am taking 'ordinaries', arriving at Delabole at 11.17am. Upwards, road boxes returning to London, Exeter and Plymouth left Delabole at 1.00pm and at Okehampton were held from 6.40pm until 8.00pm for transfer to the Plymouth-Nine Elms overnight goods (arriving 3.53am). A second goods left Delabole at 6.55pm and worked its way up to Okehampton dealing with purely local traffic until 10.55pm. Okehampton engine shed was under enlargement and able to cope with increased working to Holsworthy/Delabole. Adams '395' 0-6-0s and a handful of Beyer Peacock single-framed 0-6-0s hauled these goods trains up and down the 1 in 73 gradients with the assistance of one (some-

The 1.15 p.m. goods from Bude having arrived at Halwill (in the distance) at 4.52 p.m. had there awaited the 12.10 p.m. goods from Wadebridge. Cattle wagons and the more urgent traffic from both lines are now seen behind the tender of 'N' Class No. 31846 on the Bude train, photographed soon after departure at 6 p.m. on 4th August 1964. These front wagons, including the cattle, would be transferred at Yeoford to the 12.45 p.m. Torrington to Feltham Yard, the remainder continuing to Exmouth Junction sidings. (P.W. Gray)

The mainstay of the freight traffic to Wadebridge in the final years was fertilizer in sacks from Avonmouth. The line of wagons on the Quay in July 1964 shows how heavily it had developed. This end of the Quay was owned by the Padstow Harbour Commissioners, the stores on the right erected about 1899. (C.J. Knowles-Thomas)

times two) 10 ton brake vans. Goods guards and travelling shunters staffed most trains, their expertise tested to the full in controlling long trains of loose-coupled wagons when descending from, say, Otterham towards Launceston. Wagon hand brakes would be 'pinned down' as required to prevent a train actually pushing its engine out of control and a guard, often called brakesman, would ever be at his wheel to avoid snatching of couplings. The latter was usually the cause of divided trains if a coupling broke under strain. In spite of regulation, or through carelessness, wagon runaways did occur at Halwill and Otterham, as recounted elsewhere. In February 1905 a goods train became divided in the section between Ashbury and Halwill Junction. The rear half, after a while, gained momentum and crashed into the front half on the level crossing at Halwill, causing damage and destruction to 22 wagons. The engine was thrust the length of the platform and the fireman sustained serious injuries.

The Devonport goods by 1896 worked into Launceston and turned around there between 7.30 and 9.00am. Then it meandered its way back to Devonport taking nearly twelve hours in the process. This cross-country train appeared in the WTT up to the First War, though by 1914 it ran only if required. Meldon Junction was an important staging place in those years, though there were only two long sidings, one on each Up side of the junction points to Halwill. Most trains stopped to exchange wagons. The noc-

turnal 1.00am from Exeter spent from 3.40 to 4.50am there in 1899 taking on wagons from the Plymouth line. What it must have been like up there, nearly 1,000 feet above sea level on the edge of Dartmoor, in bad weather and in darkness, is beyond conjecture. The reason for its existence would seem the need to avoid taking trains into and out of Okehampton. Certain down trains were booked for banking assistance up the 1 in 77 from Okehampton. Meldon Junction sidings ceased to figure in the 1920s (though retained as refuges for goods

trains) probably after the arrival of the more powerful 'N' engines and 25 ton brake vans, and with more use made of Okehampton.

When at last the North Cornwall line opened into Wadebridge in June 1895, the LSWR could establish a suitable terminal for goods operation - a sizeable engine shed with turntable, some new sidings and use of the existing B & W Quay sidings. Bodmin, Wenford Bridge, Ruthern Bridge, and an exchange point at Boscarne Junction (although GWR goods trains ran into Wadebridge), also offered poten-

The 1.30am ex-Waterloo, with a train of through coaches, Newsvan and Road Boxes, snaking its way across country near Port Issac Road in May 1956. (Rail Archive Stephenson)

128

A new role for Exmouth Junction's versatile 'N' Class (working from Wadebridge depot) in 1964, concerned haulage of Wenford and Marland clay from Boscarne Junction to Lostwithiel. Here is No. 31849 climbing up to Bodmin General, assisted by No. 31840 at the rear on 5th May 1964. (S.C. Nash)

tial i.e. inward merchandise, coal, manure, cattle and, at this stage, limited china clay traffic. Of the latter, that which came down from Wenford was shipped mostly from the Quay but, additionally, granite blocks from the De Lank Quarries above Wenford began to be routed over the North Cornwall to London. Fish from Padstow (by road until 1899) and Port Isaac, and the Delabole slate joined the already thriving general goods traffic upwards from Launceston. Movement of cattle, fairly sparse in 1895 but soon to increase considerably, and the beginnings of a fresh meat and produce trade to London completed the picture. Adams 'Jubilee' 0-4-2 mixed traffic engines were sent to Wadebridge to assist the existing '395' 0-6-0s. The 'Jubilees' were equipped with steam sanding gear, much appreciated on the steep hills up to Otterham and Halwill Junction.

Two down morning, and two up, set a general pattern on the North Cornwall for the rest of its existence. Based on Exeter Queen Street (later Exmouth Junction sidings) Okehampton and Wadebridge, these trains exchanged wagons into the Nine Elms 'fast' services, with the North Devon line at Crediton (later at Yeoford), at Okehampton/Meldon

Junction with the Plymouth line, and locally for Bude at Halwill Junction. Although traffic passed to the GWR at Exeter, the LSWR would primarily route Midland counties wagons via Templecombe and the S&DJR, but otherwise Basingstoke served for the GWR and from the 1920s wagons went via Woking and the new Feltham yard (vice Willesden LNWR) to the northern and eastern lines. Padstow was served locally from Wadebridge, but the Bude line had its own services to and from Okehampton and Exeter.

From the beginning of the century long distance movement of cattle from west Devon and North Cornwall grew considerably. The Exeter dealer William Harris began buying in livestock from the existing markets at Holsworthy, Launceston, Camelford and Wadebridge; the LSWR encouraged it and, in due course, was taking store cattle to eastern England (private sales) and to Chichester market. Fat cattle were destined for Maiden Lane LNWR where the London (Smithfield) abattoirs were located. In 1909, special-notice empty wagons were sent down from Exeter at 5.50am (Launceston 10.09 arrival). At 2.30pm a special worked through to Crediton and Exeter (arrive 5.23pm) where wagons were put on a Monday night spe-

cial leaving at 6.15pm for Fratton LSWR, to be taken on by the LBSCR to Chichester fortnightly market. A second 3.00pm left Wadebridge to take Exeter-bound cattle and to clear ordinary goods wagons as far as Halwill, thence Crediton, for the Midlands and London, the engine returning light to Wadebridge. These special arrangements still applied in 1914 and into World War One - vitally in 1917, for the German submarine menace was seriously threatening Britain's food supplies in that year. Both a 2.40pm Launceston, and a 2.55pm Wadebridge Special were augmenting the regular goods services, as well as from the Bude line. By 1919 only one 'special notice' running survived, a 2.00pm relief from Wadebridge to Launceston only. After 1921 cattle sales declined considerably, not to revive until the early 1930s.

Goods Services between the Wars 1920-1939

In the mid-1920s the Goods and Mail train left Exeter Queen Street at 12.05am (it still called briefly at Meldon Junction in 1924) and entered Launceston at 5.55am. The second goods, with transferred Nine Elms, Plymouth and Exeter road boxes, left Okehampton at 5.55am arriving at

		am	pm	pm
Torrington	dep			12.45
Wadebridge	dep	11.43		
Bude	dep		12.55	
Halwill Junction	arr	5.35pm	4.54	
Halwill Junction	dep	6.05	5.50	
Okehampton	arr	7.10	6.25	
Crediton	dep		7.10	7.27
Exmouth Junction	arr		8.30	
Nine Elms	arr			2.58am

Wadebridge at 1.53pm. There was some re-organisation to services from 1925 when the new 'N' Moguls were introduced, and Exmouth Junction sidings to the east of Exeter became the focal point for London and west of England exchanges. The up morning goods, formerly Launceston to Devonport, and later Wadebridge to Exeter, ceased to run, replaced by an afternoon service. The main Up services from Bude and Wadebridge were timed to exchange wagons at Halwill Junction. The importance of these trains should be seen in the context of the road box system, shortly to be described. Upwards, there was livestock for the Midlands (via Templecombe) Salisbury, Basingstoke, Woking and Maiden Lane (LMSR), market produce for Nine Elms, fresh meat (Launceston and Halwill) to Nine Elms, with 'ordinary' wagons transferred at Crediton. The Halwill loops were filled as rafts of wagons were taken from the Wadebridge train and placed on the back of the 12.55pm Bude. This went on six days a week, year in, year out, until the end of freight working in 1964, though most 'perishable' traffic and two primary Nine Elms road boxes were speeded up from the 1930s by attachment to the two mid-afternoon passenger trains from Padstow and Bude.

These 'road boxes' or 'road vans', long employed by most railway companies, carried sundry merchandise such as groceries and perishable goods of an urgent or semi-urgent nature. The earlier LSWR 10-ton brakes were also goods vans for this purpose - the guard having direct charge of their contents. However with increased business and a need for a heavier brake-force, the use of this type of van died out by the 1920s, though 18 and 20-ton vans (of 1906-11) still retained a goods compartment. During the early 1920s 24-ton vans, referred to as 'New', were put on to certain North Cornwall line trains, concurrently with heavier loading provided by the 'N' 2-

6-0s. They were followed by the familiar SR 25-ton brakes termed 'New Heavy' vans. The midnight Exeter - Launceston Goods and Mail was an example, using a 'New Heavy' on Nos 4 and 5 services and returning on the 5.00pm up Goods from Wadebridge. LSWR box vans, fitted with vacuum brake and oil-filled axle boxes (i.e. not grease) took on the role of the road boxes. With ventilators they were suitable for market produce and, with modification, the meat carcase traffic. Introduced about 1910 they lasted until replaced by SR versions in the 1930s.

The Road Box System

In 1930 the down 'Tavvy', the 9.32pm (8.33pm SO) from Nine Elms included road boxes for stations Launceston to St Kew Highway (No 26), Ashbury/Halwill (No 27), Okehampton and stations to Bude (No 28). Arriving at Okehampton at 4.53am, No 26 working, a box from Exeter for Launceston and all stations to Wadebridge (No 242), and a box from Plymouth Friary (No 288) were made up into a 5.55am departure. It called only at Halwill and Launceston, then all stations to Wadebridge, except Tresmeer. The latter station was served by Egloskerry. A road box (No 209) from Templecombe (3.52pm) was transferred in the early hours to the Launceston goods and Mail at Okehampton leaving at 4.00am, thence from Launceston on the 8.38am to Wadebridge. In this case it was a non-vacuum van. Lastly the 3.26am from Exmouth Junction to Bude left Okehampton at 7.38am taking No 27, the London - Halwill box with goods for Ashbury, Ashwater, Tower Hill and the stations on the Torrington branch; No 28 was London - Bude; No 243 Exeter - Bude and No 286 Plymouth - Bude. A similar system operated in the up direction, the principal trains being the 11.15am from Wadebridge, the 12.53pm from Bude and the 7.27pm from Crediton to Nine Elms. An interesting Road Box

working (No 275) concerned a through van from Bude (6.57am dep) to Bristol LMS. It spent a long time getting there, lingering at Exmouth Junction and Honiton between transfers, and arriving at Bristol about 48 hours later!

Cattle, Meat, Fish and China Clay

Cattle, or livestock as the Southern Railway termed it (to cover sheep/lambs and horses for slaughter as well as cows) began moving again in quantity from about 1932. Pigs, not good travellers, were rarer and in any case were more likely to be killed locally on farms and their carcases sent by rail - therefore pork! There was a steady trade of 'baconers' to Harris' factory at Calne. Carriage of horses for slaughter was spasmodic. They were strictly regulated (as to numbers per wagon) and were never a popular loading task for station staff. Best horses, the gentrys' and farmers' pride, went by special horse boxes to the numerous shows. It was said that farmers wouldn't let them walk far on these occasions and a box would be taken merely from Egloskerry into Launceston. Most horse box wagons were attached to passenger trains, but for big events such as Launceston Horse Show, the Holsworthy and Stratton Agricultural Show, or the prestigious Royal Cornwall (then movable year-to-year) there would be much rail activity. The LSWR and SR provided 'Prize' or special cattle wagons (with owner's compartments) from wherever, not just locally, as well as demonstration agricultural machinery on flat wagons. If the Royal Cornwall was at Launceston or Wadebridge, extra shunting power came from Exmouth Junction (often a 'K10' 4-4-0). The normal cattle market aftermaths are described in the stations chapter. Again, an extra shunting engine would be needed for the constant marshalling into the cattle pens, and making up specials. Pathways for the livestock specials rarely now showed in the WTT, for they were timed by Special Notice. During World War Two the Ministry of Food was the sole buyer of livestock, and slaughtering was permitted only in selected inland centres. Consequently the number of livestock specials increased at the expense of fresh meat forwardings. The late afternoon goods would take as many wagons as possible, even the 3.15pm Padstow Perishables and Passenger would take some (within the limit of the T9's capability) from Launceston to Halwill. Otherwise a special would run, headed by a 'K10' or 'L11' through to Exeter. Empty wagons were held at Yeoford for distribution as required.

Post-1945, cattle were dispatched to Boston (for sea transport to Europe) and Easingwold (Yorks). Ministry controls eased in 1954 and local slaughtering was again permitted. A new enlarged slaughterhouse opened at Halwill, and Jaspers of North Petherwin started loading at Launceston for London (Smithfield). Demountable rail/road containers appeared in the late 1930s, but it was from the 1950s that exclusive use was made of them for fresh meat traffic. The 3.15pm from Padstow would take some (as did the similar 3.13pm from Bude). The locomotivemen's strike in 1955 caused the first dent in this lucrative traffic, though it remained buoyant into the 1960s. With the freeing of road licensing restrictions, and the withering of rail freight traffic generally, cumulating with withdrawal of services in September 1964, the juggernaut took over. Today, the meat trade is quite different, being concentrated on only a few large abattoirs in the west of England, and dependent completely on road transport.

Significantly five fish vans were involved in the Tresmeer accident in November 1898 and the Up goods had been delayed by their attachment at Port Isaac Road. The previous year, in October, 150 tons of herrings had been dispatched, presumably in some fifteen wagons, brought up from Port Isaac quay in carts and wagons by local farmers. As long as the autumn herring seasons lasted, certainly into the 1930s, both Port Isaac and Padstow were well served by the LSWR and SR taking this highly perishable trade to Exeter, London and the Midlands. Although there were undoubtedly fish 'specials' before this date, not until 1927 did the timetable show conditional train runnings. Empties from Exeter arrived at Padstow at 10.25am and were loaded for despatch at 4.40pm, passing Okehampton at 7.27pm. The up train was re-engined at Exmouth Junction (in 1932 this apparently took only nine minutes between 8.13 and 8.22pm). The 1938 timetable shows no fish special times. The herring seasons declined but Lowestoft and Grimsby trawlers were still producing catches of white fish for auction in Padstow Fish Shed up to the early 1940s. A mid-afternoon passenger train ran for many years from Padstow and Bude, but from 1924 the portions were separated into two trains, available to take rail traffic of a perishable nature. Both ran through to Exeter Queen Street behind 'T9' or 'S11' 4-4-0s. As far as goods traffic was concerned, any attached vans were 'passenger' rated (referred to as 'XP') so that fish vans from Padstow, rabbit vans serving almost all North Cornwall stations, and some meat vans, mainly from Wadebridge, Launceston and Halwill, were accorded a faster and guaranteed run to Exeter for the overnight fast goods services. Very little tonnage of china clay went to the east by rail. Most of the output from Stannon Pit (piped to the driers at Wenford) was taken via Boscarne Junction, and the GWR to Fowey after 1946. Only small coasting vessels could use Wadebridge and Padstow and, although the LSWR was co-operative, at one time even supplying special containers for transit, transhipments never rose above a weekly shipload or so. Oddly enough, in the 1960s, a considerable tonnage of clay was traversing the whole length of the North Cornwall on the way from Meath, in North Devon to Fowey, following the demise of Fremington Quay near Barnstaple.

Although livestock forwardings had declined in the 1920s, there was a rising demand for fresh meat in the cities. The Southern Railway speeded up overnight delivery to the markets from 1927. A new service at 7.30pm from Exeter Queen Street Goods Yard was in to Nine Elms at 12.51am, two hours earlier than the 12.45pm Torrington, the principal carrier west of Exeter. The exchange of vehicles at Halwill around 5.00pm continued, whereby Bude and Wadebridge/Launceston market-vans were in due course forwarded for attachment to the Torrington train at Crediton (7.29pm). However a number of vans, mostly of meat but some flower and horticultural products, were now put on the rear of the 3.06pm Padstow passenger and

About to pass under Delabole Barton bridge in June 1957 is 4-6-2 No. 34033 'Chard' working the 11.15 a.m. Wadebridge to Okehampton goods. Use of the light Pacifics on goods working was not uncommon on the North Cornwall line. (Photomatic)

131

'perishables' at Halwill. This train left at 5.17pm arriving at Exeter Queen Street at 6.32pm in time for the above-mentioned 7.30pm fast goods. The 11.35am Wadebridge in fact had road boxes or vans for Nine Elms, Plymouth Friary and Exeter, continuing to Okehampton. The Exeter boxes, also from Bude and a Bude to Bristol (LMS), went forward on the 10.10pm from Okehampton (the 5.00pm Wadebridge to Salisbury, calling at Templecombe). All these operations were subject to prompt despatch by local staff, as for passengers, but with the added element of some smart shunting. To assist, the SR published summaries of wagon formations in the WTT.

The revival of cattle sales traffic in the 1930s was indicated by a Special Notice pathway on Tuesdays (Launceston Market) at 2.36pm, to relieve the 11.35am Wadebridge, and to run to Exeter if necessary. This was in the summer of 1938, with the 11.35 itself retired on Saturdays to leave at 10.50am. These amendments, and on the Bude line, below Halwill, were to accommodate the extra holiday trains from Waterloo to Padstow/Bude in the afternoons. The down London newspaper traffic expanded in the 1930s concurrent with a 'circulation war'. Although passenger-rated, specially allocated bogie vans served Bude and the North Cornwall stations. The 5.55am Okehampton goods attached these vans from the 1.30am Waterloo to Plymouth News. Together with the Nine Elms and Friary for stations to St Kew and Wadebridge Road Boxes and a limited tail of wagons, it was smartly timed down to Launceston, in 25 minutes from Halwill. Ashwater's tablet to Launceston was left in a special box, and signals lowered the night before by departing signalmen - an uncommon arrangement. The newsvan was transferred to the 7.45am Launceston to Padstow (arrive 9.03am). Otherwise in 1938, apart from the time-honoured early down (and the afternoon up) trains with their 'vacuum' wagons, there ran a 10.15am goods from Okehampton and a 5.00pm back from Wadebridge. Both meandered through north Cornwall and west Devon picking up and setting down 'ordinary' wagons, reminding us of the very local nature of rail transit in these times. A truckload of hay might go only from St Kew to Launceston, or a load of bricks from Whitstone (on the Bude Branch) to Otterham, and there were always the 'empties' for return to a distant colliery or - by 1938 - a tank wagon to a petrol distributor.

Wartime Pressures
No part of Britain really escaped the Second World War. The North Corn-

wall in 1940 lay well within the range of German airfields in Brittany and a number of raids occurred as well as numerous 'alerts'. Bodmin was hit but the local lines escaped. The 1941 Blitz on Plymouth, however, had a direct reaction on Wadebridge and the NCR's useful alternative way round the destruction. It happened in April and the GWR was severely blocked. For a total of eleven days, in five periods, passenger and goods trains were diverted off the Cornwall main line at Bodmin Road, reversals taking place there, at Bodmin GWR, at Wadebridge and, eventually, at Exeter St Davids. GWR engines could not work on the North Cornwall (until 1943) a matter of footsteps and outside cylinders fouling the gauge. The ubiquitous 'N' 2-6-0s therefore stood in, Wadebridge bearing the brunt of these operations while the GWR 2-6-2Ts and 0-6-0Ts, having brought their trains over the hilltop at Bodmin, were replaced by the 'N's or SR 4-4-0s with the necessary re-arrangement of goods trains. The prolonged 1 in 75 gradients up to Delabole - 650 feet to be climbed in ten miles - proscribed loads in excess of 29 wagons and brake van.

Even in 1939 building materials and Government stores started to arrive at Wadebridge and Padstow for an Anti-Aircraft Practice Camp established at St. Eval, later an RAF Coastal Command base. St Merryn airfield, above Padstow, and a gunnery range at Treligga (Delabole) followed. In 1942 runways were laid on Davidstow Moor, rail-served from Otterham. Most wagons were sent by normal goods services, but the smaller NCR station yards were sorely tried. This was when Tower Hill came to life again, regaining its loop and two new gated sidings. The ammunition and stores were for the US army, preparing for the Normandy Invasion in June 1944. Once again the 'N's shouldered the burden. The spur between the two Launceston stations, also opened in 1943, was for these trains to pass from Tower Hill (and Halwill) to Tavistock Junction yard and Plymouth. The 'N's would take them into Launceston SR, a pair of GWR 45XX 2-6-2Ts then attaching to the rear to take the spur directly towards Lifton.

Livestock traffic continued, and increased until by 1944 it was double that of 1939 with many more sheep, even the difficult pigs. Ironically, fresh meat was being sent into the west, such was the slaughtering policy and food rationing system. Coal was diverted by rail and none arrived by sea at Padstow or Wadebridge after 1940. As a precaution a large coal dump was laid down at Delabole - there was plenty of room in the yard and demand for roofing slate rose as a result of

bomb damage in England. Normal exchange traffic between the companies was prohibited at Launceston, only special traffic as above, but the situation altered after Nationalization in 1948, as detailed elsewhere.

It is recounted that one evening there were three trains to be brought into Launceston from Tower Hill. The SR driver said he would bring the last two down as one, providing Launceston was clear. This done, two pairs of 45XX took the wagons on to Plymouth.

Road Transport Triumphs
Freight traffic remained quite heavy into the 1950s, in fact bulk commodities - coal, grain (maize) and animal feeds - actually increased. Outwards a flow of sugar beet started to East Anglia and Kidderminster, a trade unknown in pre-war days. With farm subsidies, especially for those fields on poorer land as might be found in the semi-moorlands, bagged artificial fertilizers came by the trainload. The number of wagons on hand sometimes reached embarrassing levels, but this was seasonal. All this time, however, such staples as building materials and general merchandise gradually seeped away to road transport. Easing of restrictive long distance 'A' licensing and abolition of 'C' licensed short-haul road transport operations from the 1950s with its unassailable door to door flexibility, was bound to have an effect. In 1938 the four big railway companies had campaigned for the relaxation of their Common Carrier requirement, that is carriage (without refusal) of many classes of goods and at published rates. It was too easy for a road haulier to study these rates and undercut them. The Common Carrier legislation was only replaced in 1963...

The two goods services in the down direction continued until cessation in September 1964. The twelve midnight Goods and Mail from Exmouth Junction with its main calls at Yeoford, Okehampton and Halwill, still terminated at Launceston but in the 1960s was later by an hour, at 7am. Letter Mail, Exeter and Plymouth road boxes, the 'Western Morning News' (ex-Plymouth) and calf traffic dictated timings. The 1.30am Waterloo Newspaper train (5.55am off Okehampton) now had through coaches to Padstow, and a collection of vacuum and loose goods vehicles to Launceston. The second goods train was more ordinary and worked all day on the North Cornwall line, finally arriving Wadebridge at 7pm.

Upwards, the 11.35am from Wadebridge, noted over the years for its 'meet' at Halwill Junction with its counterpart from Bude between 5 and 6pm, continued in the post-1945 period to forward North Cornwall livestock exports to London and eastern England. As mentioned elsewhere, fresh meat was regarded now as passenger-rated insofar as the vans were taken by the respective 3.15pm Perishable and Passenger trains from Padstow and Bude. The vans were away from Exeter at 7.30pm to Templecombe and Nine Elms, whereas cattle wagons went on to the 12.45am Torrington at Crediton. Latterly Feltham Yard received them, via Woking, being the main sorting yard on the Southern for north and eastern England. Alas, here too the traffic declined, accelerated by the footplatemen's strike in 1955, and had all but ceased by 1964. Meat vans were succeeded by demountable containers soon after the war and by 1960 the abattoirs at Launceston, Wadebridge, Halwill (and Holsworthy) were producing a sizeable tonnage for rail transit. The development of specialized refrigerated road transport of meat sealed the fate of the insulated containers and they ceased running from the west in 1965.

Blocks of wagons of fertilizer from Avonmouth would appear in season on the down morning goods trains, and there was a rise in coal carryings in the 1960s around July and August, the NCB offering 'summer prices'. The empties from these trundled back on the 5.00pm goods from Wadebridge, reaching Okehampton about 9pm. This train terminated at Exmouth Junction and later Salisbury.

The value of diversionary routes was proved again in 1963 following a slip at Wivelscombe between St Germans and Saltash. GWR goods trains were again sent via the North Cornwall line to Exeter.

Consternation at proposals by the Western Region to withdraw all freight services from the North Cornwall and Bude lines from September 1964 brought visits by Launceston and Holsworthy traders to Paddington to protest. Launceston's goods facilities would be retained, but the locals were concerned at the loss of Ashwater and Camelford. Launceston could be reconnected to Lydford, as will be seen, and Wadebridge was still linked to Cornwall via Boscarne Junction. The Western Region was adamant on closure. The bulk traffic which loomed so large in the 1960s was obtained by BR at a below cost contract. Total losses per month were running at £6,000. Worse, local road hauliers, aware of the prices, were undercutting even at loss to themselves. For bulk agricultural feeds and fertilizers, eight-ton lorries were stationed at Launceston and Wadebridge to deliver to existing warehouses along the line, or direct to farms. The Sundries traffic had ceased in the 1960s, victim again of road transport.

Matters at Launceston was complicated. From 31 December 1962 WR passenger services Plymouth-Launceston had ceased to run. At first the portion from Tavistock South to

Lifton was retained for milk traffic (including Ambrosia's) and henceforward served from the SR main line via the wartime connection at Lydford. The Lifton-Launceston (North Goods) track was retained, though closed. A bizarre situation now arose whereby the Launceston engine (now an Ivatt 2-6-2T) ran light to Meldon Junction, reversed to Lydford to work the Tavistock South Goods, thence to Lifton to collect milk tanks for Plymouth. Freight from Exmouth Junction ceased to run west of Okehampton from 9 September 1964 (and to Tavistock South from 26 September). However as Launceston was to be retained as a railhead for wagonload traffic, to serve it the Lifton-Launceston line re-opened. Wagons were brought from Tavistock Junction, on the outskirts of Plymouth, via Bere Alston and across at Lydford. By this time trains were in the hands of the NBL 63XX diesels. This service lasted until 28 February 1966, the North (ex-GWR) sidings being clipped out immediately. The South (ex-SR) yard was taken out of use in the following July. Both places (and the Launceston passenger stations) have been obliterated by spreading industrial premises.

Wadebridge retained full load facilities until 17 December 1978, served by a daily train from St Blazey which also handled the china clay from Wenford Bridge. A Class 08 diesel shunter was employed on this, the clay traffic lasting until September 1983.

The 6.00 a.m. limited stop goods to Launceston from Okehampton eventually reached Wadebridge about 1.00 p.m. in May 1935. Here, 'N' Class No. 1829 brings it past the North Cornwall Down outer home signal. At the rear were overnight Nine Elms to St. Kew local, Friary/ Wadebridge, and Templecombe/Wadebridge 'road boxes'. (H.C. Casserley)

Chapter Seven

MOTIVE POWER ON THE NORTH CORNWALL

'Steamroller' (380 Class) at Exmouth Junction in 1923. No. 0162 (ex-388) was built by Beyer Peacock in 1879 and was commonly seen in the 1890s, during World War I, and just after, at Okehampton on mixed-traffic duties. It was withdrawn in 1925. (Stephenson Locomotive Society)

Initially goods trains on the Okehampton to Holsworthy branch were in the hands of Beattie 0-6-0s, the turntable at the terminus being only 42ft in diameter. William Adams had provided three new Class '46' 4-4-0 tank engines at Okehampton in 1879 to work passenger trains, but these were replaced by Beyer Peacock 4-4-0Ts soon after. On the opening to Launceston in 1886 a 50ft turntable was installed there, matched by another at Halwill Junction. One of the first engines to try it out was a newish Adams '445' Class 4-4-0, No.448. It hauled the Directors' train and was obviously a show piece for the day, as its big driving wheels were unsuited for general work locally. In the photograph of this event what looks like one of the Beattie 2-4-0s rebuilt as a tender locomotive, possibly No.195, stands in the yard. One of this class was allocated to Launceston in 1887 (No. 215) with No. 185 at Okehampton. In their original 2-4-0 well tank configuration, three of these Beattie engines were destined for remarkably long lives at Wadebridge.

The sheer length of the North Cornwall (from Okehampton) dictated a tender engine policy. Water was available only at Halwill, Launceston, Delabole and Wadebridge, and the coal capacity of the earlier tank engines was very limited. Until the arrival of the Adams 'Jubilee' 0-4-2s the motive power supplied by the LSWR was somewhat elderly. For goods work there were a few Adams '395' 0-6-0s but, more often during the early 1890s Beattie 0-6-0s (both the double and single framed Beyer Peacocks), and even lightweight 'Ilfracombe' goods engines, toiled up the long slopes and were serviced at

the little sheds at Delabole and Launceston. A '395' could head a passenger train if required (after 1889 most LSWR engines had the vacuum brake) and, in the mixed traffic role, shared duties with the Beyer Peacock 4-4-0s coming on the scene about 1893. These '380' Class - the 'Steamrollers' nicknamed for their disc bogie wheels (or, it is said, for their propensity to flatten out curves) and the Adams '460s' were the regulars through the later 1890s, and up to

Adams Class '415' 4-4-2T No. 125 at Okehampton on 14th July 1924. At this time, the '415s' were working the Bude branch, as the headcode denotes. (H.C. Casserley)

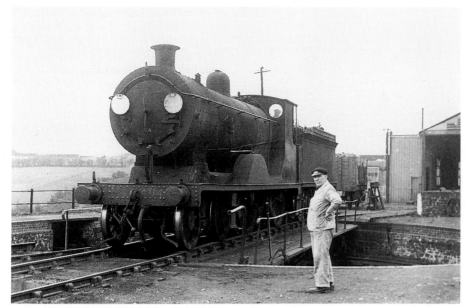

On 2nd August 1945 'S11' Class No. 404 stands on the original 50ft turntable at Okehampton. She was one of ten in the Class and had lately been loaned to the LMS (1941-44), hence the 21A (Saltley) code. Two 'S11s' were allocated to Wadebridge pre-1914 and again in the 1920s to work the heavier trains from and to Exeter, and were to be seen on the Bude and Padstow 'Perishables' in the 1930s. (H.C. Casserley)

Drummond '700' Class 0-6-0s occasionally worked on the North Cornwall line. Here at Okehampton on 14th July 1924 No. 694, rebuilt with an 'Eastleigh' type superheater in 1922, awaits its next duty. (H.C. Casserley)

as required, to Okehampton. At Halwill they would pass by a '460' from Barnstaple after the Torrington line was opened in 1925.

Whatever tank engines were employed on the Holsworthy (later Bude) branch services, few of them went on to the North Cornwall line. Over the years, until the 1950s, '02', 'T1' and finally 'M7 0-4-4Ts (but including a period of '415' 4-4-2Ts), attached or detached Bude coaches at Halwill from Okehampton/Padstow trains. The '460's from Barnstaple were replaced by 'Brighton' rebuilds (the 'E1/R' 0-6-2Ts) from 1928. The latter never ventured onto the North Cornwall, but over the years a Bude 'M7' would work into Launceston on Saturdays, and regularly on Sundays in the 1940s. The South Western end of the North Cornwall was tank territory again, principally the Wadebridge to Bodmin/ Wenford and, to a certain extent, Padstow. After the realignment works on the Bodmin branch the '02' were permitted to work it, Nos. 182 and 219 being allocated from 1896. On and off there were always a couple of '02's at Wadebridge until their demise in the 1950s. The railmotor (1906 - 1918) and the '415' periods (1918 - 1926) were exceptions. Apart for a brief motor-control interlude in 1918 the '02's always ran round their trains at Bodmin, Wadebridge and Padstow. The 'M7's and 'T1's were not permitted between Wadebridge and Bodmin owing to axleweight restrictions (as were most of the 4-4-0s), though in the very last years 'N' 2-6-0s and 'West Countries' were allowed. Thus the lighter '02's persisted alongside the antique Beattie well tanks. Goods working to Wenford Bridge called for the latter's services (severe curvature was the problem here). The story of the Beattie tanks is well known, and were continually photographed in their various

1914. The 'Jubilees', and Drummond's newer breeds of 4-4-0s, the 'K10's and 'L11's, could also be noted on North Cornwall trains in this next decade.

Of the '380s', Nos. 386, 390 and 391 were sent to Wadebridge in 1895, and there were five others at Exeter. No. 386 was involved in the Tresmeer collision on 19 November 1895. The 'Steamrollers' soldiered on, their lives prolonged by the 1914-18 war, and two were still at Okehampton in the early 1920s. The Adams '460s' became the passenger workhorse for many years. The new shed at Wadebridge received a couple on opening, capable of working the lengthier summer trains emerging at the end of the century. Nos. 474 and 526 were there in 1914 and 0464, 0469, 0471 and 526 in 1924. By that time they were relegated to the ordinary stopping passenger trains, and the Padstow fish specials

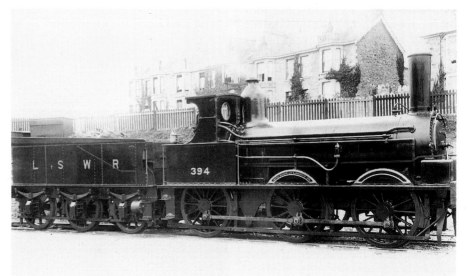

A Beyer Peacock 0-6-0 No. 394 at Wadebridge c.1900. one of the 'Ilfracombe Goods' class dating from 1880, she was eventually sold in 1918 to the East Kent Railway and, as its No. 3, lasted until the 1930s at Shepherdswell. (L.T. George Collection)

Beattie 'Well' tank No. 0254 at Wadebridge soon after arrival by ship in May 1893. The LSWR renewed the track at Wadebridge in 1888 and the 80 lb/yard double-head rails with bracketed fishplates date from then. No. 0254 returned to Nine Elms by rail in 1895. (NRM)

guises. Suffice to say the first one was shipped into Wadebridge from Southampton in May 1893 (No. 248) and the last (No.30587) left in September, 1962. As far back as 1900 their replacement was mooted. A local '02' (No.228) and 'Ilfracombe Goods' No. 301 were tried out, as was an SECR 'P' Class 0-6-0T, and PD & SWJ 0-6-0T 'A.S. Harris' in 1929, but the curves defeated them. The well tanks were noted as station pilots at Wadebridge and chuntered along to Padstow and back, often on the 'mixed' trains.

The not unduly steep gradients of the Bodmin - Wadebridge - Padstow lines prompted the LSWR to introduce railcars, or railmotors, i.e. single carriages powered by steam and two of the later Drummond H13 Class, Nos.13 and 14, commenced running on 1 June 1906. An extension to Wadebridge engine shed housed them overnight. They were expected to provide an economical service in this somewhat rural area. In 1914 nine return trips ran to Bodmin between 5.50am (ex-Wadebridge) until the 9.29pm from Bodmin. None then appeared to be running to Padstow, compared with several in 1909. The surviving three LSWR cars, 3, 4, and 10, carried on until March 1918 when they were replaced, only for a while, by '02's equipped for motor train control.

The 4-4-2Ts were not seen at Wadebridge until about 1919, but they were familiar sights at Halwill at the turn of the century working from Okehampton and Bude. Displaced by 'M7's and electrification in London and suburbs, these elderly tanks (1883 - 5) decanted to the Bodmin/Padstow local workings, Nos. 050, 054, 0169 and 0522 being there at Grouping in 1923. They also reappeared on the Bude branch. All had gone by 1927, their

Bodmin duties once again in the hands of the '02's, while the Bude - Halwill shuttle had firstly 'T1's, and then 'M7's from 1926. Other tank engines entering Wadebridge from the east, but then going no further, were on GWR trains from Bodmin Road. The one-time 0-6-0 saddle tanks eventually gave away to Churchward 2-6-2Ts shedded at St. Blazey. Some seven return (one 'mixed') passenger services were recorded in 1932.

The 45XX GWR 2-6-2Ts were not only at Wadebridge (and working to Padstow as well post-Nationalization) but at Launceston. The Laira engines kept very much to the Western side until 1951, but then with the closure of the ex-GW station in June 1952 they commenced using the ex-SR station (but not the SR shed as yet). A reported shortage of tank engines for an extended Sunday service to Delabole brought quite a surprise in 1953. In

Steam operation was dirty and smoky as this picture of 'T9' No. S283 at Wadebridge on 21st July 1948 illustrates. The smokebox is being cleared of ash, and coal dust surrounds the mobile conveyor, but there is a gas lamp for the dark hours. No. 283, built at Nine Elms in 1899, was allocated at this time to Exmouth Junction, working from Okehampton. It was withdrawn in December 1957. (A.E. West)

During the 1920s individual Adams X6 4-4-0s were sent to Bude and Wadebridge to assist with summer extra passenger workings. No. E662 is seen at Wadebridge on 6th August 1928. (K.A.C. Nunn/LCGB)

Steam 'Railmotors', in vogue on some railways in the period before the 1914 War, appeared at Wadebridge in 1906. Their employment on services to Bodmin also included occasional trips to Padstow, where 'H13' Class No. 10 is seen in that year. The LSWR withdrew the last ones from Wadebridge (nos. 3, 4 and 10) in March 1918. (Real Photographs)

New 'West Country' Class 4-6-2 No. 21C112 'Launceston' being named there on 1st November 1945. For the Southern Railway's Directors and Officers the train (in the Up loop) was formed of saloons and a borrowed LNER sleeping car. (Author's collection)

Mention of the Drummond 4-4-0s underlines the fact that during the summers up to 1914 the Waterloo/Padstow through train, and some of the locals with attached through coaches, presented some haulage problems on the 1 in 73 grades. Keeping time and crossing at loops in the right order was quite a task. While the 'K10's were adequate for the local three-coach trains of the period, (up to five including through coaches) they shared with the '460s' and the 'Jubilees', the eight-coach 'North Cornwall Express' was a different proposition. In 1906 two mixed traffic 'S11' Class 4-4-0s (of 1903) were stationed at Wadebridge for this express. After superheating in the early 1920s two were sent to Exmouth Junction and one, No.401, to Wadebridge for similar duties, though they could work goods trains when required. The 'K10's at Exmouth Junction in 1903 were Nos. 152, 153, 383, 385 and 389 along with ten 'A12's and four '460' Class, any of which could be subshedded at Okehampton for working the North Cornwall line. Wadebridge always had two 'A12's until the 'N' 2-6-0s arrived in 1924. Very popular engines, especially with their steam sanding gear, these 0-4-2s could be seen on anything from a passenger train to a fish special. By the 1930s the '395' 0-6-0s were rarely seen farther west than Okehampton, if so it was probably on an Engineer's train. No. 29, then 029, then 3029 in SR days and finally BR No 30564, was a familiar example for many years (usually Okehampton pilot), but had been seen on the Bodmin Branch in the 1920s. The Drummond 4-4-0 type, the 'Large Hoppers' of his 'L11' Class, started

the spring a 45XX was given clearance tests from Okehampton to Bude and Delabole. On 26 July No. 4583, subshedded at Launceston, set off on that Sunday morning at 9.50am to Halwill. From there she took the 10.29 to Bude, returning to Halwill at 11.51am. At 12.19 she arrived back at Launceston, then went on to Delabole. After running round (and taking water) 4583 simmered at Delabole before taking the 12.55pm back to Launceston, going an shed at 2.40. During August, though, Standard Class 3 2-6-2T No. 82013 was found from the Bude Branch to take the afternoon working to Okehampton from Launceston, going on at 4.15pm to Delabole (6.06pm) before going back to Launceston. 4583 was back again on 20 September doing the whole turn Launceston - Halwill - Bude - Halwill - Delabole - Launceston between 9.15am and 2.45pm. The steps had to be cut back and the ATC shoe clipped up to operate on the SR lines.

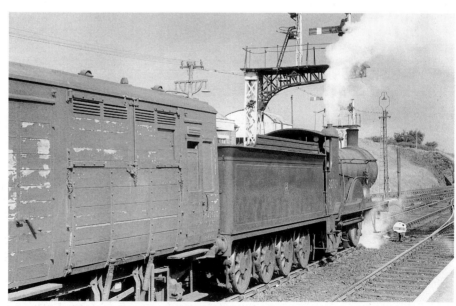

On a warm August morning in 1960, the 9.56 a.m. Okehampton to Padstow has the road to Ashwater en route to Padstow. Dubs-built '79' No. 30709 leads an ex-LMS horse box with its groom's compartment. Such vehicles were usually conveyed in passenger trains. The Down Main and Bay Starting signal pairs on their brackets dated from 1934 when the heights of the arms were altered. Up on the cutting is the large water tank for locomotive supply and cattle wagon washing points. (R.A. Lumber)

In July 1949 one of the Drummond 'T9' 4-4-0s sits well within the 70ft diameter turntable provided by the SR at Padstow in 1947 for the 'West Country' 4-6-2s. The vacuum pump is connected to the turning mechanism. This engine, built by Dubs & Co. in 1899 and superheated (the extended smokebox) in 1927, was one of the last four working the North Cornwall and Bude in 1961, being withdrawn in July. (H.C. Casserley)

working on the North Cornwall when new from 1904-7. The usual stud at Exmouth Junction until the 1920s was about six to eight. Neither the 'K10's or 'L11's received superheating, as did (eventually) the 'S11's and the 'T9's, so they were to be found principally on goods.

Double heading on the LSWR and SR was not commonplace, though the Bude branch was an exception, probably because of the steep rise from sea level to 660 feet at Halwill (and nearly 900 feet at Meldon) in 19 miles. There were also operational problems at Bude which called for piloting in the down direction. Sixteen-coach trains were not unusual in World War Two and after! Not that double-heading was *unknown* on the North Cornwall line, though weight restrictions over Meldon Viaduct prohibited two 2-6-0s, or a 4-4-0 and a 2-6-0 coupled together. As the Padstow summer expresses became heavier in the 1930s it was the custom to schedule two 4-4-0s all the way to Okehampton or Exeter. This is where the 'K10's and 'L11's came in useful as pilots, though a pair of 'T9's was usual. On Saturdays, even before World War One, scheduled non-stop running from Exeter St Davids to

Launceston was timetabled. In the reverse direction a stop at Okehampton was inserted, probably to release the pilot engine. In this respect the eight-wheeled Drummond 'water cart' tenders on the 'T9's were more than welcome in the 1930s. Some of the remaining Adams 'X6' 4-4-0s were pressed into service in the 1920s on local passengers or as pilots, though the Bude-Halwill portions of the summer 'Atlantic Coast Express' was usually their employ.

The sight of a '700' Class 0-6-0 was relatively uncommon west of Okehampton, occasionally sharing goods duties with the 'Jubilee' 0-4-2s on the North Cornwall or on Sunday engineers trains at the Halwill end. There was usually one at Okehampton on station pilot or local Plymouth line goods turns in the week. There was even a report that No. 30691 hauled the 3.13pm Padstow 'Perishables' in October 1960.

The Drummond 'T9' 4-4-0s will always be associated with the North Cornwall line, yet they were quite late on the scene. When built in 1899/1901 they were the LSWR's principal express engines and remained so until displaced, partially by Drummond's 4-6-0s before World War One, and completely by Urie and Maunsell 4-6-0s from the 1920s. Even then a number were transferred to the Eastern and Central Sections of the SR. However they could be seen at Okehampton

A light load for 'N' Class 31855 approaching Maddaford Moor Halt over the high ground at East Bowerland on Saturday 11th July 1964 with the 5.51 p.m. Okehampton to Wadebridge. The 'N' Class were nicknamed 'Woolworths' on the Southern, attributed to their acquisition at a bargain price from Woolwich Arsenal in 1924. (R.A. Lumber)

In the last year of steam in 1964, BR Class 3 2-6-2Ts were taking turns on the North Cornwall trains. No. 82030 calls at Delabole on 19th September with the 11.05 a.m. Padstow. The goods yards connection into the Down loop has already been spiked following closure on 7th September. (R.A. Lumber)

working on the Plymouth main line from 1901. All the sixty six engines received superheated boilers in the 1922-29 period, and during this time the first regular workings to Padstow occurred as the Adams 4-4-0s were withdrawn. There were ten at Exmouth Junction in 1932, seven of them 'Dubs' engines built in Glasgow in 1899/1900. Wadebridge received its first soon after and in 1939, according to Bradley, Nos. 703 and 710 worked as follows: one daily duty to Okehampton and return, Saturdays: Exeter and return, piloting Atlantic Coast Express to Exeter, returning on a passenger to Wadebridge. Launceston's No. 732 worked Padstow - Okehampton passenger turns. Okehampton's No. 723 was working to Bude, Exeter and Plymouth. Exmouth Junction had six engines and these were more widely used, and were available for a Saturday duty working to Padstow and Bude amongst others. Piloting the summer through trains has been mentioned. By 1939 ten coach trains were in vogue, hauled by 'U1' 2-6-0s allocated to Exmouth Junction from 1937, but double-heading by 4-4-0s persisted. On the outbreak of war in 1939 the number of 'T9's increased by eight (three retaining six-wheel tenders after transfer from the Eastern Section). Long passenger trains continued during the war, firstly evacuation specials and then troop trains. The 'N's took some share in this, whereas it was uncommon for one to be seen on passenger duties in pre-war days. The

'T9's took on goods duties, and the mixed trains (Bude/Holsworthy and Launceston/Wadebridge/Padstow) mainly to cope with increased cattle traffic. The introduction of 'West Country' Pacifics curbed their activities somewhat from 1945, but as troop trains continued on the Bude line (not suitable for 'West Countries', as explained later) the seven 'T9's at Exmouth Junction had plenty to do. Nearly all the stopping passenger trains Okehampton/Padstow were now 'T9' turns worked by Okehampton or Wadebridge engines (in 1948 Nos. 703 and 717). Until 1961 the enthusiasts were busy photographing them hauling their usual pair of coaches, or perhaps the up 'Perishable' and its tail of vans and meat containers. By 1959 the eight serviced by Exmouth Junction (including three at Okehampton and one each at Launceston and Wadebridge) were vir-

Displaced by electrification in Kent and Sussex, BR 4MT 2-6-4Ts reigned on the Bude Branch in the early 1960s, though the North Cornwall, previously a tender engine preserve, shared their services. On 18th September 1964 the 11.12 a.m. Okehampton had No. 80037, while No. 80043 (right) would take the rear two coaches to Bude. The Halwill signalman holds the Ashwater Tablet in its looped pouch. (R.A. Lumber)

139

'Battle of Britain' 4-6-2 No. 34069 'Hawkinge', on the 8.30 a.m. 'Atlantic Coast Express' from Padstow, passing 'T9' No.30709 heading the 9.56 a.m. from Okehampton 29th August 1960. The cross rails in the Down line cess (right) and the pedestal in the 'four foot' were for manoeuvring the Tower Hill motorized permanent way trolleys. (R.A. Lumber)

tually the only runners left on the Southern, but the end was nigh. 30313, 30709, 30715 and 30717 were at Okehampton until July 1961 when they were withdrawn, latterly working the 1.00pm Okehampton to Bude, returning at 3.15pm. The Bude and Padstow 'Perishables' then passed to the 'N' Moguls, as with other locals.

The Arrival of the 'Woolworth' N Class 2-6-0s

Quite a sensation took place on the locomotive scene in 1924 when a 2-6-0 tender engine arrived for trials, initially to Ilfracombe. The SR had been looking for a more powerful class than the 'Jubilees' and 4-4-0s, especially for goods working to Bude and North Cornwall, for passenger working to Ilfracombe and Plymouth, able to use the 50ft turntables. As it happened the Government was anxious to dispose of a quantity of their SECR-designed 2-6-0 tender engines manufactured at Woolwich Arsenal for the Ministry of Munitions, post-1918. Because of the bargain price, as whole or in parts, they became popularly known as 'Woolworths'. Later in 1924 they were tried out to Wadebridge and Bude. After some troubles with hot axleboxes on the tenders, etc. they came to be accepted by local crews. Put on to

North Cornwall goods workings straight away the 2-6-0s involved, in the A826 to A860 number series (from 1931 onwards 1826 to 1860) started working the midnight Exmouth Junction to Launceston Goods, the 6.00am and 10.00am Okehampton to Wadebridge, and the 11.30am and 5.00pm from Wadebridge. One always worked to Bude, leaving Exmouth Junction at 3.30am and arriving back at 9.00pm that night. With a heavy 25-ton brake van, a maximum 40 loaded wagons was allowed for the 'N's, tempered by length restrictions in some places. The steep gradients from Wadebridge to Delabole limited trains to 34 for instance, though in some places it reflected concern for control of unbraked wagons. ('New Heavy' 25-ton brake vans were mandatory). Other 2-6-0s of the 'N' Class appeared in 1933 i.e. Ashford-built Nos. 1406-9, also 'U' Class Moguls rebuilt from the ill-fated 'River' Class 2-6-4Ts from 1928. Between 1937-9 ten 3-cylinder 'U1's were allocated to Exmouth Junction to assist in the ever-increasing length of the Waterloo/Padstow/Bude summer trains. For various reasons the 3-cylinder engines were not over-popular, and they were not seen again in the west until 1961 when Nos. 31901-4 came to replace the 'T9's, staying only one summer. The 'N's returned in numbers again by 1945. In 1946 they were pressed onto passenger trains more often, particularly to Bude on the heavy summer trains, and single handed at that! One heavy

Ivatt Class 2 2-6-2Ts appeared in many corners of the Southern in the 1960s, including Wadebridge for working Padstow/Bodmin North. No. 41272 is in the engine spur at the west end on 21st June 1962. The plaque below the BR totem denotes that she was the 7000th engine built at Crewe - it had spent most of its life working from Bedford on the LMR. (R.C. Riley)

load for a 'Woolworth' by this time was the 5.55am from Okehampton. It was now a 'mixed' train of sorts i.e. passenger coaches and a Newspaper bogie van off the 1.30am Waterloo, and anything up to twenty goods vehicles plus a brake van. Between 1957 and 1961 as a consequence of distortion cracks, about half the 'N's underwent frame rebuilding. No doubt the curves on the North Cornwall had something to do with this. Most rebuilds arrived back with BR Class '4' chimneys and blast pipe alterations, which altered the exhaust from a 'crump' to a sharper bark. After 1961 they took over all the T9 turns, including the two 'Perishables', but the "West Countries" were also involved (except to Bude) as we shall see. From December 1962 the Western Region, taking control acquired the following 'Woolworths' 31834-49/53/55/56/60/74/75 also ex-SECR 'N' 31818 and SR No. 31406. During 1963 31812/21 (ex-SECR) and 31854/59 arrived at Exmouth Junction. Only a small number withdrawn by the start of 1964, with 21 remaining there in this last year of freight services west of Okehampton. All had gone by September, the remaining duties covered by Standard Class 4 2-6-4Ts and 4-6-0s. No. 1874 survives, the only true 'Woolworth', preserved on the Mid Hants Railway.

The Light Pacifics in North Cornwall

Replacement of the 4-4-0s in the west Country had been foreseen in pre-World War Two days. In April 1941 twenty passenger engines had actually been ordered, and a 3-cylinder 2-6-0 design drawn up. After progressing through a 2-6-2 it became a 4-6-2.

Perhaps the growing burden of the summer through trains had been in mind, though at the time (1943) the only lengthy trains were troop specials. Whatever decisions were made by O.V.S. Bulleid and the Southern Railway management as to their use in the west, and by now for the Eastern Section as well, the 'West Country' light Pacifics were born. A further ten, to make the order to thirty, were ordered in September 1944. The first ones seen west of Okehampton were 21C107 and 21C108 arriving on 31 October 1945 to be named 'Wadebridge' and 'Padstow' by the respective Urban District Council Chairmen. The following day 211C112 was named 'Launceston' by the Mayor. The local turntables were not long enough, so they worked back tender first with their trains of saloon, a Pullman Car (the first seen in North Cornwall?) and a borrowed LNER sleeping car. 21C106 'Bude' was also named on 1 November. 21C116 'Bodmin' was allowed to run specially down the branch for naming on 26 August 1946, still unturnable. This shortcoming was remedied in 1947 by the provision of a 65ft 'table at Padstow. The 'West Countries' were however suitable for tender-first working (with high sides), and did so from Bude in October 1947 when the Okehampton 'table was replaced by one of 70ft diameter. Neither did the 50ft turntable at Bude deny the 4-6-2s working on goods trains as required in the 1950s and 1960s. They were, of course, designated mixed traffic engines (7P6F latterly) and once the Padstow turntable was in commission they would haul North Cornwall goods or passenger trains.

Initially the newcomers worked the up 'Atlantic Coast Express' - only two or three coaches in winter - the 8.30am from Padstow, the engine coming down on the 10.10am goods from Okehampton, staying overnight at Wadebridge. During 1947 21C107/108, 21C111, and 21C120 were usually to be seen on the North Cornwall line. Further 'West Countries' were ordered in 1945, among them 21C132 'Camelford' (June 1946) without a naming ceremony. There were no ceremonies either for 21C125 'Rough Tor' (April) or 21C139 'Boscastle' in September. One more local name occurred in the lists, 'Trevone' with its BR number (34096) built November 1949. 'Rough Tor' carried that name in April 1948 only, being renamed 'Whimple' in May.

The sight of these unusual engines, with their 'air-smoothed' casings and 'boxpok' wheels, their original bright malachite green (with yellow lining) livery, (Brunswick green from mid-1949), and the sound of their multiple-jet exhaust, became well known on the sun-drenched (or rain-swept!) hillsides at Otterham, or shunting in Launceston yard on occasion. They were not popular on these latter duties, inclined as they were to wheel slip, or in the shed at Wadebridge with their obscured 'innards', as the Cornish would put it. Nevertheless when it came to hauling the six-coach through trains up the 1 in 73 gradients they were in their element. A maximum of ten could be taken, but there were difficulties in the loops, especially at Launceston and Egloskerry, in passing other trains. Over the twenty years of their active existance a great variety of engines could be noted e.g. 34110 '66

Released from its train No. 34066 'Spitfire' moves forward to the stop blocks at Padstow in July 1964, thence to run back via the crossover. The oil lamp has been placed above the electric lamp for some reason. No. 833 was a five-coach Bulleid Set working in Waterloo/West of England Southern Region trains in this last summer of through services. (C.J. Knowles-Thomas)

A goods train from Bodmin Road running into Wadebridge on 14th July 1964 behind NBL No. D6348. After withdrawal of freight services on the North Cornwall in the following September, the remaining traffic at Wadebridge continued to be routed this way until the latter's closure in 1978. (C.J. Knowles-Thomas)

Squadron' in 1962, 34036 'Westward Ho' in 1959, and 34015 'Exmouth' in the last days of local steam in 1964. From 1957, however, when many were rebuilt (including Boscastle', 'Bodmin', 'Trevone' and 'Camelford') and their driving axle weights increased from 18 tons 15cwt to over 20 tons, they were prevented from working from Meldon Junction into North Cornwall. The weak underbridges (of old rails) between there and Launceston are understood to be the reason. 27 of the non-rebuilt engines were transferred to the WR at Exmouth Junction from 1 January 1963. The WR withdrew freight services in September 1964 beyond Meldon Junction, and steam haulage generally from 3 January 1965, leaving Exmouth Junction with a rapidly declining allocation, vanishing altogether when Ivatt tank 41321 was withdrawn in the July. The last 'West Countries' at Padstow were 34015 on the down 'ACE' (4 September 1964) and 34023 on the final up train. It is pleasing to note that 34016 'Bodmin' is preserved (as rebuilt) on the Mid-Hants Railway, and 34007 'Wadebridge' is being restored on the Plym Valley Railway.

BR Standard Engines.
The Bude Branch lost its 'M7' tanks within a few years of Nationalization, BR Class 3 and LM Ivatt Class 2 2-6-2Ts moving in from 1952, though the BR tanks ruled the roost there until 1964. The North Cornwall, on the other hand, saw few 'Standards' until the 2-6-4Ts in 1962. In May and June Nos. 80035-43 and 80059-64/67, redundant from Tonbridge and elsewhere, were sent to Exmouth Junction to augment

the Class 3s. It was not the first time 2-6-4Ts had appeared locally. In 1951 some Central Section (LMS-type) Fairburn tanks (42099/102/103/105) were used in place of 'T9's on the afternoon Okehampton/Bude passenger while the shed pits at Bude were under repair. The BR 2-6-4Ts were doing the much reduced 'Perishables' train duties from Okehampton in 1964 and on the Halwill/Bude (from 1962) in place of the Class 3s. They were also involved in goods working with the Ns and 'West Countries', but were principally to be found on the 10.12am, and 5.50pm from Okehampton and the 3.13pm and 6.00pm from Padstow. It is interesting to note they were turned at Padstow to give 'collar' to the uphill return journey. Those not withdrawn were transferred to Yeovil Town, Templecombe, Bath and Bristol, before and after the end of steam working in early January 1965.

Working with the North Cornwall line the 4MT tanks was an occasional 3MT 2-6-2T, and one would therefore appear at Wadebridge (e.g. 82042 on the last day of steam, 2 January 1965). The Ivatt 2-6-2Ts were more common. Allocated to Bude from time to time but found wanting in power for any more than the two coach sets, they were more at home on the Torrington/Halwill lightweights, (where they replaced the 'E1/R' 0-6-2Ts), and they found a niche on the Bodmin Branch from 1962-64. Those involved were taken from Exmouth Junction's allocation and latterly (replacing the '02' pairs and the succeeding WR pannier tanks) Nos.41270/72/75 and 41320 could be seen on Wadebridge shed. The restrictions on six-coupled en-

gines were eased to Bodmin North from Boscarne Junction in the 1950s. The circuitous trips for a Launceston - based Ivatt tank in 1962/3 is described in elsewhere.

When new in 1955/56 ten BR Class 4 4-6-0s (Nos 75070-79) were allocated to Exmouth Junction. Unfortunately at 51ft they were too long for the Launceston and Bude turntables, and although their high sided tenders were suitable for reverse running, this sort of working was unpopular. The Class 4s which reappeared in 1964 on passenger working (Nos 75005/08/22/25) could not fit the 50ft turntables though their BR 2 tenders with inset sides gave a better look out. The last inhabitant of Launceston shed was one of these, working the North Cornwall in December 1964. They also went down to Bude on the Okehampton afternoon service, a duty shared with the new WR diesels, Hymeks or NBL Type 2s.

There had been a variation on the Bodmin Branch in 1961, involving Padstow as well. Two ex-GWR pannier tanks, Nos.4666 and 4694, were substituted for the '02's. At that time under Southern Region control, they were not quite 'at home' in Wadebridge shed. Further ex-GWR engines arrived in 1962. The Beattie well tanks, showing their extreme age, were withdrawn. To hand were displaced Weymouth Quay 0-6-0 pannier tanks Nos. 1367-69; although six-coupled, short wheelbases permitted them on the Wenford branch. Meanwhile the Churchward 45XX 2-6-2Ts soldiered on from Bodmin to Wadebridge/Padstow, though they were still not seen at Bodmin North.

Chapter Eight

THE TRAINS, STRUCTURES, PERMANENT WAY AND SIGNALLING

In 1879 a passenger for Okehampton would have climbed aboard a four or six-wheel coach at the Holsworthy terminus. At the head of the train would be a 4-4-0T engine and three or so vehicles, one of which was solely for the guard and his parcels. This last vehicle had a large caboose raised above the roof and from here the guard could observe the engine and apply his handbrake as necessary, as these were the days before the automatic vacuum through brake. There was communication of a sort if Clark's patent cord system was present. At night oil lamps were let into the roofs of the coaches but there was no heating unless 'footwarmers' were available (possibly not at Holsworthy!). The old LSWR varnished teak or dark green livery was about to be replaced by the unusual 'salmon pink' and brown. Platform heights were being increased to 2ft 6ins and the new branch was built to this standard, though by 1900 heights were set at 3ft (eg Padstow).

These collections of 4 and 6 wheelers, 24, 25 and 28-foot long and dating from the 1870s, gave way to bogie stock about 1895. The North Cornwall appeared to be re-quipped with 42-foot Thirds, 42 or 46-foot Tri-composites (1st/2nd/3rd Class) dating from the 1880s, but some of the older 6-wheel 30-foot Guards Brake Vans were retained, supplemented by new 44-foot bogie vans. These were formed into more-or-less permanent 'sets' and were the last of the Victorian low arc-roofed coaches, though they lasted locally until about 1910. At this time the LSWR dropped the use of the separate vans and formed two-coach sets with inclusive brake/luggage compartments. Identifying Set numbers were now applied to the coach ends and generally speaking, those traversing the North Cornwall and Bude lines were within the 186 to 229 series. Each set now consisted of a 42-foot Brake Third (1890-4) rebuilt from an all-Third, and a 45-foot Brake Composite (1892-3) rebuilt from a Tri-composite. After 1923 the SR renumbered these sets in the series 34 to 55.

In the 1930s there was another small cascade of LSWR elliptical-roofed stock to local services and after 1936 SR Sets 7 to 21, 42 to 46, 51 to 54 and 56 might be noted west of Meldon Junction. Carriage workings took them to Honiton and also to Plymouth in the course of a week. The sets most used on Padstow and Bude trains were Nos.7 to 21, originally consisting of a 48-foot Brake Third (ex-1896 Tri-composites) and 56-foot Brake Composite (1st/3rd Class) dating from 1912. In 1936 the 48-foot coaches were rebuilt and lengthened to 58-foot, and these non-corridor equipped with lavatories in some compartments (from their main line days) lasted another twenty years on the local scene. Each set would seat

An LSWR corridor brake Third at Okehampton in 1948, and in Southern Railway green livery. These post-1900 vehicles were the mainstay of the best West of England services until the advent of the new Maunsell stock in the mid-1920s. The gangways were incompatible with the latter's Pullman style and adapters were needed. There were also complications with matching screw couplings on the LSWR coaches to the buck-eye arrangements of the Maunsells; none of this was very helpful to the shunters at Okehampton and Halwill on busy Saturdays. (A.E. West)

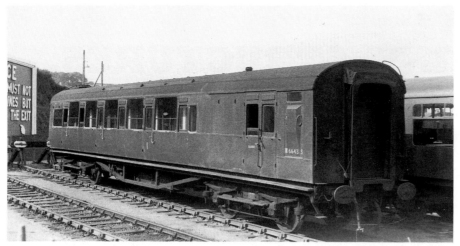

The former LSW non-corridors were withdrawn in the 1950s, but the pairing arrangements in numbered sets continued West of Exeter until dieselisation in 1965. Maunsell corridors of 1920s vintage were their replacements and they passed to the Western Region in 1965. Brake Composite No. W6643S was probably used to strengthen the morning and afternoon Wadebridge and Bodmin schools trains in 1964. (C.J. Knowles-Thomas)

Tower Hill was the quietest of the Devon stations, the nearest habitations being St. Giles and Broadwoodwidger. Included in this train bound for Launceston on 19th August 1957, behind 'T9' No. 30712, is an ex-LNER vehicle (second) converted to a Cafeteria car. 'Loose' coaches such as this, and the Maunsell 3rd corridor (leading), were probably going to Padstow for weekend holiday train formations, the usual local 'P' Set bringing up the rear. (K.J. Rea collection)

about 100 Third and 10 First Class passengers together with fairly liberal guard/luggage/parcels compartments to for the large amount of personal luggage in those days (eg commercial travellers and their samples) and rabbits, calves, boxes of fish, even seaweed destined for medical use.

Some of the old 6-wheel carriages and many guards vans were sold off to become chalets, some surviving to be rescued by the preservationists - at least the bodywork! The Southern Railway introduced wooden-bodied vans, long wheelbase with two axles, and bogied vehicles. Best known, and still to be seen today relegated to tool and mess vans for the engineers, were the 'Utility' Parcels and Mail vans (PMVs). Very common on the North Cornwall and the western lines generally, especially during the years of the lucrative rabbit trade, these too had scheduled duties laid down in the working books. Guards' compartments with hand brakes (and periscopes to observe signals) were provided in a number of these vans, particularly the

bogie vans carrying the newspapers from London which actually had roof boards 'NEWSPAPER TRAFFIC'. In due course BR 4 and 8-wheel vans appeared, along with the odd ex-LMS, LNE or GW examples. No complete parcels trains ran on the North Cornwall. 'Tail' traffic sufficed, often lengthy behind 2-sets, consisting of these van types, returning Road Vans (latterly branded 'XP'), and meat containers on flat wagons - making quite formidable loads for the 'S11's and 'T9's.

The GWR stock working into Wadebridge in the 1890s was made up of four wheelers; the LSWR's inherited Bodmin & Wadebridge open 'trucks' being discarded after 1888 (one survives at York). The re-opened LSWR Bodmin services in 1895 utilized similar coaching to the North Cornwall, until the advent of the Railmotors in 1906. After 1918 the latter were converted into pure carriage stock and coupled to suitably equipped 'motor' tank engines. Thus '02' 0-4-4Ts could be seen at Wadebridge with

their 'push and pull' trains, but only for a while. It would seem that they and the '415' 4-4-2Ts involved with mixed trains, and thus shunting, were inconvenienced by the LSWR's complicated rod and wire system. Trains reverted to engine run-rounds each time at Bodmin, Wadebridge and Padstow. The converted Railmotors figured in 3-coach workings until the late 1940s, sharing with the 2-sets, single LSWR non-corridors and even the odd SR corridor (from a London working) pressed into use.

While the Bodmin local service had variety, the North Cornwall locals were almost exclusively 2-sets until the end of steam. The only extra coach working to be seen was the Meldon Quarrymen's daily shuttle from Okehampton and the single example to Launceston on Saturday afternoons. In the 1930s it was an ex-SECR all third bogie, but usually a LSWR vehicle (S2611S in BR crimson livery in 1958). The ND & CJLR's single coach from Torrington appeared at Halwill three times a day, twice on mixed trains.

The SR (and the LSWR) kept much of their coaching stock in sets and numbered. The LSWR salmon pink and brown, abandoned in the First World War, had given way to dark green, perpetuated by the SR until Nationalization. Lining out and stock numbering was applied in yellow or gilt.

In the period before the Night Newspaper train from Waterloo included through corridor coaches to Padstow, there was accommodation (of a sort) for those in the know. In 1938 a 2-set went down on the 5.21am (MO) goods from Halwill, and from Okehampton at 4.00am goods on other weekdays. This early morning train started as the 12.01am Goods and Mail from Exmouth Junction (to Launceston). At Launceston the 2-set became an advertised train at 7.44am on to Padstow. It returned with vans as the 2.55pm 'Perishables' through to Exeter. On summer Saturdays in 1938 its duties were quite different. As with other sets it had to fit in with through Waterloo/North Cornwall workings. On these Saturdays it left Okehampton at the back of the 11.00am Waterloo through coaches to Bude at 3.30pm, eventually gaining Exeter Central on the 7.12pm local from Bude. On Sundays it worked to and from Honiton/Exeter Central.

Although during the Monday to Friday period six sets were employed part of their day on the North Cornwall and Bude lines on ten local services, their rotas became quite complicated on summer Saturdays. In 1938 several Waterloo/Plymouth extras shed portions, to Bude particularly. From the 1.00pm and 3.06pm Waterloo 2-sets were added at Okehampton, keeping the station pilot busy. The 3.06 (Okehampton 7.47pm) had one to Delabole arriving at 9.25pm, returning ECS to Launceston. The workings

The Southern Railway introduced a 25-ton goods brake in the late 1920s. Several were soon allocated to Exmouth Junction yard for North Cornwall trains, their movements specified in the working timetables. Use of the new 'N' 2-6-0s from 1925 enabled haulage of up to 40 unbraked wagons, the long and steep gradients calling for careful control by engine crews and guards. In some places (e.g. Otterham to Launceston) wagon standing brakes were also pinned down to assist. (Real Photographs)

of these 2-sets were not confined to North Cornwall. Some went to Plymouth, and Diagram 173 was a working to Sidmouth from Exeter Central before arriving at Okehampton to form the 1.00pm to Padstow. Only Bude was getting a Sunday service in 1938 involving a set, but on several August Sundays a berthed overnight at Padstow was used on an excursion to Exeter. The decanting of main line stock to local passenger services is noted above when the LSWR 2-sets arrived in the 1890s. The same thing happened in the 1940s when Maunsell's SR main line coaches were relegated.

There seems no doubt that excursions from London (see Chapter 2 on the Wadebridge opening) ran through to North Cornwall in the 1890s, particularly at Christmas and Easter. Patrons probably had to make do with whatever stock was available, and timings appeared to be very liberal to allow for personal needs at stations en route! The 1890s non-corridors did have limited lavatory accommodation and these possibly figured as the experimental single through coaches of 1902 and 1904 and again 1905, when regular services started. In 1907 the first purpose-built through brake tri-composites (1st/2nd/3rd) appeared, 56ft long, with corridors and now gangways (see below). They even had steam heating. The luggage compartment was generous as well, reflecting the amount Edwardian travellers took with them. The 11.00am Waterloo (and 8.54am return next day) included one for Padstow along with individuals for

Sidmouth, Exmouth, Torrington and Bude. In these pre-1914 summers the 1.00pm Waterloo also included one each for Bude and Padstow.

For the 'North Cornwall and Bude Express' of 1907 the LSWR converted the 1892 'Eagle' boat train saloons. The six for Padstow (including a dining car pair) and the four for Bude had central vestibules and gangways within each set. By the lack of connections at the ends Bude passengers were deprived of access to the dining cars! This was rectified in 1908. These, and their 56-foot corridor successors were a heavy load for a '460' Class in the Up direction, which by 1914 was non-stop from Halwill to Exeter St Davids. LSWR corridors were still appearing in holiday trains just after 1945.

New Corridor Stock from 1926
For the 'Atlantic Coast Express' that year ten Brake Composites were built at Eastleigh in 1926 - Nos.6565-74. They were 59ft over ends and 9ft wide (Restriction 1), with four Third and two 1st Class compartments seating 32 and 12 respectively. An end-lavatory and a guard/luggage compartment (14ft 9ins) completed the accommodation. These coaches were equipped with Pullman gangways and buckeye automatic couplers. From this date the shunters at Okehampton and Halwill etc. had to be conversant with coupling them from the existing screw hooks of older stock, retracting buffers and using gangway adapters where necessary. While they were designed for the individual services of the ACE formation at this date, other Maunsell

59ft stock was appearing in through trains. The summer 1930 10.24am (SO) Waterloo to Bude was all new SR stock except for one LSW corridor brake third at each end. None of these coaches were in 'Sets', and the formations were from 'loose' vehicles generally formed up each summer season. Interestingly, the 10.24 included a new Maunsell kitchen dining saloon and open saloon for Bude, as did the Up 10.45am SO from Bude, arriving empty the previous day. The Padstow portions were no more than four coaches out of ten. As the decade progressed the Restaurant Cars were diverted to the North Cornwall line, with new SR three and six-coach sets. One of the new dining cars, No. 8000, was displayed at Wadebridge for the Bodmin & Wadebridge Centenary exhibition in September 1934. Increasing traffic on Saturdays caused the SR to run separate trains to Bude and Padstow, let alone Ilfracombe and east Devon resorts. A further 40 brake composites were built in 1930 as well as the new Kitchen/Dining Saloons (20). All these were part of a large number of corridor coaches ordered by the SR at that time, and included three car 'P' Sets and 'loose' vehicles, many of which appeared in the North Cornwall summer through trains in the 1930s, and well into the 1950s.

A Waterloo wartime working (October 1941) surprisingly served Padstow by a through three-car Restaurant Set. The 10.59am (SO) had a 3rd brake for Plymouth and a brake composite each for Sidmouth, Exmouth and Bude. A brake composite detached at Salisbury worked all stations to Exeter. Even wartime circumstances did not prevent the daily 'ACE' coaches arriving off the 10.50am Waterloo, and the provision of Saturday trains such as above. By May 1946 the 'ACE' was a very heavy train, comprised of three-car sets for Ilfracombe and Plymouth. Padstow had two Brake Composites while Seaton, Sidmouth, Exmouth, Bude and Torrington had one each. A Dining car twin set was detached at Exeter. At this time the 1.35am Waterloo Newspaper train detached a Newsvan and two corridor thirds for Padstow from the Plymouth main train at Okehampton. The Southern Railway embarked on new coach building after 1945, with O.V.S. Bulleid, better known for his 4-6-2s, responsible for the overall design. His Brake Composites, following the traditions of the through Waterloo/Atlantic Coast workings, appeared in 1948 under BR guise but retained the SR malachite green livery. Nos. 6713 to 6752 followed the earlier Maunsell layout except the lavatory compartment was in mid-coach, between the 1st and 3rd accommodation. An adjacent cross vestibule largely accounted for a longer length of 64ft 6ins. These comfortable coaches, with curved sides and windows, were three inches wider inside than the Maunsells (though still at an overall 9ft) and saw out steam haulage until 1964. There were also two and three coach sets, 'R' and 'L' to be seen on Padstow summer trains, though it is doubtful if Bulleid Restaurant cars infiltrated west of Exeter. As BR Mark 1 corridor stock became available in the 1950s, the last of the 'ACE' workings acquired them, usually in three car formations. In spite of the predilection for set working, 'loose' corridor vehicles often made up the summer Saturday Up trains, and local trains would include one or more en route for Bude or Padstow.

Local 'P' Two Coach Sets from 1948
The LSWR two coach sets were phased out in 1948 in favour of demoted Maunsell corridors - none other than erstwhile 'ACE' through Brake Composites coupled to other brake thirds. Eight of these, Nos 22 to 29, fulfilled the duties required by the five or so each-way services Okehampton/Padstow/Bude. They lasted until the early sixties, all but one (No. 28) passing to WR control in January 1963. Already in 1958 a further eleven sets - 'W' - were put together and numbered 100 to 110. The difference from the 'P' Sets was the substitution of the Brake Seconds by open saloons. Only Nos. 102/3 and 110 passed to the WR. There were yet more local sets: two in 1962, Nos. 30 and 31 conforming to the earlier 'P' sets, and another nine original 1936 main line pairs demoted in 1960/1. The latter, Nos 168, 172, 178-180, 196, 198-200 were not confined to this area but also worked on the east Devon and Callington

Signal arms facing in opposite directions on one post were not uncommon. Halwill Down advanced starter to Ashwater in March 1966 was an ex-LSWR lower quadrant arm (left), and its Up home from Ashwater an ex-SR upper quadrant (right). The slender old rail assemblies needed strong guying, but a substantial steel bracket was erected to site the Up home signal from Dunsland Cross (Bude) on the right. Noteworthy was the new 109 lb/yd flat bottom rail on pre-stressed concrete sleepers, laid in by the WR at this late hour. (A.E. West)

branches. Six of these passed to the WR as well as over 40 Bulleid Composite Brakes (1st/2nd, and 3rd). (All third class accommodation was renamed second in 1956). After January 1963 many of the Maunsell coaches were withdrawn and Bulleid Composites substituted, so that by the end of the steam working few of the original SR sets were recognisable. There was increased use of three-coach sets on the North Cornwall line at that time - the SR 'R' sets and their BR equivalent Mark 1s. Finally, Torrington trains into Halwill employed every sort of coach from LSWR Corridors, ex-railmotor 'gate' stock, Maunsell Corridors to Bulleid Composites, usually one only - two sets were never seen however.

'Foreign' coaching stock was fairly rare on the North Cornwall, the Bude branch seeing more because of the military Anti-Aircraft Practice Camp at Cleave, (Morwenstowe) and the Sec-

ond World War movement of firstly British, and then US army personnel. Troop trains were frequent in the summer for the AA camp until the 1950s, thus trains of LNER, LMS and GWR stock (but never their engines) appeared at weekends. The terminus at Bude was uniquely able to handle up to sixteen coaches. Such lengths were virtually unknown on the North Cornwall due to the many loops to be negotiated. There were, however, numerous Prisoners of War specials to Launceston and Wadebridge, and it is known that an Ambulance train was at Delabole, though whether it was hauled by the usual ex-GER 'B12' 4-6-0 cannot be confirmed. The greatest occasion occurred on 9 May 1956 when the Royal train of eleven heavy coaches left Launceston in charge of 'N's 31830 and 31845. It had previously worked empty stock from Plymouth (via Meldon Jn). The LNWR examples in this train were not the first seen on the North Cornwall, as one was parked at Wadebridge, and one at Launceston, as enginemen's dormitories in the 1950s. On the change from WR steam to diesel locomotives in mid-Cornwall the 45XX 2-6-2Ts and NBL 63XXs invariably came into Wadebridge from Bodmin Road with a two-coach ex-GWR 'B' set - similarly Launceston 'South' after 1951, though the 45XX and their Plymouth trains were more likely to consist of a pair of ex-GWR corridors.

Goods Rolling Stock

The four-wheel wagon with its short base has almost disappeared from the BR scene, but a century ago thousands were on the move, or lying in sidings (some for days on end), throughout Britain. The LSWR could not compare with its northern neighbours as a major freight carrier, yet almost all its stations had a yard and goods shed. The classification of certain box wagons as 'Express Passenger' (dating from the 1930s) has been noted. They were equipped with the vacuum brake (and oil axle boxes) for inclusion in passenger trains and fast running. Many cattle wagons, all container flats and all horse boxes were similarly treated. Other box wagons with the vacuum brake (or 'piped' to run with these) were the staple of the overnight Nine Elms/Exeter/Plymouth fast freights. Carrying mostly household merchandise and foodstuffs, on detachment (e.g. at Okehampton) they would be shunted to the front of local goods trains, providing added brake force for the usual collection of loose wagons. None of these refinements graced the earlier Beattie or Adams wagons, almost four-square in shape, though spring buffers and a hand brake were provided. These brakes served not only for the obvious purpose of parking, but would be 'pinned down' by the guard to assist the driver in controlling a heavy train down a gradient (e.g. Otterham to Launceston). The rise in cattle forwarding to the east of England, very much concerning the North Cornwall line, resulted in the LSWR producing a standard type of 10-ton wagon with vacuum brake (or 'piped'). 430 of Diagram 1506 were taken over by the SR in 1923 and the latter continued to reinforce the fleet until Nationalization. Allied to the cattle trade, the meat carcase traffic developed by the LSWR and SR was carried in ventilated vans, again equipped for a fast running. After 1945 this meat was taken in containers (insulated) on flat wagons. Readers are referred to the 'History of Southern Wagons, Vol. 1' (Oxford Publishing Co 1984) for a comprehensive coverage of LSWR wagons. Fuller details of china clay, granite, fish and ballast wagons (and brake vans) may be studied therein. Other company's wagons were, of course, commonly seen on the North Cornwall and British Railways new stock from 1951 figured largely in the block fertilizer trains in the 1960s. During this decade the slate dust filling from Delabole was being carried in ex-'Presflo' wagons (latterly from Wadebridge). No trace has been found regarding coal wagons owned by local merchants, though the china clay firms' vehicles occasionally, earlier on, travelled east from Wenford and colliery wagons (e.g. Stephenson Clarke) were familiar up until World War Two. Roadstone from Hoare Bros. of Wilminstone, and possibly by Betty & Toms in their own wagons from Port Isaac Road, occasionally appeared in local goods trains, as did oil tank wagons from Regent, Esso or Royal Daylight.

Signalling & Telegraph

The LSWR was already installing the Block Telegraph system on its lines when the Meldon Junction to Holsworthy branch opened in 1879. Signalling was still comparatively primitive even then, and the four single line sections were equipped with Train Staffs and Tickets, albeit under Block Telegraph control. Semaphore signals for the drivers were not universal (the Inspecting Officer asked for them to be placed at the loop entrances on the branch, rather than ground signals). The principle of the Block Telegraph was to prevent two trains being in a section at the same time, the adjacent signalmen using bell codes and visual instruments to notify the approach, passage and exit of each train. This was in addition to the Train Staff already used for many years. A staff was allocated to each section between signal boxes, each differing by shape and colour to reduce the risk of a driver proceeding with the wrong one. Between Meldon Junction and Ashbury the Staff was blue and diamond-shaped for Ashbury to Halwill whilst Beaworthy was red and circular. An obvious inflexibility of one Staff per section was overcome by the issue of 'Train Tickets'. If two (or more) trains were to follow in the same direction a separate Train Ticket was obtained from a special box in the signal cabin. This was given to the driver of the first train and the Train Staff shown to him. The Staff was given to the driver of the second (or last) train.

As the North Cornwall progressed Block Telegraph and Staffs were provided for each section:

Halwill Junction		
and Ashwater	AAA	Green
Ashwater and Tower Hill	BBB	Yellow
Tower Hill and Launceston	CCC	Blue
Launceston and Egloskerry	DDD	Green
Egloskerry and Tresmeer	EEE	Red
Tresmeer and Otterham	FFF	Yellow
Otterham and Camelford	GGG	Blue
Camelford and Delabole		Not known

It was essential to keep trains in the right order under this system. Hence the heading notes in the working timetables of this period. 'Train No. - to pass Train No. - ' at the appropriate passing loop. Indeed the LSWR stipulated that where drivers should exchange Staffs, and which should have Tickets. Surprisingly, in the event of late running, where the all-important Staff was at the wrong end of a section, adjacent Station Masters could agree over the telegraph to permit a driver of a train to proceed without it, but in possession of a 'Train Order'.

The continual development of electrical communication led to the invention by Edward Tyer of his Electric Train Tablet system in 1878. Instead of a Staff, the authority to proceed was a small metal tablet, circular shaped, but with distinguishing holes and the section signal box names inscribed. Adjacent boxes housed machines capable of holding 30 Tablets for each direction. Only one could be released at a time, an action coordinated by the two signalmen using bell codes and the Block Telegraph apparatus. Thus a succession of trains could be passed in one direction providing the Tablets were restored correctly in the machine in advance. Should all the Tablets (or too many) end up in the advance box, only the Signal Lineman could retrieve them and carry them back to the box in the rear. It was not uncommon for this to happen on the North Cornwall, especially in the summer season.

In 1893 the LSWR authorised the replacement by Tyers No. 3 Tablets for the Staffs between Meldon Junction and Holsworthy/Delabole. It is not known how quickly this was done (it is believed the Ashbury-Halwill Staff survived into the 1900s). The only thing the passenger perceived was a wire hoop, passing to and from signalmen/engine crews, which carried a small pocket for the Tablet. The four sections, Delabole to Port Isaac Road/ Port Isaac Road to St Kew Highway/ St Kew Highway to Wadebridge Junction/Wadebridge Junction to Wadebridge, were equipped with Tyers No 3 Tablets from opening in 1895. The drawback of the No.3 Tablet was that it could not be returned to the issuing machine but had to be carried through to the next. Tyers No.6 system allowed restoration to the issuing machine ('Returnable'). Patented in 1892, Tyers No 6 was provided between Wadebridge West and Padstow on opening in 1899. At this date the new Wadebridge West and East signal boxes communicated by Preece 3-wire double line instruments. Following the closure of Wadebridge Junction in 1907 the St Kew Highway to Wadebridge East section was re-equipped with No.6 Tablets. They also eased the working between Camelford and Delabole, and Delabole and Port Isaac Road as from November 1923. The latter enabled the siding at Tom's Quarry to be operated by a ground frame, released by the Tablet and the train allowed to return to Port Isaac

Road. It is not known which types were provided in the new Maddaford Loop Box in 1899 but on closure in 1919, a No.6 safe-guarded the restored Meldon Junction to Ashbury section. The closure of Tower Hill between 1920 and 1943 extended the No.3 Tablet between Ashwater and Launceston, but on its re-opening in 1943 No 6 Tablets were installed for each direction.

Already the Electric Key Token was making its appearance. In 1943 Ashbury to Halwill was converted, in this case to ease the situation at Halwill ground frame 'C' where trains could be 'shut in' to the new lower yard by restoration of the Key Token in an auxiliary machine. With successive abolition of signal boxes and extended sections, the situation in October 1966 was perceived to be:

**Meldon Junction
to Ashbury** E. Key Token (WR pattern)

Ashbury to Halwill "

Halwill to Launceston "

Launceston to Egloskerry No 3 Tablet

**Egloskerry to
Camelford** E. Key Token (WR pattern)

**Camelford to
Port Isaac Rd** No 6 Tablet

**Port Isaac Rd to
Wadebridge E** E. Key Token (WR pattern)

**Wadebridge
East to West** Preece 3-wire (double line)

**Wadebridge West
to Padstow** Annetts Key on Train Staff

The Block Telegraph was separate to the other station-to-station communication - the Single Needle Telegraph operated by booking clerks. Before the advent of speaking instruments (the telephone) messages were tapped out in Morse code adapted for the railway use, though the system was visual to an extent, using a deflecting needle. Like the telephone which replaced it, the circuits were organised into 'omnibus' systems. Consequently all and sundry could eavesdrop; no wonder news travelled fast on the railway! Resulting from these instruments were miles of telegraph wires supported on poles about 55 yards apart. The maintenance and repair of these lines was never ending on the North Cornwall, particularly on the high ground from Otterham to Delabole open to the salty ocean gales and rain. The LSWR and SR employed a lineman and a mate at Okehampton, Launceston and Wadebridge for all the signal and telegraph work. Their Inspector was at one time in the District Engineer's department, but by the

These permanent way men in this pre-World War One photograph may be from the Launceston area. On the right is an Inspector and another is in the back row. The gangers also wore soft-brimmed hats; the lengthmen wear the caps. They are sitting and standing on a demountable trolley (then known as 'lorries') and the two men in front are lying on 'jim crows' used for bending or straightening rails or point blades. The large group indicates an important job was in hand - there is a carpenter present (2nd left standing) and a ganger (top right) wears a lookout armlet. (R.L. Goodman Collection)

time of SR renewals in the 1930s the 'S & T' had its own.

The Structures and Permanent Way
Mention of 'standard' North Cornwall station building should in reality refer to LSWR architecture dating from the 1870s. The same applies to the supply of signalling equipment and permanent way. The NCR had little to say in these matters as Galbraith and Church were the LSWR Consulting Engineers and the LSWR would 'work' the line by agreement. This also applied to the Devon & Cornwall Railway. On the latter, although Okehampton and Holsworthy stations followed the LSWR standard generally (though with detail changes) Ashbury, Halwill, and Dunsland Cross housed the station master and staff in unadorned single storey edifices. The NCR rural stations were (only Tower Hill was demolished after 1966) strictly

utilitarian. The circular lintel of the upper storey windows and the grey and brown stone give them a rather sombre look. Portland stone quoining cheered their appearance, and none of them ever became blackened - the rain, sun and clean air from the Atlantic saw to that. Nearly all were constructed in local dressed blocks, varying from brown sandstone at Ashwater to grey/blue slate stone at Port Isaac Road. Egloskerry and Tresmeer, however, were built of brick. There appeared to be a shortage of stone in this area and the proposed Treneglos viaduct was not built for this reason, an embankment being substituted. The SM residences were quite commodious, though without bathrooms, and the WCs were in the back yard. The size was deceptive, as the ladies' waiting and cloakroom occupied one of the ground floor rooms. The general waiting area was within the book-

The location of these platelayers cannot be identified with certainty, but they are perhaps in the Higher Shipyard area at Padstow and may show contractor's temporary way under removal. Protection for the men seems to be under the watchful eye of a traffic department handsignalman (right). (H. Hambly collection)

Tower Hill's trolley shed, solidly built of sleepers, on the Down side in March 1966. It could house the Ashwater and Launceston permanent way trollys if required, and a trailer outside. (A.E. West)

ing hall in the single storey end, the remainder housing the booking office, parcels office and porters' room. The SM also had an office. Launceston and Wadebridge (not NCR) stations were quite different, though somewhat similar in appearance and layout, the Station Masters living in separate accommodation. Awnings were attached to these station buildings, (also at Padstow and Camelford). Camelford was intended as the railhead for the gentry and visitors to the coast, recognising at the same time the rainfall here is one of the highest in Cornwall! All platforms were constructed in local stone with various edge copings. Slate slabs were used at Delabole and Port Isaac Road, and it is interesting to note that some Waterloo platforms still have them, quite likely from Delabole Quarry.

Goods sheds, where provided, followed LSWR country style and with similar stonework to the stations. Okehampton, Launceston and Wadebridge goods sheds were larger, and differed according to the LSWR's contemporary designs. This principle also applied to signalboxes, though all from Ashwater to St Kew adopted the

mid-1880s 'glasshouse' appearance. Many terraces of three or six houses were erected by the LSWR for P.W. staff and are readily noticeable near most stations at the present day. Brick also appeared in the arches of the mainly dressed stone bridges west of Launceston. Wrought iron girders were employed on the wider river crossings and some roads, but apart from the skew span over the GWR at Launceston, none approached the size of the Little Petherick Viaduct at Padstow. The restrictions on locomotives passing over Meldon Viaduct have been mentioned, but other insignificant underbridges contributed to the ban on rebuilt 'West Country' 4-6-2s from Meldon Junction westwards. Apparently this was due to a number of cattle creeps laid with old rails on their sides, though with wheel timbers under the running rails.

The LSWR developed a concrete products works at Exmouth Junction which was extended by the SR from 1923 to supply the whole system. Every form appeared, from footbridges to mileposts. They soon emerged on the NCR, starting with station name boards. Concrete fencing panels

hardly enhance the scenery and the utilitarian slabs of the new Wadebridge footbridge compared poorly with the original timber structure graced with its finials. One thing is certain, if all else disappears Exmouth Junction concrete fencing posts will be found in the undergrowth along the NCR.

Concrete sleepers in the track were first installed in the 1930s, not like the sophisticated ties seen today in our main lines but simply reinforced for use with bull head rails in the lower speed range. In the 1880s the 'permanent way' by contrast was comparatively complicated. The rails were double-headed and laid in cast iron chairs, then wedged tight by oak or elm 'keys'. The chairs, in turn, were spiked to the wood sleepers by wood treenails, or hollow treenails and iron spikes. The Holsworthy line through Halwill had been laid with 75lb to the yard wrought iron rails, only 18ft long under 2ft 8ins sleeper centres. The fishplated rail joints were 'suspended', a form adopted by the LSWR only since 1860. For the opening to Launceston in 1886, new 82lb/yd double-head steel rails in 24ft lengths were stipulated by the LSWR. The same sort of material was laid on the Padstow extension in 1899, only second hand. It was not long (1908) before new 90lb/yd bull head 45 ft rails were laid here! Nearly all the North Cornwall had been relaid by 1910, though the earlier (1879) line through Ashbury had been relaid with 87lb/yd double head 45ft lengths in the mid-1890s.

To maintain the length from Halwill Junction to Padstow (the contractor handed over after twelve months following each opening) were nineteen gangs, each of five men for approximately 2 1/2 miles of route. From 1895 the existing Wadebridge gang looked after the stretch from the new junction to the end of the embankment at Polgammon, including several miles of sidings in the yard and quay. Between Meldon Junction and Halwill were four gangs, and two between Wadebridge and Padstow. Most of the men taken on were local, probably learning their skills on the contractor's work before-

			Permanent-way			
Gang No.	From (m.ch)	To (m.ch)	Home Station	Ganger	Trolleys	Notes
71	200.00	209.73	Ashbury	W. Wonnacott	Meldon Jcn, Halwill	a
80	209.73	218.60	Ashwater	F. Northey	Halwill, Tower Hill	
89	218.60	227.70	Launceston	T. Rickard	Tower Hill, Egloskerry	b
91	227.70	236.00	Tresmeer	G. Drew	Egloskerry, Otterham	
97	236.00	250.00	Delabole	S. Horrell	Otterham, Camelford	
103	250.00	259.44	Wadebridge	G. Warne	St Kew Highway, Padstow	b

a   Also maintained part of the Bude branch (209m 71ch to 210m 20ch)

b   Also maintained part of the 1943 Launceston spur (GWR) 31m 48ch to 31m 55ch

c   Plus parallel single lines from 253m 15ch to 253m 63 ch (Bodmin branch) and the sidings at Wadebridge and Padstow Quays.

The lamp room on Camelford Down platform, clad in the modish corrugated iron of the late Victorian period, was a vital part of station working. Herein was stored paraffin for the signal lamps and, until 1966, the platform, office and house lighting. (C.J. Knowles-Thomas)

The original aqueduct carrying the mill leat at Newport, Launceston in 1991. The narrow gauge track was laid on the North Cornwall formation in 1983 by the Launceston Steam Railway and takes its diminutive trains several miles out to New Churches. (Author)

and capable of towing a trolley. Except from between Ashwater and Launceston up to 1943, no facilities for side-tracking were provided and the tablets were required to be carried as a normal train between signal boxes.

A relaying gang was based at Launceston, originating at Halwill in the 1930s when much renewal was undertaken; in the 1950s its ten men would prepare the 'road' for renewal by throwing out the old ballast to the sides. This took place during the week, followed on Saturday nights/Sundays by removal of the rails and sleepers and replacement by new material. All this work was by hand, even to the loading of spent ballast - though new ballast would be run out from hopper wagons. If points and crossings were involved, a crane would be supplied from Exeter, and some mechanization crept in finally, principally to handle heavy concrete sleepers.

Although traffic volume was relatively light, the advent of the six-coupled 'N's and later 'West Country' Pacifics increased the wear and tear on the rails. The 50mph limit (later 55mph) was achieved over the 30 and 40 chains radius curves by superelevating the higher rail. Most curves were uprated in the 1930s to a maximum five inches in conjunction with the extensive renewals. New 45ft rails of 95lb/yd, with resleepering, replaced the old LSWR material. Many sidings were relaid with the best of the latter. Some American 39lb rails (BH) were laid in below Delabole in the last war, and after Nationalization new BR 'flat-bottom' rails (98lb) were laid in at Halwill, Halwill - Ashwater, Tower Hill, Launceston, and Wadebridge. There was always a good supply of ballast hereabouts, either from Meldon Quarry, Hingston Down (Callington Branch) and from Tom's Quarry at Port Isaac Road.

hand. It was attractive work, paying better than agriculture rates, and many were favoured with housing at reasonable rents. In the 1920s Ganger Trewin, based at Otterham, maintained the exposed section over the 860ft summit, while Ganger Lawry's length down through the damp Tilleslow woods at Ashwater, was a place always at risk from washouts, from the adjacent River Carey.

These small gangs lasted until the 1930s. The four main line companies were adopting motorized trollies on single lines for 'economic maintenance' and the gangs from Meldon Junction to Padstow were re-grouped, each consisting of Ganger, Sub-Ganger, Trolley Driver, Patrolman and two or three Lengthmen.

The original trolleys were simple, belt-driven from a JP motor, open to the elements but with front screens. They could be turned and run off to the cess by an under lift-jack. In BR days replacements came in the form of Wickham trolleys of higher power

St. Kew Highway waiting shed on the Down platform, together with oil lamp. The platform copers were slate slabs from Delabole - some of these may be seen at Waterloo to this day. (C.J. Knowles-Thomas)

The LSWR No. 2 country goods shed at Ashbury, constructed in local brown stone in 1879. By 1966 it had not been used for small consignments for some years and the cattle pen had been stripped of bars and gates. In the distance are the LSWR staff cottages. (A.E. West)

are valid today. The chain measurement, although now declared obsolete, is still regarded as a useful division by BR's engineers and the provision of mile and quarter mile posts remain requirements of the 1845 Consolidation Act.

Opening, closing and alteration dates have been verified as far as possible, but the reader should be aware that official published versions could be postponed, or facilities even used in advance! Attention is drawn, particularly, to when trains 'last ran' and 'on and from' closure dates. In the case of Meldon Junction to Bude and Wadebridge the track remained in situ, even used (e.g. wagon storage), for varying periods after 3 October 1966 before lifting.

SUMMARY OF EVENTS

23 May 1832 Bodmin & Wadebridge Railway Act (B&WR).

4 July 1834 B&WR opened from Wadebridge Quay to Bodmin.

30 September 1834 B & WR opened from Dunmere Junction to Wenford Bridge.

12 May 1851 Cowley Bridge Jn. (Exeter) to Crediton opened.

1 August 1854 North Devon Railway (NDR) (Crediton to Fremington).

19 July 1860 London & South Western Railway (LSWR) opened line to Exeter Qn St. from east.

Two Permanent Way Inspectors directed track maintenance in this area, Halwill's extending from Meldon Junction to Delabole (in BR days to Otterham), also the Bude Branch and four miles of the Torrington-Halwill line. The remainder came under Wadebridge (taking in the Bodmin and Wenford branches). In 1966 Mr Bill Geach was the Halwill Inspector, and until 1963, Mr Charles Mitchell at

Wadebridge (still with us as a nonagenarian in the 1990s).

Notes
Track plans are based on LSWR, SR and BR originals or, where those are not available, from the Ordnance Survey 1/2500 series. Derived scales in chains/feet are appended to most of these and it should be noted that the statute mile and chain (80 to the mile)

The restricted headroom of the bridge over the A39 trunk road became untenable in the new motor age. After the railway closure in 1966 the road was straightened (to the right) but the bridge remains today in a cu-de-sac. Unusually at this end of the line, the arch is of dressed stone. The signal is St. Kew Highway's Down home. (C.J. Knowles-Thomas)

1 February 1862 LSWR Exeter Queen St to Exeter St Davids, B & E Railway.

17 July 1862 Okehampton Railway Act. Coleford Jn. to Okehampton.

13 July 1863 Okehampton Railway Lidford (sic) Extension Act.

29 June 1865 Okehampton Rly renamed Devon & Cornwall Railway (DCR). Worked by LSWR.

1 July 1865 Launceston & South Devon Railway (L & SDR) (Tavistock to Launceston) opened (GWR) from 31 January 1876).

1 November 1865 DCR Yeoford (separate line) to North Tawton opened.

8 January 1867 DCR North Tawton to Okehampton Road (Belstone Corner).

3 October 1871 DCR Belstone Corner (Sampford Courtney) to Okehampton opened.

1 January 1872 DCR Coleford Jn. to Okehampton purchased by LSWR.

7 July 1873 DCR Meldon Junction to Holsworthy (Railway No.1) authorized.

12 October 1874 Okehampton to the L&SDR at Lidford (sic) opened.

9 January 1879 Line doubled Sampford Courtney to Meldon Viaduct (excl.).

20 January 1879 MELDON JUNCTION TO HOLSWORTHY OPENED.

1 November 1879 Line doubled Meldon Viaduct (incl.) to Meldon Jn.

18 August 1882 NORTH CORNWALL RAILWAY ACT (NCR). Worked by the LSWR for the owners (Agreements December 1882).

28 July 1884 NCR Launceston to Halwill Separate Undertaking (Railway No.5) authorized.

5 June 1886 GWR granted future running powers Boscarne Jn to Wadebridge.

1 July 1886 B & WR legally acquired by LSWR.

21 July 1886 HALWILL JUNCTION TO LAUNCESTON OPENED.

1 November 1886 Wadebridge to Bodmin closed for re-alignment works (re-opened 1 November 1895).

3 September 1888 GWR Bodmin to Boscarne Junction opened.

3 September 1888 LSWR Wadebridge new station opened.

21 July 1891 NCR Launceston to Delabole (Separate Undertaking Railway No.2) authorized.

28 July 1892 LAUNCESTON TO TRESMEER OPENED. (Egloskerry from 3 October 1892).

27 July 1893 NCR Delabole to Wadebridge (Railway No.2) Separate Undertaking authorized.

14 August 1893 TRESMEER TO CAMELFORD OPENED.

18 October 1893 CAMELFORD TO DELABOLE OPENED.

26 July 1894 LSWR lease NCR as built, and yet to open, for 999 years.

1 June 1895 DELABOLE TO WADEBRIDGE JUNCTION OPENED.

1 November 1895 B & WR re-opened for LSWR trains Wadebridge to new terminus at Bodmin.

20 July 1896 NCR Wadebridge to Padstow Separate Undertaking (Railway No.1).

11 August 1898 Holsworthy to Bude opened.

12 March 1899 Enlarged Wadebridge station and Signal Boxes opened.

23 March 1899 WADEBRIDGE TO PADSTOW OPENED.

27 March 1899 Public train services started to Padstow.

3 February 1907 Wadebridge Junction abolished. Two separate lines to Wadebridge East.

1910 - 1915 Padstow Harbour new works.

World War I (August 1914 - November 1918)

1 January 1923 North Cornwall Railway acquired by LSWR. LSWR amalgamated with LB & SCR and SECR to form Southern Railway Company (SR).

27 July 1923 North Devon & Cornwall Junction Light Railway (ND & CJLR) Torrington to Halwill opened.

**World War II
(September 1939 - August 1945)**

22 September 1943 Launceston Junction between SR and GWR opened (connected SR 30 May/GWR 19 September).

1 January 1948 Southern Railway Co. became British Railways (Southern Region). Great Western Railway Co. became (Western Region).

1 July 1950 Southern Region commercial and civil engineering responsibilities west of Exeter (Cowley Bridge Jn.) transferred to Western Region.

1 January 1951 Former SR and GWR stations at Launceston renamed (South) and (North) respectively.

30 June 1952 WR trains from Plymouth diverted into Launceston (South).

1 January 1958 Southern Region regained most of the 1950 transfers.

31 December 1962 WR passenger service Plymouth to Launceston withdrawn and line between Lifton (excl.) and Launceston (North Goods) closed.

1 January 1963 Western Region took over all functions west of Wilton (Salisbury).

April 1964 BR propose to withdraw passenger services Okehampton to Wadebridge (and Bude) from 5 October.

7 September 1964 FREIGHT SERVICES WITHDRAWN FROM OKEHAMPTON WADEBRIDGE (EXCL.) AND PADSTOW. Lifton to Launceston closed line re-opened for freight trains. Wadebridge served by freight trains from Bodmin Road.

7 September 1964 Passenger services on North Cornwall and Bude lines start connecting into WR Paddington/West of England trains at Exeter St Davids. 'Atlantic Coast Express' ceased to run.

25 September 1964 Transport Users Consultative Committee meeting to hear objections to withdrawal of passenger services between Okehampton and Wadebridge.

1 January 1965 Okehampton, Launceston and Wadebridge (and Bude) motive power depots ceased steam operations.

1 March 1965 Passenger trains withdrawn from Torrington to Halwill. Line closed from Meeth (excl.) to Halwill.

28 February 1966 Launceston freight services withdrawn (from Lifton) and line closed.

1 October 1966 Last passenger trains run from Okehampton to Bude and Wadebridge/Padstow. LINE CLOSED FROM MELDON JUNCTION TO WADEBRIDGE (EXCL.) AND TO BUDE as from 3 October 1966.

28 January 1967 Last Passenger trains run from Bodmin Road to Padstow and Boscarne Junction to Bodmin (North). WADEBRIDGE (EXCL) TO PADSTOW CLOSED COMPLETELY as from 30 January.

4 September 1978 Last train (freight) Boscarne Junction to Wadebridge. Remained operational until 31 December.